EVERYTHING IS SACRED

THEOPOLITICAL VISIONS

SERIES EDITORS:

Thomas Heilke
D. Stephen Long
and C. C. Pecknold

Theopolitical Visions seeks to open up new vistas on public life, hosting fresh conversations between theology and political theory. This series assembles writers who wish to revive theopolitical imagination for the sake of our common good.

Theopolitical Visions hopes to re-source modern imaginations with those ancient traditions in which political theorists were often also theologians. Whether it was Jeremiah's prophetic vision of exiles "seeking the peace of the city," Plato's illuminations on piety and the civic virtues in the Republic, St. Paul's call to "a common life worthy of the Gospel," St. Augustine's beatific vision of the City of God, or the gothic heights of medieval political theology, much of Western thought has found it necessary to think theologically about politics, and to think politically about theology. This series is founded in the hope that the renewal of such mutual illumination might make a genuine contribution to the peace of our cities.

OTHER VOLUMES IN THE SERIES:

Gabriel A. Santos
Redeeming the Broken Body: Church and State after Disaster

Nathan R. Kerr
Christ, History and Apocalyptic: The Politics of Christian Mission

Stanley Hauerwas & Romand Coles
Christianity, Democracy, and the Radical Ordinary: Conversations between a Radical Democrat and a Christian

Everything Is
SACRED

Spiritual Exegesis

in the Political Theology

of Henri de Lubac

BRYAN C. HOLLON

CASCADE *Books* • Eugene, Oregon

EVERYTHING IS SACRED
Spiritual Exegesis in the Political Theology of Henri de Lubac

Theopolitical Visions 3

Cascade Books
A Division of Wipf and Stock Publishers
199 W. 8th Ave., Suite 3
Eugene, OR 97401

www.wipfandstock.com

ISBN 13: 978-1-55635-857-9

Cataloging-in-Publication data:

Hollon, Bryan C.

Everything is sacred : spiritual exegesis in the political theology of Henri de Lubac / Bryan C. Hollon.

x + 214 p. ; 23 cm. — Includes bibliographical references and index.

Theopolitical Visions 3

ISBN 13: 978-1-55635-857-9

1. Lubac, Henri de, 1896–1991 — Contributions in hermeneutics. 2. Lubac, Henri de, 1896–1991 — Contributions in doctrine of the church. 3. Political theology. I. Title. II. Series.

BX4705. L7918 H63 2009

Manufactured in the U.S.A.

For Suzanne

Contents

Acknowledgments

This book began as a dissertation, which was completed during the spring of 2006 at Baylor University. Although I have cut several chapter sections and tried to strengthen the scholarship in several areas, the outline of the argument has not changed. Accordingly, I continue to owe a great deal of thanks to my dissertation supervisor, Barry Harvey, who offered encouragement, counsel, and camaraderie from the conception of the project through its completion. He was an ideal mentor and continues to be a good friend. I am indebted to Ralph Wood not only for reading and editing the manuscript but also for his continuing friendship. Thomas Hibbs was on the original dissertation committee and offered advice, especially in the area of Thomist philosophy. Dan Williams read the work and made helpful corrections and recommendations in the area of patristic thought. I also want to thank Mikeal Parsons, not only for reading the dissertation but also for supporting and encouraging me in many ways during my years at Baylor.

I am grateful to Thomas Heilke, D. Stephen Long, Chad Pecknold, and Charlie Collier for their enthusiasm about seeing the book published in the Theopolitical Visions series. Chad Pecknold read several chapters when we were both still working on our doctorates, and he has been a great dialogue partner and continues to be a cherished friend. The library staff at Malone College has been very helpful in retrieving obscure books and articles. Jan Anderson, in particular, but also Barb Shallenberger and Stan Terhune, were not only capable, but eager to help each time I made a request.

I am extremely fortunate to have a supportive family. My parents, Cynthia and Bill, have been entirely selfless in their encouragement of my academic pursuits. The same is true of my in-laws, Judith and the late

John Bryant. I am grateful to my children, Harrison, Claire, and John, for filling my days with joy. Above all, I am grateful to Suzanne, my wife and companion, without whom neither this book nor a career in academia would have ever been possible.

PART 1

Secular Politics and Sacramental Ecclesiology

CHAPTER 1

Henri de Lubac and the "New Theology"

"All nature," according to Henri de Lubac, is an "infinitely vast and diverse symbol across which the Face of God is mysteriously reflected. A man is religious to the very degree that he recognizes everywhere these reflections of the divine Face, that is, that he lives in a sacred atmosphere."[1] When he spoke these words in 1942, de Lubac was concerned that this "sense of the sacred" was hard to find in the modern, secular world of twentieth-century Europe. He was also concerned that early twentieth-century Catholic theology was doing too little to restore it.[2] Indeed de Lubac was critical of all theology that assumes God to be a being, though of much greater power and proportion, like other beings. He believed, of course, that God is not one being among others but rather the total context within which all creatures "live and move and have [their] being" (Acts 17:28, NRSV). De Lubac believed that Christian theology, at least since the late Middle Ages, has too often proceeded as though the natural world were cut off from its divine context—from the God, who is its beginning and end.

Moreover, de Lubac feared that some of Catholicism's most important constitutive practices, such as the sacraments and the spiritual exegesis of Scripture, had been obscured and stripped of their vitality by extrinsicist and historicist conceptions of the faith. Accordingly, his entire career focused on a revisioning of both theology and philosophy unencumbered by rationalist and historicist presuppositions.

---

1. De Lubac, "Internal Causes," 231. This essay is the published version of a lecture given to a group of youth-camp chaplains in Saint-Baume, from April 14 to 17 in 1942.

2. For his personal reflections on these years, see de Lubac, *Christian Resistance to Anti-Semitism.*

Like many of the twentieth century's most notable philosophers, de Lubac affirmed, "human knowledge is never without an a priori." He suggests, "man is made in such a way that he cannot give meaning to something without choosing his perspective."[3] De Lubac argued that critical biblical scholars and neoscholastic theologians both assume an ahistorical, disincarnate, and impossible objectivity.[4] In order to overcome the twin problems of rationalism (which, following Maurice Blondel, he often called "extrinsicism") and historicism, de Lubac advocated a *Ressourcement*—a return to the sources of the great Catholic tradition and specifically a retrieval of the best insights of patristic and medieval exegesis. He believed that the ultimate goal of theology is not the identification and explication of a static body of revealed knowledge but rather the cultivation of Christ's wisdom and love within the church through a christological reading of signs.[5] While de Lubac was clearly interested in helping the church overcome the dualism of post-Cartesian philosophy and theology, he affirmed consistently that spiritual exegesis mediates the church's ontological participation in Christ.[6]

De Lubac argued that, unlike historical-critical biblical scholarship, that the allegorical approach of the Fathers sought not scientific knowl-

3. De Lubac, "Mysticism and Mystery," 39.

4. Notably, de Lubac did not reject the contributions of historical-critical scholars. Indeed, he understood well that there could never be a return to the days of pre-critical exegesis. For de Lubac, the methods of critical scholars have become indispensable in the never-ending effort to understand the literal sense of Scripture. Moreover, de Lubac never advocated a new exegetical method based upon the fourfold sense of Scripture. He did, however, advocate a retrieval of the participatory ontology and philosophy of history that under girded patristic and medieval exegesis. See de Lubac, *Scripture in the Tradition*, 67–68.

5. In one essay, de Lubac ridiculed Catholic neoscholastic theologians who "stroll about theology somewhat as if in a museum of which we are the curators, a museum where we have inventoried, arranged and labeled everything; we know how to define all the terms, we have an answer for all objections, we supply the desired distinctions at just the right moment. Everything in it is obscure for the secular, but for us, everything is clear, everything is explained. If there is still mystery, at least we know exactly where it is to be placed, and we point to this precisely defined site" (de Lubac, "Internal Causes," 233).

6. Consider the following statement: "the two Testaments are always considered in tradition as the place of operation for all sacraments, and the place of concealment for all mysteries." Moreover, "the sacrament would play, therefore, the role of package, or envelope in relation to the mystery which hides in it" (de Lubac, *Corpus Mysticum*, 57–58). The mystery of which he speaks is the "mystical" or "spiritual" sense of Scripture.

edge but a sapiential and thoroughly christological wisdom to guide the church in its inherently social and political mission to the world. In a certain sense, his entire career was focused on returning the Catholic Church to a way of doing theology that, like the exegetical approach of the Fathers, serves both to draw the church into the mystery of Christ and salvation history while extending the reach of the church into the fullness of Christ where all of humanity is reconciled and redeemed.[7]

The Purpose of this Project

The purpose of this work is to examine the centrality of Henri de Lubac's retrieval of patristic and medieval exegesis within the context of his broader efforts to inspire a more faithful and robust Catholic engagement with the secular world. It is well known that de Lubac's groundbreaking and highly controversial work on nature and grace had important implications for the Catholic Church's relationship to culture and was intended to remove a philosophical obstacle hindering Catholicism's witness to the world. This book will address a too-often neglected dimension of de Lubac's thought by examining the centrality and indispensability of spiritual exegesis in his *oeuvre* and making explicit its social and political significance in the church's worship and witness. While de Lubac's major preconciliar works are the primary focus of this study, recent theological movements such as postliberalism and Radical Orthodoxy will serve as helpful interlocutors, especially in the final chapters. Placing de Lubac in a critical dialogue with some of his recent interpreters will highlight the continuing relevance of his work and put some distance between *la nouvelle théologie* and more recent theological programs such as Radical Orthodoxy.

Nouvelle Théologie and Radical Orthodoxy

Certainly the "post-modern critical Augustinianism"[8] of John Milbank and others constitutes the most explicit (and controversial) recent appro-

---

7. This is the theme of the first chapter of his first book, published in 1938. For a more recent English translation, see de Lubac, *Catholicism*. It is widely agreed that de Lubac's entire publishing career was foreshadowed in this book, whose individual chapters were expanded to become the basis for nearly all of his major works.

8. See Milbank, *Theology and Social Theory*, 225–37.

priation of de Lubac's work.[9] In the introduction to *Radical Orthodoxy: A New Theology*, John Milbank, Catherine Pickstock, and Graham Ward suggest that their own "perspective is in profound continuity with the French *nouvelle théologie*,"[10] and elsewhere they acknowledge a special appreciation for the work of Henri de Lubac. Milbank suggests that Radical Orthodoxy has a greater "alliance" with *la nouvelle théologie* than with neo-orthodoxy. "Radical Orthodoxy," he writes, "considers that Henri de Lubac was a greater theological revolutionary than Karl Barth, because in questioning the hierarchical duality of grace and nature as discrete stages, he transcended, unlike Barth, the shared background assumption of all modern theology. In this way one could say, anachronistically, that he inaugurated a postmodern theology."[11]

Like their French Catholic forerunners, the proponents of Radical Orthodoxy intend a careful retrieval of the patristic and medieval sources, and they are especially intent on a recovery of the "Augustinian vision" that rejects any dichotomy between nature and grace or reason and faith. The Radical Orthodoxy project shares with *la nouvelle théologie* a desire to engage the secular world with the gospel, but "where radical orthodoxy wishes to reach farther is in recovering and extending a fully Christianised ontology and practical philosophy consonant with authentic Christian doctrine."[12]

---

9. It is of course true that de Lubac has always been of interest to readers of and contributors to the International Catholic journal *Communio*, which was founded by de Lubac, Hans Urs Von Balthasar, Joseph Ratzinger, and others. *Communio* is currently published in fourteen countries and languages, and has continued to publish translations of de Lubac's shorter writings as well as various articles by contemporary theologians on all aspects of his thought. *Communio*'s American editor, David L. Schindler, is inarguably the most important figure on the American theological landscape when it comes to carrying on the legacy of *la nouvelle théologie*.

10. Milbank et al., *Radical Orthodoxy*, 2.

11. Milbank, "Programme of Radical Orthodoxy," 35.

12. The authors write that "the consequences of modern theological decadence for philosophy and the wider culture were never fully considered by *nouvelle théologie* (and indeed it sometimes uncritically embraced various modes of secular knowledge)" (Milbank et al., *Radical Orthodoxy*, 2). It is somewhat inaccurate, I believe, to suggest that de Lubac failed to fully consider the "consequences of modern theological decadence." See for example, de Lubac, *Drama of Atheist Humanism*. Milbank and the others may be faulting *la nouvelle théologie* for failing to propose a theological engagement with culture along the lines of Radical Orthodoxy. I will argue, especially in chapters 5 and 6, that the program of *nouvelle théologie* remains the better approach.

The recovery and extension of a fully Christianized ontology is the main thrust of the Radical Orthodoxy project, and the initial volume in the Routledge Press series contains essays on diverse topics such as desire, language, friendship, music, the city, and knowledge.[13] This effort has continued through the publication of books and articles that offer a theological perspective on issues where "secularism has invested heavily—aesthetics, politics, sex, the body, personhood, visibility, space," economics, and more.[14] Certainly, de Lubac and others associated with *la nouvelle théologie* never addressed many of these topics in writing, so Milbank, Pickstock, and Ward are correct in claiming that their project goes farther in this direction.[15]

However, there are other, perhaps more important differences between *la nouvelle théologie* and Radical Orthodoxy thus conceived. One difference is obvious in light of de Lubac's sustained efforts to illumine and retrieve the participatory ontology and distinctively Christian philosophy of history that under girded patristic and medieval exegesis. Although he is best known for his works on the social nature of Catholicism, the relationship between nature and grace, and the eucharistic nature of the church, de Lubac wrote more pages on the history of biblical exegesis than on any other single issue. In contrast, the proponents of Radical Orthodoxy have had little to say about the role that biblical interpretation should play in the church's struggle for a "fully Christianised ontology."[16]

13. "The central theological framework of radical orthodoxy is 'participation' as developed by Plato and reworked by Christianity, because any alternative configuration perforce reserves a territory independent of God. The latter can lead only to nihilism (though in different disguises). Participation, however, refuses any reserve of created territory, while allowing finite things their own integrity. Underpinning the present essays, therefore, is the idea that every discipline must be framed by a theological perspective; otherwise these disciplines will define a zone apart from God, grounded literally in nothing" (Milbank et al., *Radical Orthodoxy*, 3).

14. Ibid., 1.

15. De Lubac did, of course, recognize the "all-encompassing" nature of theology. See, for example, de Lubac, "Authority of the Church in Temporal Matters," 214.

16. Although biblical exegesis is lacking in Milbank's work thus far, he acknowledges in his recent book on de Lubac that spiritual exegesis is fundamental in de Lubac's theology (see Milbank, *Suspended Middle*, 56–59). It is unclear, however, whether Milbank thinks spiritual exegesis is a viable alternative for Christians today or whether it is merely an interesting, though dispensable, dimension of de Lubac's *Ressourcement*. One wonders, moreover, whether Milbank would amend any of his earlier christological proposals, especially those found in *The Word Made Strange*, given his more recent comments in *The Suspended Middle* about the christological dimension of de Lubac's spiritual exegesis.

In a critical review of the initial Radical Orthodoxy volume, David Ford suggests that "Graham Ward's essay on 'Bodies' is interesting and provocative, but it is the only one of the twelve essays to try to interpret Scripture as part of its argument." He explains: "I find all this very disturbing, because I do not see a good theological future for the movement unless this is urgently addressed. Scripture is so intrinsic to the traditions, practices and theologians they espouse that without it their claim to be in continuity with these is hopelessly compromised."[17]

Whereas Radical Orthodoxy theologians have been criticized for neglecting biblical exegesis, de Lubac's *nouvelle théologie* makes spiritual exegesis fundamental and constitutive for the church in its engagement with secular culture and in the ultimate extension of a "christianised ontology." Although Radical Orthodoxy's commitment to a theological engagement with secularism is laudable, it will remain too separated from the life of the church unless it embraces the centrality of spiritual exegesis, as de Lubac did.

An Outline of Forthcoming Chapters

In chapter 2, I examine the historical and philosophical context of de Lubac's work, beginning with a summary of late nineteenth- and early twentieth-century atheism and secularism. In particular, I argue that de Lubac saw a connection between the atheist humanism of the nineteenth century and the various sociopolitical crises of the early twentieth century, and that he believed the Catholic Church's response to atheist humanism and its social and political manifestations was insufficient.

Chapter 3 considers the social and political context within which de Lubac wrote two of his major works on the church: *Catholicism* (1938) and *Corpus Mysticum* (1944). Whereas his first book, *Catholicism*, set out a grand vision for a renewed Church, his subsequent genealogical works sought to overcome a series of obstacles that he thought were obscuring the Church's identity and preventing its faithful engagement with the world. *Corpus Mysticum* offered a somewhat-veiled challenge to the

---

I will return to a comparison of de Lubac and Milbank in chapters 5 and 6 below.

17. Ford, "Radical Orthodoxy and the Future of British Theology," 398. In a response to David Ford's essay, Catherine Pickstock expresses sympathy with the concern regarding scriptural engagement, and she writes that "this should be remedied in the future" (Pickstock, "Reply to David Ford and Guy Collins," 411).

extrinsicism of Catholic sacramental theology and ecclesiology as well as to the dialectical method of Scholastic theology.

Chapter 4 focuses on the efforts of de Lubac and several other *nouvelle* theologians who worked hard from the 1930s through the 1950s to enrich and revitalize Catholic theology.[18] Although the battle between *la nouvelle théologie* and neoscholasticism did not begin in 1946, de Lubac's *Surnaturel* (1946) became the central and most controversial work in the debate, since it challenged an entrenched neoscholastic dualism that considered the sacred and secular as two distinct realms with separate ends. After reviewing this mid-twentieth-century conflict, I will illustrate how de Lubac's work on spiritual exegesis should be considered in relation to these earlier debates over the nature of theology and theology's engagement with secularism.

Chapter 5 examines several recent proposals for a philosophically sound christological hermeneutic to guide the church in its engagement with secular culture and politics. It includes a survey of several recent theological attempts to address and overcome the deficiencies of historical criticism. The work of postliberal theologians Hans Frei and George Lindbeck is assessed, and John Milbank's hermeneutic alternative to postliberalism is considered and evaluated as well.

In chapter 6, I argue that de Lubac's retrieval of spiritual exegesis offers a needed correction to the work of postliberal and Radical Orthodoxy theologians. Specifically, I argue that the hermeneutical theories of postliberal and Radical Orthodoxy theologians fail to overcome the problem of extrinsicism, while de Lubac's retrieval of spiritual exegesis succeeds. I argue that the key to de Lubac's vision of Catholicism fully engaged with contemporary secularism, and the factor that makes it preferable to postliberalism and Radical Orthodoxy, is its christological mysticism, which is grounded in spiritual exegesis.

The seventh and concluding chapter offers a brief summary of de Lubac's theological program and makes a number of suggestions as to how contemporary biblical scholars and theologians can and should appropriate his work in service to the church and the world. Specifically, I discuss de Lubac's hope for a revitalized approach to spiritual exegesis—one that makes good use of the contributions of critical biblical scholarship. I ar-

---

18. I first encountered the phrase, "*nouvelle* theologians," in a conference presentation by Hans Boersma, "Nature and the Supernatural in *nouvelle théologie,*" 1

gue that such a development will strengthen the church's sociopolitical witness, since recent exegetical methods like literary, social-scientific, and rhetorical criticism offer helpful means of gaining insight into the social and political contexts of biblical stories. By synthesizing critical scholarship with contemporary approaches to participatory/spiritual exegesis, the social and political dimensions of Scripture's literal sense are preserved without accommodating the church's witness to secular social and political ideologies.

CHAPTER 2

Atheist Humanism and Neoscholasticism:
The Background of de Lubac's Work

The turmoil that enveloped Europe during the early twentieth century had a significant influence on the theology of Henri de Lubac. Born in Cambria in northern France in 1896, the young Frenchman entered the Society of Jesus in 1913.[1] He was conscripted into the French army in 1916 and sent to the Battle of Verdun, the longest and deadliest conflict of the First World War.[2] During the battle, he fought at Éparges, where Pierre Rousselot died in battle in 1915, and he sustained an injury that afflicted him for the rest of his life.[3] After the war, he began studies for the Jesuit priesthood and was ordained in 1927.

In 1929, de Lubac became professor of fundamental theology and history of religion at the Catholic University of Lyons and soon thereafter joined the Jesuit faculty at Fouviere.[4] He was also actively involved in the French resistance to Nazism during World War II, and later he played an important role in the proceedings of Vatican II.[5] Although his profes-

1. The most recent introduction to de Lubac's life and work can be found in Grumett, *De Lubac.*

2. It is estimated that five hundred thousand French soldiers were killed or wounded in the Battle of Verdun, while the German toll was closer to four hundred thousand. See Marshall, *World War I*, 248.

3. De Lubac mentions the death of Rousselot in his memoirs, and he discusses his own continuing struggle with headaches, earaches, and dizziness resulting from his military service. See de Lubac, *At the Service of the Church*, 15–19.

4. Wagner, *Henri de Lubac*, 12.

5. For his personal reflections on the World War II era, see de Lubac, *Christian Resistance to Anti-Semitism.*

sorial role ended in 1961, his service to the Catholic Church as priest, theologian, and eventually cardinal, continued until his death in 1991.[6]

There is little doubt that de Lubac was deeply committed to the Roman Catholic Church throughout his life.[7] Even during the years of his forced silence,[8] he remained faithfully obedient to the hierarchy and published his most affectionate work on the Church, *The Splendor of the Church* (1956).[9] However, he was also deeply concerned from early in his career that the theological vision of early twentieth-century Catholicism was too narrow to speak effectively to the social and intellectual crises of early twentieth-century Europe.[10] Accordingly, much of his theological career was focused on enabling the Church, through a renewal of the Spirit that inspired its great tradition, to reengage the surrounding culture with the gospel.[11]

6. For a more complete biographical treatment, see Wagner, *Henri de Lubac*, 11–27. See also Balthasar and Chantraine, *Le Cardinal Henri de Lubac*.

7. While he was in his mideighties, de Lubac completed a manuscript "which explains the genesis, meaning and fate of his books and situates them within the course of the various stages of his life, his studies, his meetings, his friendships as well as his legendary exiles and banishments" (Chantraine, foreword to *At the Service of the Church*, 7). Overall, the book portrays a life devoted to the Church. The nature of the church was a subject that de Lubac returned to again and again.

8. When de Lubac published his controversial *Surnaturel* (1946), neoscholastics especially in Rome and in southern France were offended at the obvious criticisms of their approach to doctrine. They aggressively sought a condemnation, and many people believed that Pius XII's encyclical *Humani Generis* (1950) contained one. However, de Lubac argues that the one sentence in the encyclical that appears to condemn his position in *Surnaturel* is in agreement with him and in fact reproduces his language exactly. Nevertheless, de Lubac was prohibited from teaching at Fouviere, and several of his books, including *Surnaturel*, *Corpus Mysticum*, and *Le Conaissance de Dieu* were censored. The affair, which involved a number of other theologians besides de Lubac, lasted for over ten years. See de Lubac, *At the Service of the Church*, 67–79.

9. De Lubac, *Splendor of the Church*, published originally as *Méditation sur L'église*. Notably, de Lubac composed this work between the years of 1946 to 1949, though it was not published until the time of his forced silence. See de Lubac, *At the Service of the Church*, 74–76. Fergus Kerr comments: "For the immediately pre-Vatican II generation of seminarians and lay people, this was a widely read and much treasured book—a reminder of just how rich pre-Vatican II ecclesiology was" (Kerr, *Twentieth-Century Catholic Theologians*, 76).

10. Cf., Komonchak, "Theology and Culture at Mid-Century," 579–602.

11. In his memoir, de Lubac describes the nature of the renewal that he worked for. He writes that "without claiming to open new avenues to thought, I have sought rather, without any antiquarianism, to make known some of the great common areas of Catholic tradition. I wanted to make it loved, to show its ever-present fruitfulness. Such a task

The purpose of this chapter is to describe the cultural and ecclesial contexts within which de Lubac was formed as a theologian. I will first examine briefly the atheist humanism and secularism that swept Europe during the nineteenth century. Next, I will consider the Catholic Church's response to atheism and secularism, paying special attention to Pope Leo XIII's 1879 encyclical *Aeterni Patris* and the Thomistic revival that ensued. In conclusion, I describe de Lubac's dissatisfaction with the neoscholastic character of the Thomistic revival.

ATHEIST HUMANISM AND SOCIAL CRISIS

De Lubac lived and worked during some of the most violent and confused years in modern European history. In addition to the losses caused by the several wars that ravaged Europe, the violent events of the early twentieth century led to an acute emotional and intellectual anxiety for many citizens of the continent. The First World War, in particular, brought European confidence in unending technological and moral progress to a halt.[12] In 1922, the French poet Paul Valéry wrote:

> The Storm is over, and yet we are still uneasy . . . anxious . . . as though it were just now going to break. Nearly all human affairs are still in a state of terrible uncertainty. We ponder on what is gone, we are almost ruined by what has been ruined; we do not know what is to come, and have some reason to fear it. We hope vaguely, but dread precisely; our fears are infinitely clearer than our hopes; we recognize that pleasurable living and abundance are behind us, but confusion and doubt are in us and with us.[13]

---

called more for a reading across the centuries than for a critical application to specific points; it excluded any overly preferential attachment to one school, system, or definite age; it demanded more attention to the deep and permanent unity of the Faith, to the mysterious relationship (which escapes so many specialized scholars) of all those who invoke the name of Christ, than to the multiple diversities of eras, milieux, personalities and cultures. So I have never been tempted by any kind of 'return to the sources' that would scorn later developments and represent the history of Christian thought as a stream of decadences; the Latins have not pushed aside the Greeks for me; nor has Saint Augustine diverted me from Saint Anslem or Saint Thomas Aquinas; nor has the latter ever seemed to me either to make the twelve centuries that preceded him useless or to condemn his disciples to a failure to see and understand fully what has followed him" (de Lubac, *At the Service of the Church*, 143–44).

12. Glover, *Humanity*, 1–3.

13. Matthews, *Collected Works*, 54.

Although war and atrocity are not recent inventions, there was something distinctive, and even surprising, about the violence witnessed during the European wars of the past century. On the one hand, people were surprised by the scale of those wars. Modern technology, which held such promise in agriculture, communications, medicine, travel, and more also enabled the production of much deadlier weapons than previous eras had known, and the millions of soldiers and civilians killed during the first half of the twentieth century were unprecedented.[14] On the other hand, the world wars were shocking because they "contrast[ed] with the expectations, at least in Europe, with which the twentieth century began," expectations of unrestrained social progress.[15] Those expectations were inspired in large part by a philosophical revolution that took place during the nineteenth century.

Whereas European civilization during the Middle Ages was relatively organic in terms of religion, government, law, art, literature, and the like, the seventeenth and eighteenth centuries witnessed the unraveling of the old order and a revolt against its authorities and institutions. In France, for example, the roles of clergy and nobility were forever diminished with the revolution of 1789. Then in the nineteenth century, philosophers set out to construct a modern replacement for the older organic civilization.[16] They did not look to theology and metaphysics, however,

14. In a fascinating book, Hillel Schwartz has documented, through newspaper articles, popular magazines, personal letters, sermons, graduation speeches, and much more, the strikingly optimistic attitude that captivated much of Western civilization at the close of the nineteenth and at the dawning of the twentieth century. Like many other commentators, Schwartz paints a picture of late nineteenth- and early twentieth-century civilization obsessed with the promise of the future. Still, he writes, "Classical Liberals, Social Darwinists, Progressives, Syndicalists, Anarchists, Marxists, and Socialists of many stripes had sharp disagreements over present intimations of the future, what could be done to shape it or square oneself with it, and who must be its avant-garde" (Schwartz, *Century's End*, 175).

15. Glover, *Humanity*, 3. On page 6, Glover adds that "at the start of the century there was optimism, coming from the Enlightenment, that the spread of a humane and scientific outlook would lead to the fading away, not only of war, but also of other forms of cruelty and barbarism. They would fill the chamber of horrors in the museum of our primitive past. In the light of these expectations, the century of Hitler, Stalin, Pol Pot and Saddam Hussein was likely to be a surprise. Volcanoes thought extinct turned out not to be."

16. The French Revolution, in particular, inspired several social movements that were intended to replace the old organic society of the Middle Ages. Charles Fourier formulated a plan for a kind of utopian civilization built around small communities of

as a foundation for modern European society. Rather they embraced the Enlightenment's turn to the subject, in the spirit of Descartes's *cogito ergo sum*, and endeavored to make a new society, built upon the methods of empirical science and the moral capacity intrinsic to human nature, in which there would be no need for the Christian religion.

The nineteenth was the century of Auguste Comte, Ludwig Feuerbach, Karl Marx, Friedrich Nietzsche, and others.[17] It was a century characterized by a great optimism in the ability of humankind to forge its own destiny unencumbered by the weight of religious authority and superstition. The nineteenth century was the zenith of the great intellectual adventure that began with the European Enlightenment, and its intellectuals had a significant influence on the growing secularization of Europe, on expectations of social progress, and on the increasing marginalization of the church.

In addition to Comte, Feuerbach, Marx, and Nietzsche, all mentioned above, thinkers such as John Stewart Mill, Charles Darwin, Bertrand Russell, George Bernard Shaw, and many others had a profound influence on the increasing secularization of Western civilization. According to Jean Lacroix, in the nineteenth century "the storm of atheism . . . burst upon the history of humanity. This atheism is both absolute and positive; absolute, for it truly denies God himself; positive, for it is an authentic anti-theism. It is an atheism which demands total commitment, and which would change the face of the earth. It appears as

---

about 1800 persons each. For the most complete account of his teachings, see Fourier, *Le Nouveau Monde Industriel Sociétaire*. Another important figure was Claude Henri de Rouvroy de Saint-Simon, founder of Saint-Simonism, who sought to "restore social and political order by rebuilding society on the basis of a scientific truth (reduction of the whole body of science to the Newtonian law of gravitation) as well as of a religious truth (the Christian law of charity understood as a purely natural truth)" (Gilson et al., *Recent Philosophy*, 266). Saint-Simon's complete works have been published along with the works of his successor, Enfantin, as follows: Saint-Simon, *Oeuvres de Saint-Simon et d'Enfantin*.

17. Nietzsche may seem out of place in this list, since he was highly critical of the modernist spirit and certainly did not share the optimistic view of history that characterized so much late nineteenth-century thought. Nevertheless his atheism, like that of the other thinkers mentioned, was influential in various ways during the twentieth century. For his treatment of Nietzsche, see de Lubac, *Drama of Atheist Humanism*, parts 3 and 4.

a radical humanism, as a tremendous effort on man's part to possess his humanity completely."[18]

Indeed, all of the above-mentioned thinkers had in common a confidence in human nature. They placed all hope for the future in humanity's ability to take control, to improve society, and to achieve intellectual and moral self-mastery. Although it would be unfair to exaggerate the direct influence of these atheist humanists on the average European during the late nineteenth and early twentieth centuries, there is good reason to believe that the above-mentioned figures were able to make explicit a pervasive cultural élan. In their philosophical works thinkers such as Comte, Feuerbach, Marx, and Nietzsche articulated and influenced a common spirit of the age. De Lubac makes a similar observation in the preface to his *The Drama of Atheist Humanism* (1944):

> Contemporary atheism is increasingly positive, organic, constructive. Combining a mystical immanentism with a clear perception of the human trend, it has three principal aspects which can be symbolized by three names: Auguste Comte, Ludwig Feuerbach (who must share the honor with his disciple, Karl Marx) and Friedrich Nietzsche. Through a number of intermediaries, and with a number of accretions, admixtures and, in many cases, distortions, the doctrines of these three nineteenth-century thinkers are, even today, the inspiration of three philosophies of life (social and political as well as individual) that all exercise a powerful attraction. . . . Positivism is an immense edifice of scientific philosophy and practical politics; that Marxism, which has received its Summa if not its Bible in *Das Kapital*, is a vast and powerful system of political and social economy; and that Nietzsche's ideas offer an extraordinary profusion of pedagogic resources (in the profoundest sense of the term).[19]

In *The Drama of Atheist Humanism* (1944) de Lubac engages the reigning secular philosophies head-on in order to expose their inherent nihilism. He writes in the preface of *The Drama* that positivist humanism, Marxist humanism, and Nietzschean humanism have a "common foun-

18. Lacroix, *Meaning of Modern Atheism*, 31.

19. De Lubac, *Drama of Atheist Humanism*, 11–12. John Milbank, who has expressed great admiration for the work of de Lubac, has also focused a great deal of attention on the need for a theological engagement with atheism and particularly with secular social theory. See Milbank, *Theology and Social Theory*. For a recently revised edition, see Milbank, *Theology and Social Theory*, 2nd edition.

dation in the rejection of God [that] is matched by a certain similarity in results, the chief of which is the annihilation of the human person."[20] The nineteenth century's most influential atheist philosophers, it seems, were compelled to reject the Christian faith because of a conviction that humankind is oppressed, held back, and negated by such faith.

The irony, according to de Lubac, is that the experience of late nineteenth- and early twentieth-century Europeans suggests the opposite. Having witnessed, several decades earlier, the devastation of "the Great War" and writing in the midst of the Nazi terror of World War II, de Lubac suggests that "the 'death of God' was bound to have fatal repercussions. Thus we are confronted with what Nicholas Berdyaev . . . has rightly called 'the self-destruction of humanism.' We are proving by experience that 'where there is no God, there is no man either.'"[21]

For de Lubac, when we view the world from an atheistic perspective, humankind loses all value and meaning.[22] Regarding the work of figures like Comte, Feuerbach, Marx, and Nietzsche, he asks:

> What has actually become of the lofty ambitions of this humanism, not only in fact but in the very way of thought of its initiates? What has become of man as conceived by this atheist humanism? A being that can still hardly be called a 'being'—a thing that has no content, a cell completely merged in a mass that is in process of becoming: 'social-and-historical man,' of whom all that remains is pure abstraction, apart from the social relations and the position in time by which he is defined. There is no stability or depth left in him, and it is no good looking for any inviolable retreat there or claiming to discover any value exacting universal respect. There is nothing to prevent his being used as material or as a tool either for the preparation of some future society or for ensuring, here and now, the dominance of one privileged group. There is not even anything to prevent his being cast aside as useless.[23]

20. De Lubac, *Drama of Atheist Humanism*, 12.

21. Ibid., 65. In statements such as this, the affinity between de Lubac and Radical Orthodoxy is obvious. Indeed Milbank and the others should be commended for emphasizing and rejecting the nihilism of secularism and for insisting that theology should combat it aggressively. See Milbank, et al., *Radical Orthodoxy*, 1–20.

22. For a recent work arguing that the world can have value and meaning in a universe without God, see Wielenberg, *Value and Virtue*.

23. De Lubac, *Drama of Atheist Humanism*, 66.

De Lubac wrote these lines not long after the Communist Revolution in Russia and at the height of the Jewish Holocaust in Western Europe. There was a clear and obvious connection, in his mind, between nineteenth-century atheist humanism and twentieth-century European totalitarianism. With regard to the lasting influence of Comte, for example, he suggests, "the positivist formula spells total tyranny." "Auguste Comte," he explains, "the worshipper of Humanity, profoundly misjudged human nature."[24] The same, of course, is true of Feuerbach, Marx, and Nietzsche who, in their attempts to rescue and redeem humankind, achieve only a negation.[25]

De Lubac claims that in contrast to the various atheist philosophies described above, authentic Christianity offers a vision and way of life that is truly humanistic.[26] Christianity and not atheist humanism understands human nature most profoundly and offers the ultimate and only lasting hope for humankind.[27] Ironically, in the early twentieth century, the social, political, and individual lives of Europeans were perhaps influenced to a greater degree by these "philosophies of life" than they were by the Catholic faith. Whether Marx and Communist Revolution in Russia, Comte and L' Action française in France, or hope for a distorted kind of Nietzschean overman in Nazi Germany, the influence of atheist humanism was profound and tragic.[28] Yet a godless humanism seems to have been the preferred option in early twentieth-century Europe. Science and technological innovation appeared then, as they do now, to offer endless possibilities for individual and social improvement. Thus the hopes and dreams of modern people were wedded to the promises of an emerging

24. Ibid., 263–67.

25. Ibid., 70–71.

26. In describing the "spiritual battle" between Christianity and atheist humanism, de Lubac suggests that "Christianity must be given back its strength in us, which means, first and foremost, that we must rediscover it as it is in itself, in its purity and its authenticity" (Ibid., 127).

27. Here again we see the affinity between de Lubac and Radical Orthodoxy, which insists that "every discipline must be framed by a theological perspective; otherwise these disciplines will define a zone apart from God, grounded literally in nothing" (Milbank, et al., *Radical Orthodoxy*, 3).

28. It is well known that Nietzsche's *Thus Spoke Zarathustra* was a favorite of Hitler's. Hitler distorted Nietzsche's vision of an overman in support of his own Aryan agenda, and Nietzsche's vision of a unified Europe was distorted in support of Nazi military campaigns. For more on this subject, see Aschheim, *Nietzsche Legacy in Germany*. Also see Golomb and Wistrich, *Nietzsche*.

technological civilization.[29] For this reason, the calamity of world wars, revolutions, and mass genocide created a profound emotional and intellectual crisis for many.

In light of the violence and devastation witnessed in early twentieth-century Europe, technological utopia and human self-mastery seem to have been an illusion, but where else could persons look for answers to the social ills plaguing modern industrial civilization? Why not the Church? According to de Lubac, the Catholic Church was ill prepared to offer the gospel as an alternative to atheist humanism because it had retreated into a kind of spiritual ghetto. In the words of Joseph Komonchak, early twentieth-century Catholicism was in exile.[30]

CATHOLIC RESPONSE TO ATHEIST HUMANISM

The atheist humanism described above was inspired by the vacuum created with the collapse of the old order in the eighteenth century, and especially in the wake of the French Revolution. The collapse of the old order also forced the Catholic Church to redefine itself in opposition to the various trends of secularization. Indeed, all the pontiffs of the nineteenth century, whether major or minor, had to contend with Catholicism's increasing loss of temporal authority and with the growing threats of liberalism, materialism, socialism, and atheism in general.[31]

---

29. Notably, of all the philosophers mentioned above, Nietzsche is the least enthralled with the promise of science and technology. For Nietzsche, "science is not a finished and impersonal system" whose truths can be mastered and technologically applied in order to overcome societal problems. Rather, Nietzsche believed that science is a "passionate quest for knowledge . . . a way of life" not recently discovered and incapable of improving, fundamentally, human nature (Kaufmann, *Nietzsche*, 68–69, 111).

30. Komonchak, "Theology and Culture at Mid-Century," 579–602.

31. The atheist humanism that swept Europe in the nineteenth century was merely the latest in a long line of challenges to Catholicism's once authoritative role in European society. For many nineteenth-century Catholics, the process of European secularization had moved through three decisive stages: "beginning with Christian heresy in the Reformation, next as developing into a secular philosophy with the Enlightenment, and finally as mobilizing a revolt of the masses in the French revolution and in its subsequent ideological expansion throughout Western Europe" (Holland, *Modern Catholic Social Teaching*, 33). Cf. Maritain, *Three Reformers*.

The Collapse of the Ancien Régime

At the beginning of the nineteenth century, Catholic resistance to secularization came as a response to the French Revolution and its aftermath. During the Revolution, the papacy hoped that the problem of liberalism would be limited to France and thus did very little to oppose it. Indeed, there was broad support for many bourgeois causes among the French clergy prior to the revolution, but when the new government drafted the Civil Constitution of the Clergy, which made "the French Catholic Church a division of the French government," tensions between the Church and the state in France intensified.[32] Although many French clergy and laity had long embraced Gallicanism,[33] the changes made in the aftermath of the revolution led to an increase in loyalty to the papacy for many Catholics.

Consequently French Catholicism became increasingly associated with the counterrevolution movement, and this led to anticlerical persecution and the execution, imprisonment, and exile of thousands of clergy. The persecution continued until Napoleon signed a concordat with Pope Pius VII in 1801 recognizing that Catholicism was "the religion of the great majority of the French people."[34] The concordat guaranteed salaries for clergy and gave the pope the right to remove bishops, a right that popes did not have in the Gallican era of the *ancien régime*. This agreement became a model for relations between the Catholic Church and secular governments in the nineteenth century, and it had several important consequences. Namely, as governments became increasingly secular, ecclesial authority was moved in the direction of the papacy, thus establishing a trend towards the Ultramontanism that would flourish later in

32. Holland, *Modern Catholic Social Teaching*, 37.

33. Gallicanism was a French tradition of resistance to papal authority and control. Beginning in the seventeenth century, French clergy claimed that local bishops had greater authority in local matters than the pope did. Advocates of Gallicanism preferred a conciliarist approach in matters of Catholic authority and tended to support the sovereignty of local princes and nobles in secular matters. In addition to French Gallicanism, there was a tradition of Josephinism in Austria, which began when Emperor Joseph II worked to subordinate the Church to his own imperial authority. For a concise treatment of the Catholic Church–state developments that began with the Reformation, see McCool, *Nineteenth-Century Scholasticism*, 21–23.

34. Holland, *Modern Catholic Social Teaching*, 38.

the century.[35] Moreover, the papacy became increasingly bureaucratic, mirroring the developing independent nation-states and interacting with sovereign nations through diplomatic processes.

With the continuing spread of liberalism throughout Europe, the papacy embraced the Congress of Vienna (1814–1815), which was essentially a "reactionary counterattack by means of a continental coalition attempting to restore the Old Regime."[36] The *ancien régime* was an aristocratic system of the prerevolutionary period within which clergy and nobility controlled all of society with an authority founded upon a highly developed theological/metaphysical understanding of reality.[37] With the Congress of Vienna, Austria's Prince Metternich endeavored to restore the *ancien régime* by force, installing the Bourbon monarchy in France and supporting monarchical rule in Austria, Prussia, Russia, and Great Britain.[38] However, the rise of liberalism could not be held back, and a wave of revolutions swept Europe in 1830. As Eric Hobsbawm explains:

> The revolutionary wave of 1830 . . . marks the definitive defeat of aristocratic by bourgeois power in Western Europe. The ruling class of the next fifty years was to be the "grande bourgeoisie" of bankers, big industrialists, and sometimes top civil servants, accepted by an aristocracy which effaced itself or agreed to promote primarily bourgeois policies, unchallenged as yet by universal suffrage.[39]

---

35. The word *Ultramontanism* comes from Latin and means literally, "beyond the mountains." The term is used to describe a nineteenth-century Catholic movement that took place in France, Germany, Spain, and England—all countries for whom Rome was "beyond the mountains (the Alps)." The movement worked for the consolidation of power in the papacy as a way to combat liberalism as well as atheistic philosophical and scientific trends. With the anti-clericalism that followed the French Revolution, and with the growing problem of nation states stripping power away from the church, the Ultramontanist movement became quite popular and was influential in the development of papal primacy and infallibility at Vatican Council I. For more on Ultramontanism, see Von Arx, *Varieties of Ultramontanism*.

36. Holland, *Modern Catholic Social Teaching*, 33.

37. For a concise treatment of the *ancient regime* (a term used only after the French Revolution), see Doyle, *Ancien Regime*. For a more thorough treatment, see Goubert, *Ancien Régime*.

38. Holland, *Modern Catholic Social Teaching*, 40.

39. Hobsbawm, *Age of Revolution*, 139.

Although the restorations of Prince Metternich were maintained temporarily in the Austrian Empire and in the papal states, the triumph of liberalism was secured fully with the revolutions of 1848 and with the loss of the papal States in 1870. At this point, "the papacy retreated to the spiritual ghetto of a religious counterculture."[40]

Interestingly, the decline of papal authority and influence in European secular affairs was accompanied by a consolidation of ecclesial power in the papacy. Gerald McCool suggests that "to make up for its weakened diplomatic and political position in relation to the national governments the Holy See began to play a more direct and aggressive role in the political and intellectual life of the individual national Churches than it had played under the *ancien régime*."[41] This more active role was perceived as a necessary approach in order to preserve Catholic unity in the face of increasing state influence in areas such as charitable service and education. As Joe Holland explains:

> As . . . ultramontanism became the all-embracing papal strategy, the Western Catholic Church was pressured by Vatican officials to become ever more Roman. Just as the Vatican bureaucracy had gained control over the episcopacy, so now it sought a standardized Roman model for all of Western Catholicism. The papal bureaucracy promoted a standardized Roman liturgy in the name of liturgical reform and the training of future bishops in Roman seminaries. It also promoted Roman devotions like Forty Hours, Roman clerical dress, expansion of Roman colleges for foreign seminarians, and extensive granting among priests of the Roman clerical title monsignor (an honorary aristocratic appellation meaning "my lord," a title normally used at the time for aristocrats, including aristocratic bishops).[42]

The papacy also became increasingly involved in setting the direction of Catholic theology in the universities and seminaries. The French Revolution and the Napoleonic Wars had left Catholic institutions in shambles, and this was particularly devastating in relation to the education of clergy. Accordingly, at the beginning of the nineteenth century, Catholic philosophy and theology were characterized by a quite diverse

40. Holland, *Modern Catholic Social Teaching*, 33.

41. McCool, *Nineteenth-Century Scholasticism*, 25.

42. Holland, *Modern Catholic Social Teaching*, 53.

set of options.[43] According to James Hennesey, "Eclecticism prevailed,"[44] since many Catholics had been influenced by Enlightenment thought, and there was no authoritative voice insisting upon unity. Thus the thought of John Locke was taught in a number of French Jesuit schools. Likewise "Cartesianism had a wide following, and so did traditionalism and fideism growing out of romanticism." German theologians, by contrast, were often heavily influenced by "rationalism and historical method," and Ontologism was popular at Louvain in France as well as in Italy under the direction of Gioberti and Rosmini. It was only in Spain among the Dominicans that the thought of Thomas Aquinas was taught with enthusiasm.[45] This widespread disunity resulted in a large number of theological disputes, and the papacy became increasingly active in resolving them. McCool explains that the papacy,

> beginning with the pontificate of Gregory XVI, began to play a dominant role in the internal direction of Catholic theology through a series of disciplinary decrees and formal condemnations. The direction of speculative theology and the pursuit of the Holy See's political designs were increasingly united in the papal response to the intellectual and political challenges to the pope's authority during the embattled pontificate of Pius IX. Rome intervened in almost every serious theological controversy during

43. Fitzpatrick, "Neoscholasticism," 838–51.

44. Hennesey, "Leo XIII's Thomistic Revival," 190.

45. Ibid. McCool has also written on the disunity of early nineteenth-century Catholic thought. He explains: "During the Catholic renaissance after the French Revolution, the philosophy taught in the Catholic schools of France, Belgium, and Italy was of two kinds. There was that associated with Felicite Robert de Lammennais (1782–1854), Joseph Maistre (1752–1821), or Joseph Bonald (1754–1840), whose characteristic thinking is sometimes called "traditionalism." This was a reaction to eighteenth century rationalism and it stressed the importance of faith as opposed to reason. Secondly, there was the approach associated with Vincenzo Gioberti (1801–1852) or Antonio Rosmini (1797–1855), commonly called "ontologism." This claimed its ancestry in the writings of Plato and Augustine and held that all human knowledge implies an immediate intuition of uncreated Truth (i.e. God). The resurgent Catholic theology in Germany during the first half of the century looked to Post-Kantian idealism rather than to traditional scholasticism for its philosophical resources. Even in the Society of Jesus (the Jesuits), after its restoration in 1814, scholastic philosophy did not make an immediate return, and, as late as 1850, the General of the Jesuits, John Roothan, complained to the Provincial of Lyons about the ontologism being taught to students of his Province" (McCool, *Neo-Thomists*, 25).

the nineteenth century, and in almost every case, the intervention was influenced by the Church-state tensions.[46]

Aeterni Patris and the Neoscholastic Revival

Roman intervention in matters relating to the direction of Catholic theology reached a new height with the papacy of Leo XIII, who "wanted . . . to realize ultramontane goals unrealized under Pius IX by intellectualizing the combat with modernity, by providing a theoretical underpinning for his policies." Leo XIII sought to "restore in the world an objective and immutable order, with the church as its most effective guardian. Renewal of Thomistic philosophy was the tool essential to his purpose."[47]

By the middle of the nineteenth century, already a number of Catholic theological centers were advocating a revival of the teachings of Thomas Aquinas. In Spain, Jaime Balmes and Ceferino Gonzalez were influential Thomists, while Joseph Kleutgen and Matthias Scheeben taught in Germany. Maurice D'Hulst was an important French contributor to the movement, and Vincenzo Buzzetti inspired a Thomistic revival in Italy. The revolutions of 1848 and the loss of the papal States in 1870 provided the movement heightened momentum, and a Jesuit journal, La civiltà cattolica, was "founded with the expressed purpose of restoring in the modern world the role played by the church in medieval Christendom." The journal's orientation was decidedly Thomistic.[48]

The revival that Vincenzo Buzzetti began in Italy was influential and attracted a number of important disciples, including the bishop of Perugia, Cardinal Gioacchino Pecci. Cardinal Pecci offered a "Lenten charge" in 1877 through which he made three suggestions for "the restoration of society: (1) only reintegration of religious values will correct social ills; (2) natural law is the foundation of civil morality and power; and (3) the church is the indispensable guarantor of this power and judge of its extension and limits."[49] When Cardinal Pecci became Pope Leo XIII the following year, he embarked on an aggressive program to apply his

46. McCool, Nineteenth-Century Scholasticism, 26.

47. Hennesey, "Leo XIII's Thomistic Revival," 190.

48. Ibid., 191. For a more thorough treatment of the history of Leo XIII's Thomistic revival, see Aubert, "Aspects Divers," 133–227.

49. Hennesey, "Leo XIII's Thomistic Revival," 192. Cf. Thibault, Savoir et Pouvoir, 138–39.

Lenten suggestions to the entire Catholic Church. His first step, which came only a week after his election, was to make the writings of Thomas Aquinas a mandatory part of the curriculum at the Apollinare Seminary in Rome.

Similar pressure was exerted in other Roman schools, such as the Urban College of the Propaganda and especially at the Gregorian University in Rome, where the influential Thomistic scholar Joseph Kleutgen was put in charge of studies.[50] This "Roman revival" was expanded to include the entire Catholic Church when Leo XIII gave his famous encyclical, *Aeterni Patris* (August 4, 1879). The encyclical is unambiguous in its assertion that a philosophical revival is necessary to cure social ills. The second paragraph suggests that

> Whoso turns his attention to the bitter strifes of these days and seeks a reason for the troubles that vex public and private life must come to the conclusion that a fruitful cause of the evils which now afflict, as well as those which threaten us, lies in this: that false conclusions concerning divine and human things, which originated in the schools of philosophy, have now crept into all the orders of the State, and have been accepted by the common consent of the masses. For since it is in the very nature of man to follow the guide of his reason in his actions, if his intellect sins at all his will soon follows; and thus it happens that false opinions, whose seat is in the understanding, influence human actions and pervert them.[51]

When Leo XIII speaks of the "evils of society," his remarks are directed especially at the problems of socialism, communism, and nihilism, and he believes these to be a direct consequence of antitheistic philosophy that denies the Church its authority.[52] These "deadly plague[s], creeping

---

50. Hennesey, "Leo XIII's Thomistic Revival," 192.

51. Leo XIII, *Aeterni Patris*, 17.

52. Leo XIII's first encyclical, *Inscrutabili Dei Consilio* (April 1878), specifically addressed what he called the "evils of society" and claimed that "the source of these evils lies chiefly, We are convinced, in this, that the holy and venerable authority of the Church, which in God's name rules mankind, upholding and defending all lawful authority, has been despised and set aside" (*Papal Encyclicals*, 2:5). In his second encyclical, *Quod Apostolici Muneris* (December 1878), Leo XIII identifies the source of society's ills as "socialists, communists, or nihilists" (*Papal Encyclicals*, 2:11).

into the very fibers of human society,"[53] he writes, are born of secular philosophies divorced from Christian theology.

Aeterni Patris was, in a sense, a call for the Catholic Church to engage in the difficult work of apologetics. Indeed, it charges Catholics with "the duty of religiously defending the truths divinely delivered, and of resisting those who dare oppose them."[54] For Leo XIII and the scholastics who helped him draft *Aeterni Patris*, the philosophy of St. Thomas employs natural reason in order to prove and justify the claims of Christian revelation. Thomistic philosophy is thus a "handmaid to revealed truth."[55] According to Leo XIII, human reason is prone to error if it is not supported by faith. "Faith," he writes, "frees and saves reason from error, and endows it with manifold knowledge." On the other hand, "philosophy, if rightly made use of by the wise, in a certain way tends to smooth and fortify the road to true faith, and to prepare the souls of its disciples for the fit reception of revelation."[56]

Philosophy also serves theology by helping it to "assume the nature, form, and genius of a true science. For in this, the most noble of studies, it is of the greatest necessity to bind together, as it were, in one body the many and various parts of the heavenly doctrines, that, each being allotted to its own proper place and derived from its own proper principles, the whole may join together in a complete union."[57] Philosophy and theology (reason and faith), for Leo XIII, are thus separate but complementary, and no figure in the history of the Church has been more successful in wedding them together than the Angelic Doctor, Thomas Aquinas. Leo continues in *Aeterni Patris*, explaining that Thomas Aquinas, "clearly distinguishing, as is fitting, reason from faith, while happily associating the one with the other . . . , both preserved the rights and had regard for the dignity of each; so much so, indeed, that reason, borne on the wings of Thomas to its human height, can scarcely rise higher, while faith could

53. Ibid.

54. Leo XIII, *Aeterni Patris*, 19.

55. McCool, *From Unity to Pluralism*, 7.

56. Leo XIII, *Aeterni Patris*, 20.

57. Ibid., 19. What it means exactly to call theology a science becomes an important question in mid-twentieth century Catholic theology. I'll return to this question several times in the pages and chapters that follow.

scarcely expect more or stronger aids from reason than those which she has already obtained through Thomas."[58]

Because Thomas offers the greatest approach to joining philosophy and theology, and because he is "the chief and master" of all the "scholastic doctors," Leo XIII called on the clergy to "furnish a generous and copious supply to studious youth of those crystal rills of wisdom flowing in a never-ending and fertilizing stream from the fountainhead of the Angelic Doctor." "We exhort you" he continues, "in all earnestness to restore the golden wisdom of St. Thomas and to spread it far and wide for the defense and beauty of the Catholic faith, for the good of society. . . . [which is] exposed to great danger from this plague of perverse opinions." Society, he explains "would certainly enjoy a far more peaceful and secure existence if a more wholesome doctrine were taught in the academies and schools—one more in conformity with the teaching of the Church, such as is contained in the works of Thomas Aquinas."[59]

According to McCool, the Catholic bishops responded to the recommendations of *Aeterni Patris* positively.[60] The social ills described in the encyclical were problems that most Catholics acknowledged, and the lack of a unified philosophical response to the various secular and atheistic philosophies associated with, for instance, socialism and communism, was a frustration. Accordingly, the Thomistic revival that had begun slowly in the early nineteenth century gained a great deal of momentum after 1879.

The Thomism that emerged in the immediate wake of *Aeterni Patris*, especially in Rome, was a coherent and closed system of philosophy and theology intended to provide the Catholic truth in opposition to the systems of modern secular thinkers.[61] In the words of William Eric Brown, neoscholasticism in the last decades of the nineteenth century was

---

58. Ibid., 23.

59. Ibid., 25.

60. McCool, *The Neo-Thomists*, 35.

61. Some of de Lubac's most important and most controversial works criticized neo-Thomists for what he perceived as their failure to appropriate the thought of Aquinas properly. See especially de Lubac, *Surnaturel*. This early, highly controversial work was revised and published later as de Lubac, *Augustinisme et Théologie Moderne*. It was accompanied by a companion volume, de Lubac, *Le Mystère du Surnaturel*. Chapter 4 of the present work will explain the thesis of these works and discuss the neo-Thomistic response to them.

a close-knit system of metaphysics leading up to arguments to demonstrate the existence of God, while in theology the dogmas were articulated to a coherent scheme of the relations of man to God, and the reasonable grounds of each of them, of analogy or suitability, were developed. The instrument of enquiry was Aristotelian logic, and the structural completeness and intellectual beauty of Thomism gave its students confidence in that instrument as great as that of scientists in their own methods.[62]

From 1879 until the end of the nineteenth century, neoscholasticism changed very little. It was above all a "clerical enterprise," and the books that were produced were principally school manuals designed to offer a clear and systematic exposition of revealed scholastic doctrines. Their purpose was not "the stimulation of original thought."[63] Thomas O'Meara explains that neoscholastic theology was

An austere linking of clear abstract terms in Latin propositions . . . [which] avoided coming too close to Scripture or to any particular theologian. . . . Its ability to inspire Christian life or to address concrete moral issues was limited. . . . Christian teaching was a timeless metaphysics . . . [in which] every facet of ecclesiastical thinking and life had its place.[64]

However, as a number of scholars have pointed out, the Thomistic revival that followed *Aeterni Patris* did not succeed in establishing a totally unified approach in Catholic philosophy. McCool explains that "when the Society of Jesus returned to the Angelic Doctor, most Jesuits, although not all, did so as Suarezians; and Franciscans could feel that Bonaventure and Scotus, as Scholastic Doctors, were representative of the common scholastic tradition."[65] Alasdair MacIntyre makes the same point when he suggests that although Leo XIII had intended a singular and integrated Thomistic revival, "what he succeeded in generating were a number of different and rival Thomisms."[66] MacIntyre contends that a diversity of Thomisms arose in the years after *Aeterni Patris* because of

---

62. Brown, *Catholic Church in South Africa*, 278.

63. McCool, *Neo-Thomists*, 38.

64. O'Meara, *Church and Culture: German Catholic Theology*, 189–90.

65. McCool, *Neo-Thomists*, 39.

66. MacIntyre, *Three Rival Versions of Moral Enquiry*, 73.

Joseph Kleutgen's strong influence both on the drafting of *Aeterni Patris* and on the Scholastic revival that followed.

Although Kleutgen was correct to see that a breach had taken place in the Western philosophical tradition that separated the ancients from the moderns, he "mislocated the rupture" and failed to see that Thomas's "immediate successors" were not able to overcome "the limitations of previous Augustinianism and previous Aristotelianism" in the same way that the Angelic Doctor had. Kleutgen mistakenly identified the thought of the later Scholastics, and especially Francisco Suarez, with the thought of Aquinas, when in fact Suarez "was already a distinctively modern thinker, perhaps more authentically than Descartes."[67] Because he assumed that Suarez was faithful to the thought of Aquinas, Kleutgen failed to see that his own philosophical work was more indebted to Suarez than it was to Thomas. This is evident in light of the fact that Kleutgen tended, following Suarez, "to make epistemological concerns central" to his philosophical system in ways that Aquinas never did.[68]

MacIntyre contends that the emphasis on epistemology in Thomistic philosophy after *Aeterni Patris* "doomed Thomism to the fate of all philosophies which give priority to epistemological questions: the indefinite multiplication of disagreement."[69] According to MacIntyre,

> Thomism, by epistemologizing itself after *Aeterni Patris*, proceeded to reenact the disagreements of post-Cartesian philosophy. Thus there were generated in turn a number of systematic Thomisms, each in contention *both* with whatever particular erroneous tendencies in modern secular philosophical thought *that* particular Thomism aspired to confront and overcome *and* with its Thomistic rivals. Often enough these two kinds of contest were closely connected. So Maréchal . . . made out of Aquinas a rival and a corrector of Kant, the work of interpretation being inseparable from that of philosophical apologetics. So Rousselot in very different fashion responded to the French academic philosophy of his day, producing a correspondingly different view of Aquinas. And so Maritain at a later date would formulate what he mistakenly took to be a Thomistic defense of the doctrine of human rights enshrined in the United Nations Declaration of Human Rights, a quixotic attempt to present Thomas as offering a

67. Ibid.
68. Ibid., 75.
69. Ibid.

rival and superior account of the same moral subject matter as do other modern nontheological doctrines.[70]

Thus rather than producing a single, unified Christian philosophy to combat the reigning secular philosophies of the day, the late nineteenth-century Thomistic revival produced several divergent Thomisms that combated each other as much as they did any secular or atheistic philosophical system. This is not to suggest, however, that the Thomistic revival was a failure. On the contrary, Leo XIII can be credited with inspiring a much more energetic Catholic engagement with secular thought, and the development of the systematic Thomisms of Rousselot, Maréchal, and Maritain in the twentieth century, combined with the historical Thomisms of Gilson, Chenu, and others, confirms that the Thomistic revival bore much fruit.

More important still is the fact that the primary goal of the revival sought by Leo XIII was social rather than epistemological. It must be remembered that his *Aeterni Patris* (itself intended as a response to the social consequences of secular philosophies) was preceded by *Inscrutabili Dei Consilio* and *Quod Apostolici Muneris* (two encyclicals devoted exclusively to addressing social ills) and was followed by a number of social encyclicals, including four on politics (*Diuturnum*, 1881; *Immortale Dei* 1885; *Libertas*, 1888; and *Sapientiae Christianae*, 1890) and his famous *Rerum Novarum* of 1891, which addressed the conditions of labor and the plight of the working poor.[71] When combined with his sustained efforts to address the social problems of modern secular society, Leo XIII's Thomistic revival must be credited with inspiring not only a more energetic engagement with secular thought, but a more energetic engagement with secular society in general.

Joe Holland suggests that the ultimate aim of the Leonine revival, which continued largely unchanged in the pontificates of Pius X and Pius XI, was to restore the old Christian civilization "with modifications adapted to the new bourgeois context."[72] Significantly, unlike his immedi-

70. Ibid., 76.

71. Beginning with Leo XIII, papal encyclicals became a more-frequent tool for pontiffs to direct the cultural and intellectual life of the Catholic Church. See Komonchak, "Enlightenment and the Construction of Roman Catholicism," 44–46.

72. Holland, *Modern Catholic Social Teaching*, 198. Joseph Komonchak explains that, during this period, "the Catholic Church constructed a new sociological form in which to give expression to its ancient Christianity. While in many respects, this Roman

ate predecessors, Leo XIII went beyond simply condemning modernism and liberalism. Indeed, taken together, his encyclicals offered a sweeping vision for a positive new relationship between the Catholic Church and modern secular society. According to Holland, the Leonine strategy had three basic elements. First, bishops and clergy were to promote "the hierarchically organic teachings of Thomism as the philosophical ground for church and society." [73] Bishops and clergy were charged with the responsibility "to teach and to educate men." [74] The content of this teaching was the close-knit metaphysical system of the Latin manuals, such as those used at the Gregorian University in Rome and elsewhere. The pope believed that the theological truths supported by neoscholastic philosophy, if they were accepted by all, would unite the various classes "in the bonds of friendship, but also in those of brotherly love. For they will understand and feel that all men are children of the same common Father, who is God; that all have alike the same last end, which is God Himself, who alone can make either men or angels absolutely and perfectly happy." [75] The neoscholastics, according to the Leonine strategy, had a part to play in the intended social renewal by clearly and systematically articulating the truths of Thomism and offering apologetic arguments in the service of epistemological justification.

The second element of the Leonine strategy was to offer "external diplomatic acceptance of moderately liberal democratic regimes and careful internal pastoral mobilization of lay Catholics to pressure these regimes in the direction of Catholic teaching." [76] Unlike his immediate predecessor Pius IX, whose ambition was nothing less than the total restoration of the *ancien régime*, Leo XIII was willing to accept the relative autonomy of liberal democratic states. However, he sought to influence the direction of liberal democracies and to combat the growing threat of state totalitarianism by supporting lay movements intended to safeguard

---

Catholicism had deep roots in earlier periods of history, nevertheless it represented a distinct and specifically modern phenomenon. It differed from the Catholicism of the *ancien régime*, of the Counter-Reformation, and of medieval Christendom, at least as much as each of these differed from its predecessors" (Komonchak, "Ecclesial and Cultural Roles of Theology," 16).

73. Holland, *Modern Catholic Social Teaching*, 197.

74. Pope Leo XIII, *Rerum Novarum*, 248.

75. Ibid., 247.

76. Holland, *Modern Catholic Social Teaching*, 197.

Catholic piety. During the pontificates of Leo XIII's successors Pius X, Benedict XV, and Pius XI, Catholic lay movements blossomed throughout Europe and in North America.[77]

The final element of the Leonine strategy involved a commitment by the Vatican to support workers' rights, unions, and limited governmental policies designed to provide the working class with "moderate social-welfare" programs.[78] This strategy was employed through diplomatic concordances much like the one worked out with Napoleon Bonaparte in the early nineteenth century. When compared with his predecessor Pius IX, Leo seems remarkably progressive, the first pope to have finally come to terms with the revolution of 1789. However, the political climate in France was consistently hostile toward the Catholic Church, and when a law was passed in 1905 "which sought to place French Catholicism under the control of the government and thereby sever it from Vatican authority,"[79] Leo's successor Pius X (1903–1914) could not help but fear the eventual "full-scale suppression of the Church."[80] According to William Bosworth, "Pius X reigned at the blackest hour for the French Church," and although he continued to deny that French republicanism and Catholicism were inherently contradictory, he set French Catholicism on a more hostile course with the French republic and condemned the only truly significant democratic Catholic organization in France, the Sillon.[81]

Leo XIII's more conciliatory policy toward secular democratic states was revived with the papacies of Benedict XV (1914–1922) and Pius XI

77. Among the many movements that flourished during this time, some of the more popular were the National Council of Catholic Men and Women, the Confraternity of Christian Doctrine (CCD), the Sodality of the Blessed Virgin, Serra International, the Catholic Interracial Councils, as well as a host of independent movements like the Catholic Worker and the Christian Family Movement. See Komonchak, "Enlightenment and the Construction of Roman Catholicism," 41–42. For a comprehensive overview of the political and ecclesial climate of early twentieth-century France, including a thorough treatment of Catholic Action, see Bosworth, *Catholicism and Crisis in Modern France*.

78. Holland, *Modern Catholic Social Teaching*, 197. The pontiff suggests that "the most important of all are workingmen's unions" (Leo XIII, *Rerum Novarum*, 253).

79. Arnal, "Why the French Christian Democrats Were Condemned," 192.

80. Bosworth, *Catholicism and Crisis in Modern France*, 18.

81. Arnal, "Why the French Christian Democrats Were Condemned," 189. See also Bosworth, *Catholicism and Crisis in Modern France*, 18–19.

(1922–1939),[82] but with the growing threat of atheistic Communism, Vatican diplomatic efforts in the 1930s and 1940s came increasingly to eschew any political movement with socialist leanings and to offer limited support to fascist regimes, including the one governing Nazi Germany, "in return for promises of governmental cooperation with the papacy to reestablish Christian civilization."[83] Holland explains that

> the fascists had been willing through concordants to grant of-
> ficial status to the Catholic Church in public life, so apparently
> in [Pope Pius XII's] view they provided the legal ground out of
> which Christian civilization could one day be restored and the
> modern world could thereby be healed of its systemic ills. . . .
> Neither liberals nor socialists had been willing even to consider
> such official public restoration, and so, presumably again in his
> view, these other political streams prohibited the restoration of
> Christian civilization and thus prohibited the Christian resolu-
> tion of what he saw as the root crises of modern liberal culture.[84]

In hindsight, the Vatican's diplomatic relationships with fascist regimes were clearly misguided. The initial hope for a reestablishment of "Christian civilization" was squelched as the regimes in Spain, Italy, and Germany committed an increasing number of social atrocities; the Catholic Church was attacked rather than empowered, and an idolatrous nationalism became the prevailing ideology. It seems that the Leonine strategy, though well intentioned, was incapable of restoring a modified, modern version of the *ancien régime*. Despite all of the Vatican's diplomatic efforts, and despite the many lay movements intended to unite citizens "in the bonds of friendship," early twentieth-century European

---

82. Pius XI is famous for, among other things, making public in 1926 Pius X's secret condemnation of the antirepublican French political movement, Action Français. See Bosworth, *Catholicism and Crisis in Modern France*, 32–33.

83. Holland, *Modern Catholic Social Teaching*, 207.

84. Ibid., 215. There have been several book-length studies on the complex relationship between the Vatican and the fascist governments of the mid-twentieth century. There is a great deal of evidence to suggest that both Pius XI and Pius XII made considerable effort to offer refuge to European Jews during the Holocaust, but they also engaged in a highly controversial effort to maintain diplomatic relationships with the governments of Italy and Germany. For a balanced and scholarly investigation, see Rhodes, *Vatican in the Age of the Dictators*. For a more sensational and less scholarly account of Pius XII's diplomatic efforts, see Cornwell, *Hitler's Pope*.

civilization became increasingly secular, and the Catholic Church became increasingly marginalized.

Henri de Lubac's "Apologetics and Theology"

According to Henri de Lubac, the Catholic Church was at least partly responsible for its own increasing marginalization. He believed that neoscholastics had become so focused on epistemological justifications of the Thomist system that they failed to engage directly with the atheistic philosophies having such a strong and dangerous influence on European society.[85] Although beginning with Leo XIII, the Catholic Church had made a concerted effort to influence the direction of European civilization, it was increasingly difficult, especially for laypersons, to understand how the Catholic faith had anything particularly distinctive to contribute to social and political life.

Among the earliest of his works was an article published in 1930, titled "Apologetics and Theology."[86] Originally delivered in 1929 as his inaugural lecture at the Faculté de théologie catholique in Lyon, the article is a call for a reinvigoration of Catholic theology and apologetics, and thus a more earnest engagement with secular thought by Catholic scholars. From de Lubac's perspective, the neoscholastic theology that prevailed after *Aeterni Patris* was too narrow in its outlook and too separated from apologetics. The result of this separation was an extrinsic theology and an apologetics cut off from the content of Christian faith. According to

85. It would be wrong, however, to view de Lubac as opposed to the Leonine revival. Rather, de Lubac's theological program offered one particular way of enacting Leo XIII's vision of a new relationship between Catholicism and culture. Importantly, De Lubac was considered, and considered himself, a Thomist when he began his teaching career. Throughout his life, he always tried to remain faithful to what he believed was an authentic Thomism. He writes in his memoirs: "When I left Jersey (I was then 27 years old), where a Suarezian spirit still reigned, I had been put down severely as a Thomist (of a Thomism, it is true, revitalized by Maréchal and Rousselot). At that time, this was called 'not holding the doctrines of the Society.' I have never renounced that fundamental orientation. I even believe that I have worked (with varying degrees of success) to lead minds back to the authentic Saint Thomas, as to a master considered ever-current" (de Lubac, *At the Service of the Church*, 143–46).

86. De Lubac, "Apologétique et Théologie," 364–65. De Lubac explains that "apart from a few earlier, insignificant lines," *Apologétique et Théologie* "was my first article" (Lubac, *At the Service of the Church*, 15). An English translation of the article, which I will cite in this chapter, appeared in a collection of essays published in 1989. See de Lubac, "Apologetics and Theology."

de Lubac, "the error," for the theologian, "consists in conceiving of dogma as a kind of 'thing in itself,' as a block of revealed truth with no relationship whatsoever to natural man." He believed that Thomistic philosophy had become so specialized and "scientific" that the profoundly humanistic nature of Christian faith was largely unintelligible for the average Catholic citizen.[87]

Clearly de Lubac's criticisms were aimed at the kind of neoscholastic theology contained in the Latin manuals and used widely for the education of clergy. The prevailing neoscholastic approach, he explains, "confines dogma to the extremities of knowledge and, hence, isolates it."[88] In a later article, written during the Second World War, de Lubac compared neoscholastic theology to museum work, suggesting that neoscholastic theologians

> stroll about theology somewhat as if in a museum of which we are the curators, a museum where we have inventoried, arranged and labeled everything; we know how to define all the terms, we have an answer for all objections, we supply the desired distinctions at just the right moment. Everything in it is obscure for the secular, but for us, everything is clear, everything is explained. If there is still a mystery, at least we know exactly where it is to be placed, and we point to this precisely defined site. . . . Thus, for us, theology is a science a bit like the others, with this sole essential difference: its first principles were received through revelation instead of having been acquired through experience or through the work of reason.[89]

87. In an essay critical of the movement, an American neo-Thomist explains the logic of *nouvelle théologie*: "the partisans of this movement are preoccupied with the 'man in the street' as we know him today. He has to be won over to Christ and to the true Church, and yet he has been brought up on the basis of a rationalistic and idealistic philosophy which has effectively sealed his mind against any approach along the old traditional lines. Scholastic philosophy will never make any impression upon him for the simple reason that he does not understand the terms and the concepts which it uses" (Greenstock, "Thomism and the New Theology," 570).

88. De Lubac, "Apologetics and Theology," 93–94.

89. De Lubac, "Internal Causes," 233. It is of course true that Thomas Aquinas called theology (*sacra doctrina*) a science (*scientia*). De Lubac himself regards it as such. See, for example, de Lubac, *Medieval Exegesis*, vol. 1, 27. However, de Lubac is suggesting here that theology does not share the positivist spirit of early twentieth-century natural sciences. It should be noted that during the middle decades of the twentieth century, de Lubac, Henry Bouillard, Gaston Fessard, Jean Daniélou, Marie Dominic Chenu, Yves Congar, Hans Urs von Balthasar, and others were engaged in a heated debate with neoscholastic

With regard to apologetics, de Lubac claimed that Catholic apologists were captivated by "a kind of unavowed rationalism, which had been reinforced for a century by the invasion of positivist tendencies."[90] Although "the apologist" during the heyday of neoscholasticism "was being reduced to a humiliated condition, he was being granted, within narrow limits, an excessive power that was bound to be disappointing."[91] That power was to offer a justification of the Christian faith by means of rational, and purely extrinsic, epistemological argumentation.[92] According to de Lubac, Christian apologists had adopted the rationalism and positivism of the age and embraced "the common prejudice that recognized no certitude or even intelligibility that was not scientific."[93] All the while, apologists had lost sight of the most important "reasons for believing" as they worked tirelessly to prove the factuality of revealed dogma.[94] In de Lubac's view, an extrinsic theology coupled with a scien-

---

scholars over what it means to call theology a *scientia*. For a then-controversial essay that criticized neoscholasticism and made recommendations for a new approach to theology, see Daniélou, "Les Orientations Présentes de la Pensée Religieuse." For an attempt to retrieve an authentically Thomistic understanding of *scientia* in Aquinas, see Chenu, *Is Theology a Science?* For a recent work attempting to correct a perceived misinterpretation in Chenu's understanding of Aquinas's interpretation of Aristotle with regard to *scientia*, see Jenkins, *Knowledge and Faith in Thomas Aquinas.* For the neoscholastic response to Daniélou and others, see Labourdette, "La Thélogie et Ses Sources." For a recent essay describing the historical context of the struggle between *nouvelle théologie* and the neoscholastics, see Nichols, "Thomism and the Nouvelle Théologie." I will return to this controversy throughout the book and attempt to show that de Lubac's theological career was, at least in part, focused on retrieving an authentically thomistic *sacra doctrina* for the Catholic Church.

90. De Lubac, "Apologetics and Theology," 93.

91. Ibid.

92. Körner, "Henri Lubac and Fundamental Theology," 714.

93. Lubac, "Apologetics and Theology," 93–94.

94. "I can only allude here in passage to that concordist apologetic that reigned—let us rather say raged—throughout the nineteenth century and of which many minds are still not completely free today. What effort has been spent to make some particular letter of the biblical account 'agree' with the 'latest state' of science! Under the appearance of triumph, the process had something sheepish about it, and the effort was always in vain, always about to begin again, because the accord was always established within yesterday's scientific theory, or day-before-yesterday's. Above all, this predominance of a wholly external apologetic involved an atmosphere of combat, and, to fight on terrain where one's defeat was assured, any effort at doctrinal penetration was left aside" (De Lubac, "Internal Causes," 227).

tific apologetics falls very far short of the Church's great tradition. Boldly he declared that

> Small-minded theology that is not even traditional, separated theology, tagging behind a separated philosophy – it is no more the theology of the Fathers than it is that of St. Thomas, and the worthless apologetics that it shaped in its image is no closer to the apologetics whose model has been given to us across the centuries: *Speeches and Letters* of St. Paul, Justin's *Apologia*, St. Augustine's *De vera religione*, St. Thomas' *Contra gentes*, Savonarola's *Triumphus Crucis*, Pascal's *Pénsees*.[95]

Against those who would defend such "small-mindedness," de Lubac argued that theology must "constantly maintain apologetical considerations" or become "deficient and distorted." Likewise, in order for apologetics to be authentic and "fully effective," it "must end up in theology."[96] At the heart of the issue is the question of whether or not Christian theology has something meaningful to say to the human condition. De Lubac believed that neoscholastic theologians had turned "dogma into a kind of 'superstructure,' believing that, if dogma is to remain 'supernatural,' it must be all the more divine." This kind of theology, he explained, acts "as though the same God were not the author of both nature and grace."[97]

De Lubac believed that theology is superficial if it fails to show how Christian dogma is a "source of universal light," that makes the world both more comprehensible and more beautiful. Thus, theologians cannot allow secular philosophies to have the last or only word on any matter that pertains to the human condition, matters involving "philosophy, the arts, even the sciences, as well as politics, the economy and diverse forms of social organization."[98] According to de Lubac, the theologian must work to illumine everything that pertains to human nature in the light of

---

95. De Lubac, "Apologetics and Theology," 95.

96. Ibid., 96.

97. Ibid., 94–95.

98. De Lubac, "Authority of the Church in Temporal Matters," 214. De Lubac remarks in an unnumbered footnote on the first page of this essay that it was originally written at some point in the early 1930s. Again, Radical Orthodoxy shares de Lubac's enthusiasm for a theological engagement with secular thought. See Milbank et al., *Radical Orthodoxy*, 2–3. In chapters 4 through 6, I will return to some of the similarities and, more important, differences between de Lubac's work and that of John Milbank.

grace. In order to do so, however, the theologian must become an apolo-gist, since the "most formidable adversaries of the Faith, who are also the most interesting, have a conception of the world and a doctrine of life that they deem to be superior to ours."[99] The challenge for the Church, from de Lubac's perspective, is to engage the reigning secular and athe-istic philosophies in order to expose their internal contradictions and inherent nihilism but, more important, to offer the Catholic faith as an alternative and more beautiful vision and way of life.

99. De Lubac, "Apologetics and Theology," 97.

CHAPTER 3

Catholicism and *Corpus Mysticum*:
The Political Implications of a Sacramental Ecclesiology

In his book *The Suspended Middle*, John Milbank notes that Henri de Lubac's theological opponents were also his political opponents.[1] This is certainly true, and it underscores the intensity of the theological debate that took place between *la nouvelle théologie* and neoscholasticism from the 1930s through the 1950s. In the pages that follow, I explain the political character of this conflict before describing de Lubac's efforts to restore a properly sacramental vision of Catholicism, which included an effort to restore the Eucharist as a potentially subversive sacramental practice.

THE POLITICS OF NEOSCHOLASTICISM

Henri de Lubac often describes his neoscholastic opponents as "integrists," and this designation illustrates a deep fracture in mid-twentieth-century French Catholicism.[2] He and others associated with *la nouvelle théologie* were involved with the French resistance during World War II, while many of the most influential neoscholastics supported Marshal Pètain and the Vichy regime, which was allied with Nazi Germany.[3] Beneath the surface of the political divisions were quite different ways of understand-

---

1. Milbank, *Suspended Middle*, 3.

2. De Lubac, *At the Service of the Church*, 64. At the height of the conflict between *nouvelle* theologians and the neoscholastics, de Lubac and a group of fellow Jesuits wrote a "Réponse" to a critical essay by Marie Michelle Labourdette, in which they remarked in highly polemical terms that "if the evil days of modernism are, by the grace of God, now far from us, the evil days of integrism are about to return" (Anonymous, "La Theologie et Ses Sources," 399–400).

3. Nichols, "Thomism and the Nouvelle Théologie," 8–9. Cf. Kerr, "French Theology," 112. See also Komonchak, "Theology and Culture at Mid-Century," 601.

ing the nature and mission of the Catholic Church in the modern world. Many neoscholastics tended toward an extreme conservatism that sought nothing less than the full reestablishment of the ancient regime.[4] They sought a return to the days when the Catholic Church had an influence over social and political affairs. Indeed, in France, the integrists never wavered from the archconservative approach of Pius IX, which had produced the Syllabus of Errors, with its fierce condemnation of all things modern, such as not only socialism but also democratic forms of government, freedom of religion, and more.

In the first decade of the twentieth century, the integrists were influential in securing the condemnation of every major Catholic democratic movement that emerged.[5] By the midtwenties, the majority of French clergy supported the antidemocratic, monarchist political movement, Action Française, which, although it promised a return to the ancient regime, was led by a self-proclaimed agnostic, Charles Mauras. Even after Pius XI's public condemnation of Action Française, a majority of the French clergy continued to be sympathetic to the movement.[6] In the nineteen-thirties and -forties, when atheistic socialism became an increasing threat to democratic European nations, many "integrists" were seduced by the promises of fascist regimes to grant the Catholic Church a limited official role in government.[7]

---

4. "Unlike the Catholic left, the Catholic right extends the spiritual sphere deep into temporal life. The principles of hierarchy and authority which govern the Church should also govern the state, and only a fully Catholic state is completely acceptable" (Bosworth, *Catholicism and Crisis in Modern France*, 319).

5. Arnal explains Catholic suppression of democratic movements: "In every instance, these condemnations followed a specific pattern. Attacks began with the integrists, the reactionaries of the French church. Sometimes the offensives were led by such powerful prelates as Henry Delassus. . . . . In other instances, prominent theologians like Emmanuel Barbier spearheaded the attack. In still other examples, the anti-Christian Democratic campaign was under the direction of laymen, notably the journalists of the *Nouvelliste de Bretagne* and *L'Action Française*" (Arnal, "Why the French Christian Democrats Were Condemned," 189).

6. Bosworth, *Catholicism and Crisis in Modern France*, 33.

7. Holland, *Modern Catholic Social Teaching*, 207–12. The word "integralist" is often used synonymously with "integrist." Gabriel Daly writes that "the word 'integralism' has had a varied history from its origins in Spanish politics in the 1890s, through the modernist period, down to the present day when it is usually employed to describe the antimodernist crusade launched in 1907 and lasting until the end of Pius X's pontificate. The fact that it often carried strong political overtones is a reminder of the overlap that often occurs between political and theological conservatism. (*Action Française* could count

Thus even during the dark days of World War II, prominent theologians like Réginald Marie Garrigou-Lagrange who had once been supporters of Action Française, gave their enthusiastic allegiance to the fascist Vichy regime, which was democratically empowered after the Nazi defeat of 1940.[8] Such was the allure of temporal power and the belief in the Catholic hierarchy's rightful possession of it.

The Politics of *La Nouvelle Théologie*

De Lubac and others associated with *la nouvelle théologie* had a profoundly different vision of the Church's influence in worldly affairs. Among de Lubac's earliest writings is an essay titled "The Authority of the Church in Temporal Matters" (1932), which outlines these conflicting perspectives on the nature of the Church's earthly mission. The opening lines offer insight into the integrist mindset in political matters:

> Even at this late date, a certain number of theologians still feel duty bound to support the idea that the Church possesses an indirect power over temporal matters, which means that she could have actual jurisdiction over them. When the requisite conditions are met—entailing at least the verification of the *ratio peccati* in a particular case (we are assuming for the sake of argument that there is an agreement on how this is determined)—the leader of the Church, could then, for example, depose (or even name) a head of state, promulgate a civil law, or act as a court of justice in a case of war. In such circumstances, it is claimed, he would be exercising a divine right. To us, such a claim seems inadmissible.[9]

---

many right-wing Thomists in its membership.) The usefulness of the term integralism to describe extreme theological conservatism during the modernist period lies in its etymological suggestion of orthodoxy as devotion to an alleged 'whole' that had to be defended against the modification of any of its parts.... Precisely because the integralists saw this whole as transcendentally guaranteed, they insisted on its segregation from the normal commerce of critical ideas" (Daly, *Transcendence and Immanence*, 187).

8. Peddicord, *Sacred Monster of Thomism*, 88–90. Eugen Weber explains that Action Français was the "theoretical background of the National Revolution of Vichy." He writes further of Action Française "The fiercest champion of the Catholic party, it was condemned by the Pope; responsible for making royalism a fashionable cause, it was disowned by the princess it professed to serve; above all patriotic and anti-German, it came into its own when France reached her lowest point since Joan of Arc rode into Bourges, and gave unreserved support to a Head of State whose policy included collaboration with the German enemies of France" (Weber, *Action Française*, 89).

9. Lubac, "Authority of the Church in Temporal Matters," 199.

The theory of indirect power, mentioned above, had a long history within Catholic thought that went back at least as far as Robert Bellarmine in the sixteenth century. De Lubac conceded that for Bellarmine, the theory "served as a dike against the flood of absolutist doctrines on royal and state power."[10] At the basis of the theory of indirect power lies the ontological distinction between two orders of reality (the temporal and the spiritual), each having a distinct end.[11] While it is granted that sovereign rulers are charged with maintaining order in relation to the temporal end, it is the responsibility of the pope and the Catholic Church to direct persons toward the ultimate good, their spiritual end.[12] Accordingly, popes have a divine right to depose kings and otherwise intercede in temporal affairs only in cases where a sovereign ruler interferes with the Church's spiritual responsibilities. In other words, popes must be able to "repress tyranny and excessive ambition," if this tyranny puts at risk "the salvation of souls."[13]

If there is any doubt about whom de Lubac's essay is directed against, all becomes clear when he quotes an essay be Charles Journet, who was, at least early on, an influential neoscholastic integrist and close friend of Réginald Garrigou-Lagrange and Jacques Maritain. According to Journet, "if the well-being of souls requires it, the Church—which should, however, resort to it only in extreme cases—can depose even pagan Caesars in view of liberating the children of God who are their subjects."[14]

To be fair, there may have been an even greater need in early twentieth-century France than there had been in Bellermine's time to build a "dike" against the excesses of secular government. This was the age of the French Third Republic, which was decidedly anticlerical and even

10. Ibid., 200.

11. Of course, this Thomist distinction between natural and supernatural ends should not be simply dismissed. Certainly de Lubac takes it very seriously and attempts to interpret it with the utmost care. I will return to an in-depth discussion of this complicated issue in a later section on nature and grace.

12. The doctrine of two distinct ends is, of course, based upon the thought of Thomas Aquinas. I will address this very complex issue in greater detail when I take up the relationship between nature and grace in chapter 4.

13. De Lubac, "Authority of the Church in Temporal Matters," 200.

14. Quoted in de Lubac, "Apologetics and Theology," 207. Although Journet and Maritain were early supporters of Action Française, and initially very close to Garigou-Lagrange, the relationship was severed as the former two were unable to tolerate the policies of Vichy France.

hostile toward the Catholic Church, perhaps even intent on its destruction. Richard Peddicord explains that "a secularist ideology imbued all of French government. It held that to uphold the revolutionary ideals of liberty, fraternity, and equality, Catholicism must be destroyed and a rationalist religion must be taught—the human person must be put in the place of God. This ideology informed foreign affairs as well as domestic politics."[15] Accordingly, it was almost a rule that "the more fervent one's Catholicism, the less likely one would be enamored of the Third Republic.[16]

For integrists such as Garrigou-Lagrange, French anticlericalism made it impossible for the Catholic Church to exercise its divine right of "indirect power" in temporal matters. Thus they resisted all Catholic attempts to reach accord with the Third Republic and instead sought to "restore the monarchy . . . [and] the Catholic Church's traditional position in French society."[17] For the integrists, the Catholic Church needed to retain at least an "indirect power" in temporal matters in order to save France from sliding into full-blown secularism and atheism and all of the evils sure to ensue. This meant, unfortunately, that neo-Thomists like Garrigou-Lagrange became supporters of fascist governments such as that of General Franco in Spain, and of course of Marshal Pétain in France.[18]

De Lubac and his friends also hoped that the Catholic Church would engage the modern world and stem the tide of secularism and

15. Peddicord, *Sacred Monster of Thomism*, 92.

16. Ibid., 91.

17. Ibid., 93.

18. "Vichy France under Marshal Philippe Pétain was fundamentally unrepublican and anti-democratic . . . . Pétain's rule overturned the anti-Catholic animus of the Third Republic. Calling his administration a *régime d'ordre moral*, Pétain suppressed the *Ecoles normales*, returned religious instruction to primary education, suspended legislation concerning religious congregations, and subsidized private schools. In light of all these developments—and in spite of his fascism—Cardinal Gerlier would proclaim: 'Pétain is France; and France is Pétain.' It is not an exaggeration to claim that not since the *ancient régime* had a French government been more hospitable to the institutional needs of the Catholic Church" (ibid., 97). Interestingly, in his memoirs of the war years, de Lubac devotes an entire chapter to Cardinal Gerlier, mentioned above. According to de Lubac, Gerlier, like many other Catholics in high position, appeared to be a supporter of the Vichy regime but was, in fact, involved in clandestine efforts to secure safe passage for Jews fleeing from the Nazis. See de Lubac, *Christian Resistance to Anti-Semitism*, 165–88.

atheism. However, *la nouvelle théologie* offered a very different vision of the relationship between Catholicism and secular society. Ironically, whereas the Catholic integrists supported the Vichy regime during the war, de Lubac and his associates favored the resistance, and those who survived the war did so only because they successfully evaded Gestapo attempts to apprehend them.[19] As mentioned above, de Lubac's vision of the Church's engagement with the world was based upon a very different understanding of the Church's authority in temporal matters. He writes of those who subscribe to the theory of indirect power, which he believes really amounts to a theory of direct power:[20]

> They do not notice that they are tempting the Church, just as Satan tempted Christ in the desert. Believing that they are justified in spreading her empire, they are ready to expose her (if that were possible) to the loss of sacred authority, to lower her—even if only temporarily and under the holiest of pretexts—to the rank of the powers of the world. . . . The Church's greatness is not a worldly greatness. She does not lower herself to this level, not even occasionally or 'indirectly.'[21]

Yet, de Lubac insists that the Church must remain concerned with all things human. "Nothing can remain alien to her." The Church's relationship to the temporal realm is analogous to the soul's relationship to the body. The soul does not act upon the body from without but instead works from within. He suggests, "grace seizes nature from the inside and, far from lowering it, lifts it up to have it serve its ends. It is from the interior that faith transforms reason, that the Church influences the State. The Church is the messenger of Christ, not the guardian of the State. The

19. De Lubac's close friend and fellow Jesuit Yves de Montcheuil was martyred by the Nazis in the summer of 1944. For his own reflections on the man, see de Lubac, *Christian Resistance to Anti-Semitism*, 215–35. See also de Lubac, *Three Jesuits Speak*, 15–60. For a recent essay, see Grumett, "Yves de Montcheuil," 618–41.

20. "Although the requisite of a superior end limits the exercise of indirect power to very particular and rare cases, the theory thus understood constitutes, in reality, a direct power over temporal matters. It assumes that the Church has real political authority, a certain temporal jurisdiction" (de Lubac, "Authority of the Church in Temporal Matters," 207).

21. "Authority of the Church in Temporal Matters," 210–11. Similarly, Milbank suggests of the Church, "when it settles and becomes objectified as mere human sovereignty, its nature is lost" (Milbank, *Being Reconciled*, 105).

Church ennobles the State, inspiring it to be a Christian State (one sees in what sense) and, thus, a more human one."[22]

For the integrists, such as Garrigou-Lagrange, when it came to the relationship between the Catholic Church and the temporal realm, a great deal of emphasis was placed on the juridical nature of the Church and its diplomatic relationships with other institutions of government. De Lubac complains that this approach is imbalanced:

> Our treatise on the Church, such as it is taught today nearly everywhere, is constituted almost solely by opposition, on the one hand, to the doctrines of imperial and royal jurists and, on the other hand, to Gallican and Protestant doctrines. Hence we have long developments, which are of course accurate but at times unilateral, on the rights of ecclesiastical authority in confrontation with civil authority, then on the prerogatives of the hierarchy and particularly of the papacy. Hence, in consequence, the obliteration of the mystical point of view; and then, when one feels the need to give some importance to this point of view again, the painful feeling that one is dealing with two parts that one has no idea how to reconcile. How much more balanced, more synthetic, was the doctrine of someone like St. Thomas![23]

De Lubac does not suggest that speculation on the juridical nature of the church is improper. However, he has grave doubts about its ability to inspire persons seduced by the promises of secular progress.[24] Indeed, de Lubac lamented the fact that modern Europeans were becoming

---

22. De Lubac, "Authority of the Church in Temporal Matters," 212. Importantly, de Lubac does insist that the church must be able to make distinctions such as between sacred and secular or nature and grace, and he credits Thomas Aquinas above all others for offering clarification in this area. See de Lubac, "Authority of the Church in Temporal Matters," 216. See also de Lubac, "Internal Causes," 231. For more on the subject of the church's relation to the state, see the section titled "Christian Vocation of France" in de Lubac, "Christian Explanation of Our Times," 446–49.

23. De Lubac, "Internal Causes," 228.

24. As mentioned above, de Lubac and others were concerned that theology speak to the real, existential reality of modern people. One commentator remarks that "there was a common interest in what is called kerygmatic theology, the theology that must be taught to non-theologians and must therefore begin with the mood and convictions actually obtaining in the milieu. The scene was the France of the 30's and 40's, when French thought was in confusion, and when the famed French rationalism was being attacked by the French as irrelevant and harmful. It was the time of French existentialism, and the 'new' theologians experienced existentialism as a fact, though they were cold to it as a theory" (Weigel, "Historical Background of the Encyclical *Humani Generis*," 220).

increasingly knowledgeable in areas of science and technology and yet increasingly ignorant of the great mysteries of the Catholic faith.[25] What was needed, in his mind, was an understanding of Catholicism and an approach to theology at once more relevant and more akin to the thought of the early Fathers.[26]

CATHOLICISM

In response to this perceived need, de Lubac's first book, *Catholicism: Christ and the Common Destiny of Man* (1938), offered a bold vision of the Church's inherently social and universal character. *Catholicism* was intended to balance, or perhaps supersede, a strictly juridical under-standing of the Church. Indeed, *Catholicism* contains no section on the pope, the magisterium, or the Catholic hierarchy at all. The book does not focus on the institution of the Roman Catholic Church but rather on the universal character and meaning of the Christian faith—its "catholicity."[27] The Catholic Church, in de Lubac's view, is not just one institution among others vying for power and influence in the temporal realm. Rather, the Church is the institution on earth through which God's subversive power

25. "There is an easily observable contrast in many men between their secular knowl-edge and their religious instruction; the former is that of a grown man, who has studied for a long time, who has specialized in some professional skill, who knows life, who is cultivated; the second has remained that of a child, wholly elementary, rudimentary, a mixture of childish imagination, poorly assimilated abstract notions, scraps of vague and disconnected teachings gathered by chance from existence. This disproportion is such that it often ends in an abandonment of faith" (de Lubac, "Internal Causes," 225).

26. Calling attention to the fact that theology in his own day had little in common with the thought of the Fathers, he remarks, "Current theology is not so much modeled on its sources, it is rather these sources that are chosen, interpreted, commented upon according to the need and the partialities of current theology" (ibid., 229).

27. It is important to remember that the various chapters of *Catholicism* were writ-ten as individual essays and then put together in book form later. De Lubac, in other words, did not set out to write a book about Catholicism that intentionally negated the importance of the hierarchy. He writes of the controversy that ensued: "They began to reproach me for omissions that, if this had been the case, would have in fact been regret-table: not a single chapter on the papacy! ... The idea that such a misunderstanding could take place from the grouping together of rather disparate pieces under a common label had never for an instant entered my mind" (De Lubac, *At the Service of the Church*, 28). However, it is perhaps instructive that his second highly influential work on the Church, *The Splendor of the Church*, also contained no chapter on the papacy. It seems that de Lubac was more concerned with the organic and sacramental nature of the Church than with its juridical constitution.

is at work redeeming time itself. De Lubac's intention was to explain "the 'social' repercussions of Christianity in the temporal order" in order to offer a "preventative against a 'social temptation' which could cause corruption in faith itself if it were to yield to it."[28]

The temptation of which he speaks is, of course, the lure of direct or indirect power in temporal affairs such as the integrists sought. Eschewing the idea that the Church might operate in the temporal realm as institutions of government do, he argued, "all action that deserves to be called 'Christian' is necessarily deployed on a basis of passivity."[29] In *Catholicism*, de Lubac demonstrates that the Church must not seek to manipulate the course of human history through force as other institutions do, since it is, in its very nature as the body of Christ, the goal of all human history; though of course the Church receives her own true nature by grace.

Catholicism was intended "to show the simultaneously social, historical and interior character of Christianity, this threefold mark conferring on it that character of universality and totality best expressed by the word 'catholicism.'"[30] De Lubac had no desire for novelty; rather, his purpose was "simply to bring out clearly certain ideas that are inherent in our faith: ideas so simple that they do not always attract attention, but at the same time so fundamental that there is some risk of our not finding time to ponder them."[31]

Primarily a compilation of previously written essays, *Catholicism* is divided into three major sections that correspond to the "threefold mark" mentioned above.[32] Section 1 addresses the inherently social nature of Christian dogma, section 2 the historical, and section 3 the interior or personal. *Catholicism* was, according to Hans Urs von Balthasar, "intended to be and actually became a major breakthrough." Von Balthasar suggests that nearly all of de Lubac's subsequent publications were anticipated in this early work and "grew from its individual chapters much like branches from a trunk."[33]

---

28. De Lubac, *Catholicism*, 17.

29. De Lubac, *Splendor of the Church*, 256.

30. De Lubac, *At the Service of the Church*, 27.

31. De Lubac, *Catholicism*, 18.

32. De Lubac, *At the Service of the Church*, 27.

33. Balthasar, *Theology of Henri de Lubac*, 35.

The Social Character of Catholicism

Catholicism illustrates that humanity was created for unity with God and other persons, that this unity was destroyed with the fall from grace, and that it is restored through Christ and specifically through his body—the Church. In contrast to the atheist humanists who saw in Christianity only an "opiate" keeping people from realizing a just and peaceful society on earth, de Lubac argues that the Church's mission is inherently social and political.

"The unity of the Mystical Body of Christ," he writes, "a supernatural unity, supposes a previous natural unity, the unity of the human race." Indeed, the doctrines of creation, fall, and redemption presuppose an originally unified human race "shattered into a thousand pieces" with the fall and brought back together with redemption.[34] "Let us abide by the outlook of the Fathers," he suggests, so that "the redemption being a work of restoration will appear to us by that very fact as the recovery of a lost unity—the recovery of supernatural unity of man with God, but equally of the unity of men among themselves."[35] De Lubac explains:

> The Church, which is "Jesus Christ spread abroad and communicated" completes—so far as it can be completed here below—the work of spiritual reunion which was made necessary by sin; that work which was begun at the Incarnation and was carried on up to Calvary. In one sense the Church is herself this reunion, for that is what is meant by the name of Catholic by which we find her called from the second century onward. . . . The Church is not Catholic because she is spread abroad over the whole of the earth and can reckon on a large number of members. She was already Catholic on the morning of Pentecost, when all her members could be contained in a small room, as she was when Arian waves seemed on the point of swamping her; she would still be Catholic if tomorrow apostasy on a vast scale deprived her of almost all the faithful. For fundamentally Catholicity has nothing to do with geography or statistics. . . . Catholicity is primarily an intrinsic feature of the Church.[36]

34. De Lubac, *Catholicism*, 24–35.

35. Ibid., 35.

36. Ibid., 48–49.

Citing Augustine, Gregory of Nyssa, Cyril of Alexandria, Origen, Tertullian, Cyprian, Ambrose, and a host of other well-known Fathers as well as more obscure writers (ancient, medieval, and modern), de Lubac argues that the Church has always understood itself, paradoxically, as not "an entirely invisible reality" but nevertheless "as a mystery surpassing its outward manifestations."[37] The Church is more than its pontiff, bishops, and priests. The Church remains incomplete until the consummation of all human history, when she will receive the fullness of herself as a gift. The Church, he suggests, "is at the same time both the way and the goal; at the same time visible and invisible; in time and in eternity; she is at once the bride and the widow, the sinner and the saint."[38]

The unity of the Church, for de Lubac, is tied to the eschatological unity of the human race in Christ, and the sacraments are instruments of this unity, since they make the eschatological reality actual in the present. Baptism, for example, is entry into the Church and thus "is essentially a social event," in that individuals enter into the fraternity of the visible church. Baptism is also a mystical and spiritual event, however, "because the Church is not a purely human society: whence comes the 'character' conferred by baptism. . . . So it is that by being received into a religious society one who has been baptized is incorporated in the Mystical Body."[39] Thus Christian baptism entails entry into the society of the visible church whose true nature and ultimate end is derived from the eschatological unity of the whole human race in Christ.[40]

37. Ibid., 64.

38. De Lubac goes on to suggest that "in the interest of refuting such chaotic concepts as those which see a divine Church only in a 'Church of the saints,' an entirely invisible society which is nothing but a pure abstraction, we must not fall into the contrary error. The Church 'so far as visible' is also an abstraction, and our faith should never make separate what God from the beginning has joined together. . . . Nor do we claim to prove this union by an explanation of it, for the mystery of the Church is deeper still, if that were possible, than the mystery of Christ, just as that mystery was more difficult to believe than the mystery of God" (de Lubac, *Catholicism*, 74). Cf. de Lubac, *Splendor of the Church*, 34–39.

39. De Lubac, *Catholicism*, 83–84.

40. De Lubac cites Irenaeus of Lyon, who understood baptism in this way: "The Holy Spirit came down on the Apostles that all nations might enter into Life. And so they are gathered together to sing a hymn to God in all tongues. In this way the Holy Spirit brought the scattered peoples back to unity, and offered to the Father the first fruits of all nations. Indeed, just as without water no dough, not a single loaf, can be made of dry flour, so we who are many cannot become one in Christ without that water that comes

The eschatological unity of the human race in Christ is also (and especially) made real, according to de Lubac, in the sacrament of the Eucharist, where the body and blood of Jesus are broken and shed and consumed in order that all who partake are united with Christ and with each other in Christ.[41] The Eucharist, according to de Lubac, is the sacrament through which the church is made, as Christians are transformed into the true body of Christ.[42] Accordingly, "Eucharistic piety . . . is no devout individualism. It is 'unmindful of nothing that concerns the good of the Church.' With one sweeping, all-embracing gesture, in one fervent intention it gathers together the whole world. . . . it cannot conceive of the action of the breaking of bread without fraternal communion."[43]

De Lubac completes part one of *Catholicism* with an explanation of eternal life as a life lived in communion with God and others: "The Christian tradition," he suggests, "has always looked on heaven under the analogy of a city" where the joy of the saints is "derived from their life in community."[44] De Lubac's discourse on the fundamentally social nature of Christian dogma offered balance to an overly juridical view of the faith. Chenu provides insight into the uniqueness of de Lubac's contribution when he suggests that

---

from heaven. That is why our bodies receive by baptism that unity which leads to life incorruptible, and our souls receive the same unity through the Holy Spirit" (quoted in *Catholicism*, 85–86).

41. For de Lubac, the Eucharist is "the sacrament in the highest sense of the word— *sacramentum sacramentorum, quasi consummation spiritualis vitae et omnium sacramentorum finis*—the sacrament 'which contains the whole mystery of our salvation,' the Eucharist, is also especially the sacrament of unity: *sacramentum unitatis ecclesiasticae*," (ibid., 88–89). Along with copious other quotations from the Tradition, he offers this from Cyril of Alexandria: "To merge us in unity with God and among ourselves, although we have each a distinct personality, the only Son devised a wonderful means: through one body, his own, he sanctifies his faithful in mystic communion, making them one body with him and among themselves. Within Christ no division can arise. All united to the single Christ through his own body, all receiving him, the one and indivisible, into our own bodies, we are the members of this one body and he is thus, for us, the bond of unity" (quoted in de Lubac, *Catholicism*, 91).

42. In *Corpus Mysticum* (1944), de Lubac describes a process, beginning in the twelfth century, when the traditional understanding of the Eucharist as a sacrament through which Christians are transformed into the real body of Christ began to wane. I will discus the thesis and implications of *Corpus Mysticum* in the following section of this chapter.

43. De Lubac, *Catholicism*, 109–10.

44. Ibid., 113.

many theological studies treat faith only as a matter of juridical assent . . . [since they provide] basic facts, and on these are built a structure of arguments, syllogisms and theses. This is hollow speculation which, in all truth and in the very strongest sense, *lacks the light* (*lumen sub quo*), since the faith is taken merely as the source of propositions and not as an interior perfection which endows the spirit with a pleasing understanding of things divine. . . . This is a regrettable separation of theological study from the spiritual life.[45]

In contrast to this kind of purely juridical account of the faith, de Lubac's portrayal is of an illuminating mystery capable of defying Christianity's philosophical detractors while challenging the pietistic and individualistic tendencies of early twentieth-century Christians, who had to a great extent surrendered the social and political realms to the forces of secular humanism.

The Importance of History

In part 2 of *Catholicism*, de Lubac explains how the history of humankind has purpose and meaning, "both direction and significance." Instead of claiming that this world will one day pass away, and that history will come to an ending, de Lubac suggests that the biblical portrait is of a world passing from time into eternity—a transformation of historical existence into eternal: "The resurrection," he explains, "which shall indicate the passing of time into eternity, will be a definitive transformation of the universe."[46]

Moreover, the transformation of time into eternity has already begun, since God has entered into the historical process: "God acts in history and reveals himself through history. Or rather, God inserts himself in history and so bestows on it a 'religious consecration' which compels us to treat it with due respect."[47] Again, it is important to place de Lubac's comments in context. He wrote these words at the height of Hitler's power, when it seemed that fascist governments had a firm grasp on the unfolding history of Europe, when Catholic integrists sought that

---

45. Chenu, "Eyes of Faith," 13, n. 7.

46. De Lubac, *Catholicism*, 142–44 and n. 24.

47. Ibid., 165.

power for themselves, and when most of the faithful looked forward to a supernatural destiny with little relation to history.

In de Lubac's account, the Church has a necessary role in the history of salvation, since the ultimate redemption of humanity is bound with the success of the mission of Christ in and through his body—the Church.[48] He holds that the Church is not only necessary for salvation but is in fact predestined in Christ. Moreover, humankind, and indeed the entire universe, is predestined in Christ and his body, the Church.[49] Catholicism, he writes, is "the only ark of salvation, within her immense nave she must give shelter to all varieties of humanity." Catholicism "is the form that humanity must put on in order to finally be itself."[50]

Catholicism and the Individual

In the final and shortest section of *Catholicism,* de Lubac suggests that many within the Catholic Church seem to have embraced the individualism of the Enlightenment to their own detriment. Thus rather than see salvation as the ultimate reunification of humans with God and each other, "many could see salvation only in a complete severance between the natural and the supernatural"—as a kind of individualistic escape from this socially and historically embodied life to something altogether different.[51] De Lubac believed that this individualistic and escapist understanding of Christian salvation was, at least in part, responsible for the Church's silence and complacency in the face of atheistic philosophies that promised their own versions of social salvation and often had no regard for the dignity of individual humans.

He argues that Christianity holds the only true promise for society as a whole, and that it does so without disregarding the dignity of persons

48. For more on the church's mission in history, see de Lubac, "Theological Foundation of the Missions." For an equally broad account of the fundamentally missionary nature of the Christian faith, see Daniélou, *Salvation of the Nations.*

49. De Lubac, *Catholicism,* 279. Hans Urs von Balthasar suggests that de Lubac's chapter on predestination "anticipates Barth's famous doctrine of predestination (K. D. II, 2) in which he inserts a weighty chapter on the election of the Church between the election of Christ and the election of the individual" (Balthasar, *Theology of Henri de Lubac,* 41).

50. De Lubac, *Catholicism,* 296–98.

51. Ibid., 313.

since individuals are completed and fulfilled as they are recreated in the image of the Trinity. He writes:

> That image of God, the image of the Word, which the incarnate Word restores and gives back to its glory, is "I myself"; it is also the other, every other. It is that aspect of me in which I coincide with every other man, it is the hallmark of our common origin and the summons to our common destiny. It is our very unity in God.[52]

This clearly distinguishes de Lubac's vision of a social Catholicism from various socialisms that would willingly sacrifice individuals for the sake of the greater good. For de Lubac, the communion of Christ's body enables individuals to achieve their greatest happiness. This is a social vision that affirms without hesitation the dignity and supernatural destiny of individuals. Also, in contrast to other social visions, and Marxism in particular, Christianity does not make humanity into an ultimate end.[53] Rather, "it is only by abandoning all idea of considering itself as its own end that mankind can be gathered together." The state of sin that characterizes humankind means that redemption is possible when human desire transcends what is humanly possible. The ultimate end and aspiration of the church transcends human nature, since it is God himself. Christianity, for de Lubac, is not mere humanism because "humanism is not itself Christian. Christian humanism must be a *converted humanism*," a humanism that seeks its final resting place only in a transcendent God. It is the nature of the Church as the body of Christ to serve human history by worshiping the Triune God, since "there is definitive brotherhood only in a common adoration."[54]

With *Catholicism*, de Lubac offered a vision of the Church as the body of Christ, mediating between time and eternity—consecrating the

---

52. Ibid., 340.

53. Fergus Kerr writes that "Against the background of the liberal-capitalist and totalitarian ideologies of the 1930s, de Lubac sought to show that, in Catholic Christianity, the claims of person and society are equally respected. Very much a tract for those times, primarily directed against the overly individualistic and introspective spirituality of his youth, as he saw it, the book is nevertheless as relevant a therapy for those who might now be inclined to over-emphasize the communal structure of Catholic piety" (Kerr, *Twentieth-Century Catholic Theologians*, 71).

54. De Lubac, *Catholicism*, 367–68, italics original.

present and directing it toward its ultimate end in the divine economy.[55] Bothered by the integrist mentality, which hungered for greater power in temporal affairs even when this entailed collusion with fascist governments, de Lubac simply wanted the Church to remain faithful as it fulfilled its mission to the world. However, there were, in his mind, a number of obstacles keeping the Catholic Church from engaging the world faithfully. Throughout the remainder of his long career, he worked to remove those obstacles.

Corpus Mysticum: Reclaiming the Mystery of the Church

As mentioned previously, *Catholicism* was a programmatic work that outlined a bold vision for a revitalized Church whose own self-understanding would necessitate a greater engagement with secular culture. De Lubac understood well, however, that the vision of *Catholicism* was not universally shared. Indeed, there were many obstacles—both philosophical and theological—that stood in the way of a more widespread embrace of *Catholicism's* vision. De Lubac's second book, *Corpus Mysticum* (1944),[56] like his major works on the supernatural and on spiritual exegesis, was intended to challenge an obstacle keeping the Church from benefiting fully from its own sacramental constitution.

The Thesis of Corpus Mysticum

Whereas *Catholicism* offers a comprehensive vision of the Church's inherently social character and mission, *Corpus Mysticum* focuses narrowly on the historical development of several phrases identified with Eucharistic piety. However, the thesis of *Corpus Mysticum* is consistent with the over-

---

55. If de Lubac's thesis in *Catholicism* seems somewhat commonsensical now, this only suggests that his theological vision was hugely influential, and that he was a precursor to the much richer ecclesiological climate that we appreciate in theology today.

56. De Lubac, *Corpus Mysticum*. In his memoirs, de Lubac explains that the text of *Corpus Mysticum* was almost finished in 1938, though its publication had to be postponed because of the war. See de Lubac, *At the Service of the Church*, 29. For the English translation, see de Lubac, *Corpus Mysticum: The Eucharist and the Church*. Although this present book you hold was written prior to the publication of the new English translation, Simmonds and the others have included corresponding page numbers to the French version at the top of each translated page. Accordingly, it should be quite easy to follow my citations with the English text.

all vision outlined in *Catholicism* and was anticipated in its chapter on the sacraments. According to de Lubac, the body of Christ was conceived in three different ways before the twelfth century. First, theologians spoke of the historical body of Jesus of Nazareth. Second, the sacramental body referred to the elements of the Eucharist, and third, the Church was designated the ecclesial body.[57] Important is that before the twelfth century, the sacramental elements were called *corpus mysticum* while the church was referred to as the *corpus Christi verum*. At some point during the middle of the twelfth century, these terms were reversed, and the church came to be called *corpus mysticum* while the eucharistic elements were designated *corpus Christi verum*.[58]

The reasons for this change are not entirely clear, but the shift may have come in part as a response to the eleventh-century heresy of Berengar of Tours, who denied the real presence of Christ in the elements. Berengar believed that he was preserving the symbolic mindset of the patristic tradition, but he failed to consider that the Fathers consistently maintained that the real presence of Christ existed in the sacramental elements (*corpus mysticum*) *as well as* in the Church (*corpus Christi verum*). De Lubac suggests that Berengar's challenge led his opponents to a greater emphasis on the real presence in the sacramental elements than had existed at any time in previous eras.[59] Before long, the patristic way of referring to the elements as both "mystical body" and "real presence" *at the same time* was lost, and medieval theologians came to believe that the two terms contradicted each other. In other words, theologians after the twelfth century believed that to call the sacramental elements *corpus mysticum* was equivalent to denying the real sacramental presence of Christ within them. Thus, after the twelfth century, the bread and the wine on the altar were designated *corpus Christi verum*, while the Church was designated *corpus Christi mysticum*.[60] This tendency took hold to such an extent that the designation *corpus Christi mysticum* was almost completely lost by the sixteenth and seventeenth centuries.[61]

57. De Lubac, *Corpus Mysticum*, 34–39.

58. Ibid., 13–19.

59. Ibid., 162–66.

60. Ibid., 229. De Lubac suggests that prior to the twelfth century, the ultimate "truth" of the sacrament resided beyond the sacrament, whereas after the twelfth century, the sacrament was its own fulfillment—it was the thing being celebrated.

61. Ibid., 285–86.

The change in usage of the terms *corpus verum* and *corpus mysticum* may have also been supported by a growing desire in the twelfth century to identify the historical body of Jesus of Nazareth with the sacramental elements present on the altar. According to Gerhart Ladner, there was a desire at that time to "connect the Church as closely as possible with the Eucharistic life in the liturgy."[62] However, it seems that as the historical body of Christ was increasingly identified with the sacramental body in the elements, the ecclesial body was neglected in Eucharistic piety. Before the twelfth century, the church (*corpus Christi verum*) and the historical body of Jesus of Nazareth were brought together mystically through the performance of the Eucharist. According to de Lubac, the ancient teaching was that while the Church makes the Eucharist, it is also, and perhaps more profoundly, true that "*L'Eucharistie fait l'Eglise.*"[63]

There was a strong connection, prior to the twelfth century, between sacramental theology and ecclesiology, since the mystical body in the performance of the Eucharist served the purpose of making, with each celebration, the true body of Christ, the Church.[64] In the biblical epistles and in the Church Fathers, the Eucharist was a deeply social/communal event. The celebration of the Eucharist meant that individuals were incorporated into the body of Christ and thus into the communion of saints—a real social body embedded in while also transcending both space and time. However, as the elements came to be designated *corpus verum,* and the Church was called *corpus mysticum*, the elements and the historical body of Jesus were more closely united while the Church's connection to the historical body of Jesus became vague— "mystical" in the sense of something hidden or less than real and knowable.[65] De Lubac explains that as soon as the ecclesial body becomes the *corpus mysticum*, eucharistic piety is separated from ecclesial unity.[66] The Eucharist becomes a matter, primarily, of individual piety, and the church's identity is tied increasingly to the present, visible institutional structures[67] and less

---

62. Ladner, "Aspects of Medieval Thought," 414–15.

63. De Lubac, *Corpus Mysticum*, 103. For more on de Lubac's eucharistic ecclesiology, and for a comparison of de Lubac's work with that of John Zizioulas, see McPartlan, *Eucharist Makes the Church.*

64. De Lubac, *Corpus Mysticum*, 162–88.

65. Ibid., 288. Cf. de Certeau, *Mystic Fable*, 82–83; de Lubac, *Corpus Mysticum*.

66. De Lubac, *Corpus Mysticum*, 275–77.

67. John Milbank suggests that the change in Eucharist language served to solidify

to the sacramental mystery that links the present church to its origin in the person of Jesus and its destiny in the ascended Christ.

Corpus Mysticum is primarily an historical investigation focused on the usage of several eucharistic phrases, and de Lubac acknowledges that twelfth-century historical circumstances may have necessitated a new emphasis on the real presence in the sacramental elements. However, it is also clear that de Lubac was uncomfortable with the separation between eucharistic practice and the church's sacramental and social identity. In deemphasizing the sacramental character of the church, theologians began to lose site of the fact that the church is a mediator and participant in the ascent of humankind to God.[68] Indeed, it seems that the aforementioned change in eucharistic language occurred at an inopportune moment in the history of Europe. For at just the time when the Eucharist might have served to subvert or counteract the trend towards secularism in European society, its power to unite Christians in a common allegiance to a transcendent body politic under Christ was undermined, since it became increasingly a spectacle and a matter of individual piety. In the mid-twentieth century, as European nation-states became increasingly totalitarian, de Lubac hoped to see eucharistic practice reinvigorated in order to unite modern Catholics in a common allegiance to a transcendent body politic under Christ.

Corpus Mysticum and Corpus Verum in Historical Context

De Lubac was not the only one to consider the implications of this change in sacramental nomenclature for the relationship between the Catholic Church and secular society.[69] For example, Gerhart Ladner explains that the church

> adopted the formula *Corpus Christi Mysticum* at a critical moment in Church history, when there was some danger of too much stress being laid on the institutional, corporational side of the

---

hierarchical authority within the Roman Catholic Church, since it disconnected the sacrament from Scripture, tradition, and the laity. See Milbank, *Being Reconciled*, 122–26.

68. De Lubac, *Corpus Mysticum*, 263–65.

69. He suggests toward the end of *Corpus Mysticum* that the current sad state of "Christendom" should lead us back to an appreciation of the Eucharist as sacrament through which the Church can learn to be made into Christ on a daily basis. Ibid., 292–93.

Church. At the moment, in other words, when, with the eclipse of the functional concept of the state and with the re-emergence of the state as body politic and, a little later, as self-sufficient community, the Papacy, too, in a world of nascent sovereign powers had to emphasize the role of the Roman Church as "corporation", supreme among all the bodies politic because of its spiritual foundation and divine institution, but not less concrete than they on the political and sociological level.[70]

To make sense of this statement, it will be helpful to review briefly the history of the relationship between the Catholic Church and civil authorities prior to the twelfth century. Whereas the early church was an often persecuted minority in the Roman Empire of the first through the fourth centuries, dramatic changes came with the reign of Constantine (d. 337). Quite suddenly, Christianity was officially tolerated within the empire except for a brief period during the reign of Emperor Julian in the mid-fourth century. Then, with the reign of Theodosius I (379–395), pro-Nicene Christianity became an official religion, and several forms of paganism were banned.[71] With the establishment of the church in the Roman Empire, Christianity spread even more rapidly throughout Europe. Thus, with the gradual disintegration of the Roman Empire in the fifth century, leaders of the new kingdoms that arose in the resulting political vacuum had already embraced Christianity on a significant scale.[72]

The breakup of the Roman Empire, like the Constantinian shift that preceded it, brought important changes in the relationship between the church and civil authorities, especially in the West.[73] Namely, whereas the early Christian churches constituted several relatively unimportant communities within the vast and powerful Roman Empire, Western

70. Ladner, "Aspects of Medieval Thought," 415. Ernst Kantorowicz explains that "under the pontifical maiestas of the pope, who was styled also 'Prince' and 'true emperor', the hierarchical apparatus of the Roman Church tended to become the perfect prototype of an absolute and rational monarchy on a mystical basis, while at the same time the State showed increasingly a tendency to become a quasi-Church or a mystical corporation on a rational basis" (Kantorowicz, *King's Two Bodies*, 193–94).

71. Thompson, *Western Church in the Middle Ages*, 3.

72. Thus "the early geographical basis of the Church was in the lands which had been part of the Empire" (ibid., 6).

73. The political unity of the Roman Empire remained more intact in the east, since the tribal invaders of Rome tended to bypass Byzantium. Ibid.

Christianity after the fifth century existed in a context characterized by numerous smaller political authorities. With the dissolution of the Roman Empire, interest in the classical political treatises, such as Aristotle's *Politics*, began to wane, as a more Augustinian understanding of politics gained popularity both in the church and among civil rulers. Ladner explains the difference between the Aristotelian and Augustinian views as follows:

> St. Augustine's concept of the City of God is a specifically Christian ideal of community life. Its true nature appears very clearly if it is confronted with Aristotle's famous definition of the state at the beginning of the first book of *Politics*: "The state or political community which is the highest of all and which embraces all the rest, aims at good in a greater degree than any other, and at the highest good." For Aristotle, then, the state is the form of community life which aims at the highest good. For Augustine the community which pursues the highest good, that is God, is not a state, but a supra-natural society, mixed on this earth, it is true, with the earthly or worldly society, but, nevertheless, extending beyond, to embrace its members in heaven.[74]

The claim that the influence of classical treatises on the nature of the state waned in the early medieval era is supported by the observation that the "literary genus" of the period dealing with political theory "consists not of works on the state such as Plato's *Republic* or Aristotle's *Politics*, but of works on government: that is true especially for the long series of 'Mirrors of Princes' or ruler's manuals of the early Middle Ages."[75] Indeed, the various principalities and kingdoms of early medieval Europe were not considered sovereign political territories. Rather, they were conceived as governments with various civic responsibilities. Moreover, governance was the responsibility of both ecclesiastical and civil rulers. This distinction dates from at least the time of Pope Gelasius I (492–496). It would be mistaken, however, to argue that Gelasius affirmed a strict separation between the sacred and the secular, because "his sense of salvation history imposed a restraint" on such a dualistic outlook. According to Gelasius, Christ was the last and only true priest-king.[76] No other human could fill

74. Ladner, "Aspects of Medieval Thought," 403–4.

75. Ibid., 405.

76. "Without in the very least usurping the role of the temporal sovereign, Pope Gelasius showed himself quite capable of reminding the emperor Anastasius that the

both roles, so for Gelasius, "the distribution of functions in Christendom is an eschatological sign, ensuring that everyone is humble, acknowledging that the priestly-royal character of the church is not for one individual alone to reflect but depends on mutual service"—at least until all things are fulfilled in Christ.[77]

Ladner explains: "from the fifth to the late eleventh century this concept of the state . . . which we might call the *functional* concept, prevailed." For example, when Charlemagne and later Otto the Great were crowned by the pope, neither of them obtained more territory or subjects. Rather, they were granted new functions of government, the most important of which was the responsibility for "the protection of the Universal Church, and especially of the Roman Church, that is to say, of the Papacy."[78]

Indeed, whereas the Church was an established institution within the Roman Empire in the fourth century, by the ninth century, the state was conceived as existing within the Catholic church.[79] According to Ladner, "this was the great political idea of Christian unity in the Carolingian age, and on the whole, in the succeeding centuries down to the era of St. Gregory VII." Kingdoms during the Carolingian era and in the Holy Roman Empire of Otto the Great were "in the Church, not beside the Church" or over the Church. During this time of the *functional* state, rulers were not so concerned with the maintenance of a nation or territory. Rather, the function of a ruler was the maintenance of justice in a world ultimately ordered to God.[80]

From the eighth through the late eleventh century, kings served dual roles. They were commonly referred to by titles such as "Vicar of Christ" and "King and Priest." Their governmental function within the universal

---

sovereign is not 'above the Church', like St. Ambrose in the case of Theodosius, or the aged Hosius in the case of Constantine" (de Lubac, *Splendor of the Church*, 192).

77. O'Donovan and O'Donovan, *From Irenaeus to Grotius*, 178.

78. Ladner, "Aspects of Medieval Thought," 405–6. Cf. Figgis, *Political Aspects of St. Augustine's "City of God,"* 85.

79. Lander explains that "while for Pope Gelasius [in the fifth century,] priestly authority and kingly power had been two forces or principles by which the world is ruled, in the Carolingian age this neutral concept of the world is firmly and clearly replaced by that of the Church which, as the Body of Christ, is the only possible all-embracing community milieu in which government temporal, that is political, as well as spiritual can function" (Ladner, "Aspects of Medieval Thought," 407).

80. Ibid., 408.

church was inscribed with christological and liturgical import.[81] Ernst Kantorowicz recalls a "little story inserted in a homily wrongly ascribed to John Chrysostom," which sums up the liturgical character of medieval kingship. The story comes from a Palm Sunday sermon focusing on the role played in the salvific economy by the donkey that carried Christ into Jerusalem before his passion. The unknown speaker says:

> It is true . . . , the animal after having made its entrance into Jerusalem Judea, was returned to its owner; but the prophecy, related to the animal, remained in Judea. For of that animal, Christ had needed not the visible, but the intelligible nature; that is, not the flesh, but the idea. Hence, the flesh was returned, but the idea retained: *caro remissa est, ratio autem retenta est.*[82]

The prophecy was from Isa 62:10 and Zech 9:9. This story was related to medieval kingship where the ruler, like the donkey, served Christ in the temporal realm and was therefore incorporated into the eternal economy of salvation. Kantorowicz explains that the "ass's messianic sempiternal body, however, its *ratio* or idea or prototype, as well as the prophetic vision it stood for helped to fulfill: these were indisputable within the course of salvation and inseparable from the image of the Messiah. Thus, the animal's immortal 'body politic' remained in the Holy City with the Messiah: it was 'haloed,' enveloped by the divine light of its Rider." Indeed medieval art often depicted the king with a halo surrounding his head. This halo was intended to communicate the idea that the king participated in the divine economy.[83]

The period of the functional state in which sovereigns were "priest and king" did not last, however, since well-balanced relationships between ecclesiastical and political rulers were hard to maintain. Trouble began when, for various often-legitimate reasons, Pope Gregory VII (1073–1085) envisaged the king as a layman and nothing more, certainly not a "vicar of Christ." There eventually developed a conflict with King Henry IV of Germany over the investiture of bishops and abbots.[84] The

81. For a multitude of examples, see Kantorowicz, *King's Two Bodies*, 42–86.

82. Translated by and quoted in Kantorowicz, *King's Two Bodies*, 85.

83. Ibid., 61–86.

84. Thus "lay investiture of ecclesiastical offices was only one of the complex issues at stake: fundamental questions were addressed concerning sovereignty in the Christian community, the relationship between temporal and spiritual power, the nature of kingship, and the status of episcopal authority as regards that of the pope and secular rulers"

investiture controversy (1075–1122) with the Holy Roman Empire signaled the beginning of a transformation in the medieval understanding of the state.[85] De Lubac suggests, "the numerous conflicts between the two rival powers, the priesthood and the Empire . . . favored the elaboration of an increasingly strict theory of pontifical theocracy. At the end of the eleventh century, the reforming energy of Gregory VII released the Church from the control of the lay nobles."[86] Oliver O'Donovan notes: "Gregory VII himself, in a dramatic text, describes kingship as an invention of violent men ignorant of God, and cites Satan's promise to Jesus (Matt 4:9) as the genealogy of all secular authority."[87] At this time, two rival political philosophies emerged. On the one hand, the popes asserted their privileged status over lay sovereigns. This philosophy, known paradoxically as "political Augustinianism,"[88] reached a pinnacle in the writings of Giles of Rome, advisor to Boniface VIII. Consider this characteristic statement from Giles:

> Royal Power was instituted by sacerdotal power; the pontiff himself, in the plenitude of his power, can be called the source of all power. In everything he is comparable to heaven (of cosmology): whatever he touches, he cannot be touched. . . . Whether heaven constructs or destroys, promotes or deposes, causes one ruler to descend and another to rise, there is nothing that can oppose it,

---

(Canning, *History of Medieval Political Thought*, 89).

85. O'Donovan and O'Donovan, *From Irenaeus to Grotius*, 240–49. The popes of the twelfth and thirteenth centuries "made it increasingly clear that for them rulers were simply leaders of peoples and holders of territories. These the Popes tried to tie to themselves in addition to the membership of all Christians in the universal Church by connecting them with the Roman Church through a special bond, which might assume various forms, but most effectively the feudal relation of vassal to Lord. In the case of the Holy Roman Empire, too, they tried to make the Emperor's protection of the Roman Church exclusively a matter of duty gradually eliminating all imperial claims of control over the papacy. Between Gregory VII and Innocent III a vast system of states subject to the Roman Church was built up. To this system belonged at one time or another almost every kingdom of Europe and also some of the city communes which began to develop political forms of their own at that time" (Ladner, "Aspects of Medieval Thought," 409–10).

86. De Lubac, "Political Augustinianism?" 257–58.

87. O'Donovan, *Desire of the Nations*, 204.

88. De Lubac suggests that the term "political Augustinianism" is problematic, since the philosophy espoused bears no resemblance to the thought of St. Augustine. "Political Augustinianism?" 259.

nothing should strive to act against it. And since this is true of the sovereign pontiff, his power can be called celestial.[89]

De Lubac suggests that Giles's ascription of all power to the Roman pontiff was "a futile attempt to rescue Boniface VIII" at a time when lay nobles were asserting their own temporal authority and doing so with the support of an increasingly influential Aristotelian political philosophy.[90]

Indeed as the popes beginning with Gregory VII rejected the earlier medieval synthesis of Church and state, the Aristotelian understanding of the state began to replace the earlier Augustinian view.[91] One of the earliest medieval political treatises to treat the state as a political body apart from the Church comes from John of Salisbury (b. ca. 1115) and his eight-book *Policraticus*. Clearly a student of Aristotle, Salisbury conceived of the state as a "body politic" composed of a sociological community that included sovereign and subjects. Although it was not his intention to limit the powers of the church, Salisbury "proclaimed the autonomy of the forms of nature, of the methods of the mind, and of the laws of society."[92] Indeed, Salisbury is an early proponent of a kind of "pure-nature" theory, and Marie-Dominique Chenu explains that "he was surely the 'modern' one in the twelfth century."[93]

However, the fact that the papacy had already begun to regard kings and their principalities as though they were ordered to a lower end than that of the church is perhaps more important than the novelty of John of Salisbury's political theory. It shows that the theory of pure nature that would develop in the sixteenth century with the work of Cajetan was preceded not only by political philosophers but also by the diplomatic

---

89. Quoted in de Lubac, "Political Augustinianism?" 270.

90 De Lubac, "Political Augustinianism?" 267.

91. In his essay, "Political Augustinianism?" de Lubac challenges an evidently common historical thesis that claimed that prior to the fourteenth century, and based upon a supposedly Augustinian political philosophy, popes exercised complete sovereignty over both the spiritual and the temporal realms. This synthesis of spiritual and temporal power under the pope remained unchallenged, or so it was claimed, until the High Middle Ages when the Aristotelian philosophy supplanted it. According to de Lubac, the Augustinian theology of history that no doubt had a significant influence in the Middle Ages afforded a much more important role to lay rulers than Giles and others allowed. See especially de Lubac, "Political Augustinianism?" 265–66.

92. Chenu, *Nature, Man and Society in the Twelfth Century*, 196. Cf. O'Donovan and O'Donovan, *From Irenaeus to Grotius*, 277–96.

93. Chenu, *Nature, Man and Society in the Twelfth Century*, 196–97.

practices of the papacy. The result of this change in the relationship between the Church and civil authorities is that the papacy increased in
power and prestige within the Catholic Church. Whereas the doctrine
of papal primacy originated in the patristic era, during the eleventh and
twelfth centuries the entire universal Church is identified increasingly
with its head, the bishop of Rome—who in earlier times had been considered "first among equals." During this era, the Catholic Church became
increasingly "corporational."[94]

According to Ladner, the rise of the papacy and the increasingly
corporational character of the church may have been necessitated by the
efforts to "lower the status of the rulers as half-clerical functionaries of
the Church." He writes further that

> It would . . . have been impossible to eliminate [the king's] influ-
> ence upon the churches in their kingdoms. There was only one
> Church which could attempt to effect this great change, that was
> the Church of the Pope, the Roman Church, which being at the
> same time universal and territorial (anchored in the Papal States),
> at the same time the Body of Christ and the "corporation" of the
> clergy, could more easily meet the nascent political bodies, that
> is to say the rising territorial and national states, on their own
> ground. Thus, the Roman and Universal Church began to enter
> into a new type of relation with the states as political bodies.[95]

In other words, as the popes began to treat secular rulers as though
they served a purely temporal role, the church had to begin engaging the
various kings and princes diplomatically. By secularizing the state, the
Church became increasingly secular in its political dealings, and increasingly corporational in its structure.[96] Kantorowicz observes that when, in
the twelfth century, the Church declared itself to be the *corpus mysticum*
rather than the *corpus verum*, the "secular world sector proclaimed itself
as the 'holy Empire.'" He comments further: "this does not imply causation, either in one way or the other. It merely indicates the activity of

94. It was during this era that the papacy began to develop an entirely novel "juridical
architecture" to deal with new political realities. See de Lubac, "Political Augustinianism?"
261.

95. Ladner, "Aspects of Medieval Thought," 412–13.

96. A number of highly complex eleventh-century developments encouraged the
trend toward a more corporational Church and a more autonomous secular realm. For
more on this subject, see McQuillan, *Political Development of Rome*.

indeed interrelated impulses and ambitions by which the spiritual *corpus mysticum* and the secular *sacrum imperium* happened to emerge simultaneously—around the middle of the twelfth century."[97]

Importantly, the concept of the *corpus mysticum* as a designation for the ecclesial body evolved into a primarily sociological designation.[98] The Church came less and less to be understood as the body of Christ created daily in the performance of the Eucharist. Rather the term *corpus mysticum* designated a political body of Christians in the temporal realm.[99] Thus Lucas de Penna could write in 1582 that "the Church compares with a political congregation of men, and the pope is like to a king in his realm on account of his plentitude of power."[100]

This sentiment is carried to an even greater extreme in the following statement by Hermann of Schilditz, who writes that "just as all the limbs in the body natural refer to the head, so do all the faithful in the mystical body of the Church refer to the head of the Church, the Roman Pontiff." Consider also the following statement from Alvarus Pelagius, who said that "the Church, which is the mystical body of Christ . . . and the community of Catholics . . . , is not defined by the walls [of Rome]. The mystical body of Christ is where the head is, that is, the pope."[101] As the term *corpus mysticum* was used increasingly to describe the Church

97. Kantorowicz, *King's Two Bodies*, 197.

98. De Lubac, *Corpus Mysticum*, 129–35.

99. Writing on the development of conciliar theory in the fifteenth and following centuries, one commentator explains that when the "Conciliarists spoke of the Church as the *corpus Christi* or the *corpus Christi mysticum* those expressions had lost for them the rich sacramental associations present in the earlier Patristic usage and had acquired in their place corporative and political connotations. Instead of the parallel being drawn with the sacramental body of Christ and *corpus mysticum* being taken to denote the incorporation of the faithful with Christ in a mysterious community of salvation, the analogy was drawn now from natural bodies or bodies in general and the expression taken to denote a 'moral and political [as opposed to a real or physical] body'" (Oakley, "Natural Law," 795).

100. Quoted in Kantorowicz, *King's Two Bodies*, 203–4.

101. All quoted in ibid., 203. Interestingly, the Conciliarists of the fifteenth and sixteenth centuries, in opposition to precisely this kind of papal teaching, argued that the mystical body of Christ is not with the pope but rather with "the general council . . . whereas the Church which is ruled by the pope as its monarchical head is but a collection of particular churches and individual members and is described as a political body . . . regarded like any other community or political society, lacking the influx of divine grace or the special influence of Christ in so far as it depends on human judgment" (Oakley, "Natural Law," 803).

as a sociological entity, a "body politic," the secular state "strove for its own exaltation and quasi-religious glorification."[102] Thus the phrase *corpus mysticum* was eventually adopted by political theorists as a designation for secular political bodies. For example, "the late medieval jurist, Antonius de Rosellis (b. 1386), enumerated . . . five *corpora mystica* of human society—the *corpus mysticum* of each: village, city, province, kingdom, and world."[103]

Whereas prior to the twelfth century, European civilization was conceived as essentially unified with the king (and his subjects) occupying a functional and liturgical role within the divine economy, after the twelfth century secular governments were ordered increasingly to a strictly temporal order and judicial end separate from the end to which the church is ordered. Kantorowicz explains that during this era, "a new halo descended from the works of Aristotle upon the corporate organism of human society, a halo of morals and ethics different from that of the ecclesiological *corpus mysticum*."[104]

The implications of this transformation from a functional and liturgical understanding of government toward a secular view cannot be overstated. As a result of the transformation that began in the twelfth century, no longer did the church look upon rulers and subjects, as though every aspect of their lives were intricately woven into the divine economy narrated in Scripture and enacted in the liturgy.[105] Rather, after the twelfth century, Europeans began increasingly to imagine that the state and not the church, was the fundamental sociological organism within which the drama of life is played out. Unfortunately, the eucharistic changes of the twelfth century complemented the developing political situation in Europe. Whereas pre-twelfth-century eucharistic practice

102. Kantorowicz, *King's Two Bodies*, 207.

103. Ibid., 209–10. De Lubac mentions the "secularizing" of the concept in the work of "Antoine des Rosiers," who distinguishes five hierarchical "mystical bodies," which are natural to all humankind. See de Lubac, *Corpus Mysticum*, 280.

104. Kantorowicz, *King's Two Bodies*, 211.

105. In the words of a prominent scholar discussing life in medieval England, not only the clergy but also "the laity were able to appropriate, develop, and use their repertoire of inherited ritual to articulate their experience of community and their own role and status within it, their personal hopes and aspirations, and their sense of the larger order and meaning of the world in which they lived and out of which they would one day die" (Duffy, *Stripping of the Altars*, 7). For a more concise introduction to this issue, see Jenson, "How the World Lost Its Story."

might have subverted the secularization of European imaginations, the developments that de Lubac describes show us that eucharistic practice, especially after the twelfth century, fit very nicely with the new political outlook and posed no theological challenges to it. Consequently, one of de Lubac's concerns in *Corpus Mysticum* was that the Eucharist had become a mere spectacle for the laity rather than the sacrament that binds members of the church to the historical body of Christ and to the entire communion of the saints—living and dead. In other words, de Lubac was concerned that the Eucharist was not "making the Church," which is the real social organism within which life takes place.

Michel de Certeau explains that as the sacramental elements come to be called *corpus verum* ("real body"), they act "as the visible indicator of the proliferation of secret effects (of grace, of salvation) that make up the real life of the Church."[106] From this point forward, the Church of the laity is a mystical or "hidden" reality while the secular realm is increasingly real. William Cavanaugh writes that "rather than linking the present with Jesus' first—and, we should add, second—coming, the mystical is now cordoned off from historical space and time. At this point in Christian history the temporal is beginning to be constructed not as the time between the times, but as an increasingly autonomous space which is distinct from spiritual space."[107]

As mentioned previously, de Lubac's *Corpus Mysticum* was a historical investigation focused on a transformation in eucharistic language that occurred between the eleventh and thirteenth centuries. De Lubac did not discuss in that work the coming of the modern secular state or the increasingly corporational nature of the Catholic Church after the twelfth century. However, it is clear that he preferred the pre-twelfth-century eucharistic identification of the Church with the *corpus verum*, because this identification entailed a conceptualization of the church as having its beginning in the historical Jesus and its telos in the ascended Christ. To call the church *corpus verum* was to recognize its mysterious nature

---

106. De Certeau, *Mystic Fable*, 84.

107. Cavanaugh, *Torture and Eucharist*, 213. De Certeau writes that "from the thirteenth century on, a new formula prevails in which the positivity of an apostolic authority (the historical body) and that of a sacramental authority (the Eucharistic body) are linked to one another and split off from the Church, which is their hidden extension" (de Certeau, *Mystic Fable*, 83).

and indispensable role as mediator between time and eternity—between fallen creation and divine economy.

De Lubac, throughout his career, advocated a return to the sources of the great patristic tradition and a theological approach that understood all of creation as though it were ultimately ordered to God, that is, sacramentally.[108] It is also important to note, however, that he was in no way recommending a return to a pre-twelfth-century theopolitical landscape (with liturgical kingships and the like). In a lecture delivered during the dark days of World War II, when there must surely have been a great deal of Catholic nostalgia for better times, de Lubac suggested that

> Medieval Christianity was not a perfect success, far from it. It had its weaknesses and its tares. All was not absolutely Christian. . . . The dreams of reaction or of restoration are utopias that are as vain and as pernicious as the dreams in the opposite direction. In making an effort to rediscover the spiritual sources of our civilization we will not forget, then, that it could not be a matter for us of borrowing ready-made solutions from the past but of rediscovering an ever-open truth so as to set ourselves to work.[109]

Rather than an interpretation advocating a return to the past, the conclusion to be drawn from *Corpus Mysticum* and other works is that de Lubac sought to retrieve the patristic and medieval approach to theology, which was, as in the above quotation, "ever-open." That is, it left no space untouched. Prior to the twelfth century, the Church envisioned no such thing as civil authority with its own secular end. Rather, everything was ultimately ordered to God and thus lay within the church's realm of interest, influence, and imagination.[110] The church prior to the twelfth century was not complacent with regard to social and political realities, because it affirmed that the natural world, and especially the world of humans, finds its completion and fulfillment only in God.

108. De Lubac, *Corpus Mysticum*, 263–64.

109. De Lubac, "Christian Explanation of Our Times," 445–46.

110. De Lubac, of course, had much to say about legitimate and illegitimate ways that the Church might "influence" the temporal realm. See especially de Lubac, "Authority of the Church in Temporal Matters," 199–233. See also de Lubac, *Splendor of the Church*, 161–201.

Corpus Mysticum *and the Ascendance of Dialectic*

Corpus Mysticum's implications for the Church's practice of theology are especially clear in the tenth chapter, where de Lubac describes the birth of a theological method founded on dialectic and increasingly inhospitable to mystery. He laments the emergence and ascendancy of the Scholastic method with its precisely formulated questions and answers since, he believes, it is unable to deal adequately with the great mysteries of the Christian faith.[111] Just as Berengar of Tours signaled the beginning of a move away from traditional eucharistic realism, so too did this eleventh-century figure represent the beginning of a new approach to theology, one that celebrates the role of reason and dialectic.[112]

For de Lubac, St. Augustine provides an excellent example of the synthesis that once existed between faith and reason, and which began to decline during the twelfth century. Whereas for Augustine, faith enabled and necessitated a search for greater understanding,[113] theologians after the twelfth century began, increasingly, to set faith and reason at a greater distance from each other. For the Fathers, the great mysteries of the faith provided the inspiration for a more earnest quest for understanding. However, beginning in the twelfth century, "the mystery to be understood fades before the miracle to be believed."[114] No longer is faith a process that leads to greater understanding. Now it becomes a problem that must be surmounted. With regard to the Eucharist, for instance, no longer is the sacrament itself a mystery that leads the faithful to a greater understanding of and hence participation in the body of Christ. Rather, the "miracle" of the bread-become-flesh must be, quite simply, "believed" by the faithful. In this context, both "faith" and "understanding" (to use Augustine's terms) are to a certain extent cut off from mystery. One must have faith in the miracle, which is clearly understood: "you see bread, understand flesh." De Lubac suggests that the only role for "understand-

111. De Lubac, *Corpus Mysticum*, 257.

112. Ibid., 255.

113. In this sense, reason and mystery are not opposed to each other. Rather, they are synonymous, or at least interdependent. This is because for the Fathers, human reason was not grounded in "identity, nor analogy, but anagogy." In other words, true reason comes only through the realization that "all sensible things are a sacrament, not necessarily demanding organization, or validation, but open to being transcended. All things reached, all things surpassed" (ibid., 264).

114. Ibid., 269.

ing" here is that it provides a clear idea of the object that must be accepted by faith.[115]

The entire sacrament and all that it signified was once an illuminating mystery, but after the twelfth century the only mystery concerns the miraculous transformation of the elements. In the new context, the only role for mystery is that it provides the opportunity for the exercise of faith. If one cannot understand the transformation of the elements, all the better, since the exercise of faith enables persons to gain merit.[116] According to de Lubac, this approach to the Eucharist was characteristic of Algerius of Liège, Peter Comestor, Innocent III, and many others, including Thomas Aquinas.[117] The expulsion of symbolism and mystery from the sacrament of the Eucharist accompanied, de Lubac suggests, a more general tendency among Scholastic theologians to devalue "signs" in a myriad of ways amid an environment that placed ever more emphasis on the importance of "things."[118]

The antischolastic implications of *Corpus Mysticism* were not lost on the neo-Thomists, who otherwise approved the scholarship of de Lubac's historical thesis. For example, M.-J. Nicolas, OP, wrote an essay for the *Revue Thomiste* in which he praised de Lubac's demonstration of the transformation in eucharistic terminology that took place during the twelfth century. Nicolas's only criticism of the entire book was with the tenth chapter, which dealt with the disappearance of symbolism and the ascendance of dialectic:

> The only thing for which we reproach Père de Lubac is that he sees in the unmindfulness of Eucharistic symbolism the necessary consequence of the scientific form taken by theology in the Middle Ages and, in this scientific form, the expression of a mentality outmoded and perhaps less accessible to modern minds, or at any rate less traditional than the symbolistic mentality of the Fathers.[119]

115. Ibid., 269–70.

116. Ibid., 271.

117. Ibid., 271–72.

118. Ibid., 274.

119. Translated and quoted in Donnelly, "Current Theology," 481. For a favorable review of the same chapter, see Glorieux, *Mélanges de science religieuse* 2 (1945) 370.

Even Yves Congar, who was largely sympathetic with de Lubac's work, reprimanded him in personal correspondence for such a blatant attack on Scholasticism.[120]

Although de Lubac denied that it had ever been his intention to attack Scholasticism, there is little doubt that his major historical projects were chosen for good reason and were intended to cut away systematically at the foundations upon which neoscholastic theology was built. Indeed, there is substantial continuity between *Corpus Mysticum* and his 1946 bombshell, *Surnaturel* (which can be interpreted in no other way than as an attack on neoscholasticism), since twelfth-century sacramental and ecclesiological developments discussed in *Corpus Mysticum* served as a prelude to the sixteenth-century development of the idea of pure nature and to the emergence of an ontological dualism.[121]

120. Cited in Nichols, "Thomism and the Nouvelle Théologie," 6.

121. A number of commentators have puzzled over why de Lubac did not write *Surnaturel* before *Corpus Mysticum*, since the former seems to be the more central, and perhaps more important, work. See, for example, McPartlan, *Eucharist Makes the Church*, 9. I would suggest, simply, that de Lubac's major historical projects were ordered chronologically in order to outline and challenge the gradual infestation of a secular mindset into the Church's self-understanding and practices. First came the eclipse of mystery in the sacraments and the ascendance of dialectic in theological method. Next came the metaphysical dualism that provided justification for the secular realm. Finally spiritual exegesis was eclipsed by a more secular approach especially after the Protestant Reformation.

PART 2

The Politics of Spiritual Exegesis

CHAPTER 4

From Scientific Theology to Spiritual Exegesis:
The Controversy over Practicing Theology in History

Henri de Lubac was certainly not alone in his condemnation of neos-cholasticism. His criticisms became part of a heated controversy after the publication of an essay in 1946 by a friend and fellow Jesuit, Jean Daniélou.[1] Like de Lubac, Daniélou argued that Christian theology must concern itself not merely with truth in the abstract, but with an illuminating truth that engages all human reality.[2] He also argued, like de Lubac, that this kind of theological orientation required a "return to the sources" of the Christian faith—the great patristic works that were a "vast commentary on Holy Scripture."[3] The neoscholastics reacted strongly, seeing in Daniélou's essay the battle cry for a revolutionary approach to theology, one very different from their own neo-Thomism.[4]

According to Marie-Michele Labourdette, a distinguished Dominican scholar and editor of the *Revue Thomiste*, the primary problem with this return to the sources, which was being called derisively and ironically *la nouvelle théologie*, was with its implications regarding the nature of theology itself and particularly with theology's claim to constitute true

1. Étienne Fouilloux, an eminent French historian, has described this controversy as "the only theological debate of any importance at least in France, between the condemnation of modernism and the Second Vatican Council" (Translated and cited in Nichols, "Thomism and the Nouvelle Théologie," 2).

2. Daniélou, "Les Orientations Présentes de La Pensée Religieuse," 7.

3. Ibid., 9.

4. Many of the neoscholastic critics detected a kind of conspiracy among the *nouvelle théologie* writers. At the center of this supposed conspiracy were three important book series: *Sources Chrétiennes*, *Théologie*, and *Unam Sanctam*. See Daley, "Nouvelle Théologie and the Patristic Revival," 366–75. See also, Greenstock, "Thomism and the New Theology," 571.

and objective knowledge.[5] Labourdette made his concerns clear when he wrote, "what we can never accept is the complete evacuation, in a perspective like this, of the idea of speculative truth." Moreover, he says, "we understand by 'truth' the conformity of the knowing intelligence with a reality which for it is a 'given,' 'never a construct.'"[6] Brian Daley suggests that Labourdette saw in de Lubac, Daniélou, and others the "rejection of propositionally formulated truth that had been the core of the modernist spirit."[7]

After Labourdette's essay, the Jesuits answered with a somewhat stinging anonymous response authored primarily by de Lubac, but with assistance from Jean Daniélou, Henry Bouillard, Gaston Fessard, and Hans Urs von Balthasar, all Jesuits.[8] The Jesuits did not try to defend themselves against all of Labourdette's criticisms but instead went on an attack against the neoscholastics, suggesting that they would do well to exercise a bit of self-criticism. In highly abrasive language, de Lubac and the others suggested that any theological tendency that defines the parameters of orthodoxy according to its own personal opinions set forth in systematic expression are not just being bold but are blaspheming.[9]

The issue was certainly not settled in 1946. De Lubac's most controversial book, *Surnaturel*, was published in the summer of that same year and focused the debate on the issue of the relationship between nature and grace.[10] According to de Lubac, a theoretical separation of the natu-

---

5. Labourdette, "La Thélogie et Ses Sources," 356.

6. Translated and cited in Daley, "Nouvelle Théologie and the Patristic Revival"; Labourdette, "La Thélogie et Ses Sources," 367–69.

7. Daley, "Nouvelle Théologie and the Patristic Revival," 367. Aidan Nichols suggests that of all the neoscholastic opponents of *nouvelle théologie*, Labourdette was the most nuanced and the least in favor of condemnation. Instead, he had hoped for genuine dialogue. Nichols, "Thomism and the Nouvelle Théologie," 17.

8. Nichols, "Thomism and the Nouvelle Théologie," 10.

9. Anonymous, "La Theologie et Ses Sources, Réponse." 401.

10. "The magnitude of the opposition that de Lubac met (*after Surnaturel*) was unexpected. The Jesuits Danielou and Bouillard, and de Solages of the Institut Catholique alone took de Lubac's position in the argument. Almost every major theologian in France, and throughout the world, soon entered his objections. The dispute became so intense in the period of 1947 to 1950 that as we shall see, the *Surnaturel* became more than a question of theology but a symbol of all that was to be resisted in the new theological revival" (Connolly, *The Voices of France*, 87). Other accounts suggest broader support for the *Nouvelle Théologie*. Indeed, there was at least moderate support throughout Europe. See Weigel, "Historical Background of the Encyclical *Humani Generis*," 218. Even before

ral and supernatural orders entered Catholic theology in the sixteenth
century, leading ultimately to an extrinsic approach to theology while
simultaneously allowing for the development of secular philosophies
based upon the idea that human nature is ordered to a natural end.[11]

For de Lubac, Action Française and other secular social and political
movements were able to thrive because theologians had long ago endorsed
a theology that separated nature from the supernatural. Describing the
consequences of this separation as they appeared in his own day de Lubac
writes:

> The supernatural gift henceforth appeared as a super-imposed re-
> ality, as an artificial and arbitrary superstructure. The unbeliever
> found it easy to withdraw into his indifference in the very name
> of what theology was telling him: if my very nature as a man truly
> has its end in itself, what should oblige or even arouse me to scru-
> tinize history in the quest for some other vocation perhaps to be
> found there? Why should I listen to a Church which bears a mes-
> sage having no relation to the aspirations of my nature?[12]

According to de Lubac, too many Catholics believed that the
Church's mission was of an entirely different order from the natural end
of humankind. The Church exists to save souls in light of an entirely extrinsic supernatural end and nothing more. Therefore, people turned to
secular philosophers, politicians, and scientists in order to find salvation
for the troubled modern world. Theologians, in contrast, were occupied
with the systemization and clarification of revealed truths. According to
de Lubac, early twentieth-century Catholic theology, often indifferent to

---

Humani Generis (1950), Pope Pius XII seems to have had concerns of his own regarding
nouvelle théologie. In addresses delivered both to the Dominicans and to the Jesuits, he
warns: "There is a good deal of talk (but without the necessary clarity of concept), about
a 'new theology,' which must be in constant transformation, following the example of all
other things in the world, which are in a constant state of flux and movement, without
ever reaching their term. If we were to accept such an opinion what would become of
the unchangeable dogmas of the Catholic faith; and what would become of the unity and
stability of that Faith?" Cited in Greenstock, "Thomism and the New Theology," 568.

11. William Cavanaugh argues that the vacuum left by Catholic theologians was filled
by enlightenment philosophers like Locke, Hobbes, and Rousseau. He suggests that religion, after the sixteenth century, was primarily concerned with extrinsic, supernatural
ends, so political philosophers stepped in to offer immanent solutions to the problems of
social and political life. Cavanaugh, *Torture and Eucharist*, 19–20.

12. De Lubac, "Nature and Grace," 32.

social issues, tended to treat the revelation of God as though it were an extrinsic and objective given. He writes:

> How little mysterious, then, is this very word "revelation" for us: God has spoken: What could be simpler? He said this and this and also this: that is clear. Consequently, one can deduce from that this and this and also this. Scripture, Tradition are only points of departure: their contribution is at times judged to be a bit rudimentary, without anyone daring to say it too loudly. . . . If doctrine increases in a way with the centuries, all is still explained wonderfully well: a major part faith, a minor part reason bring about a theological conclusion. The theologians lay in a stock of them, and they hand them over to the Magisterium, which will solemnly define those it judges appropriate according to the need. They are the proprietors of sacred doctrine. An elementary catechism teaches the rudiments, then there are more and more complete expositions at greater and greater depth, up to the large theological treatise, which comprises the science in its entirety. . . . Lord, Lord! There we have what men make of your Mystery![13]

Following the lay Catholic philosopher Maurice Blondel, de Lubac referred to this kind of theology as extrinsicism because it was separated from the concerns of everyday life. Theology was a science unto itself, and its objects of study were ancient texts and creeds which, when understood correctly, yielded the truth in the form of clear propositions and historical facts. De Lubac remarked facetiously that the only real difference between the dominant neoscholastic theology and other sciences was that theology's "first principles were received through revelation instead of having been acquired through experience or through the work of reason."[14]

The way to overcome this extrinsicism, in de Lubac's view, was to return to a more traditional understanding of the relationship between nature and grace. De Lubac believed that the entire tradition, before the sixteenth century, was consistent in its affirmation that nature is incomplete apart from the supernatural, and that grace reaches into nature to direct it towards its end. He thus set out to demonstrate, beginning with *Surnaturel*, that the true teaching of the Church, and especially of St. Thomas and St. Augustine, is that grace completes and perfects nature.

13. De Lubac, "Disappearance of the Sense of the Sacred," 233–34.
14. Ibid., 233.

Surnaturel created an enormous amount of opposition and led to aggressive attacks on *la nouvelle théologie*, such as those of Réginald Garrigou-Lagrange, who wrote an article suggesting that the movement, with its emphasis on a truth that must conform to the exigencies of human life, was simply a return to modernism.[15]

The Debate over Nature and Grace

The truth, however, is that de Lubac had no interest in a return to modernism. Rather, and as always, his hope for the church was a thoughtful *resourcement*. As mentioned above, de Lubac was especially inspired by Blondel, who in his doctoral dissertation, *L'Action* (1893), dealt specifically with the insufficiency of secularizing philosophies that placed total confidence in the ability of human reason to understand reality without reference to the transcendent.[16] Although Blondel's work was groundbreaking and had a significant influence on de Lubac, the reigning neoscholastic theology was largely unaffected.[17] Nearing the end of his career, de Lubac explained that

> Latin theology's return to a more authentic tradition has taken place—not without some jolts, of course—in the course of the last century. We must admit that the main impulse for this return came from a philosopher, Maurice Blondel. His thinking was not primarily exercised in the areas proper to the professional theologians, nor did it base itself on a renewed history of tradition. Still, he is the one who launched the decisive attack on the dualist theory which was destroying Christian thought.[18]

Although Blondel was the pioneer on the nature/grace issue, the traditionalism of the Church meant that the most effective way to change minds was through a reconsideration of the tradition of Thomist

15. Recognizing the influence of Maurice Blondel on the movement, he complained that with *nouvelle théologie*, truth is no longer the "compliance of judgement with the extramentally real and its immutable laws, but the compliance of judgement with the requirements of action and human life which always evolves" (Garrigou-Lagrange, "La Nouvelle Théologie," 144).

16. Blondel, *L'action*, 300–302. For a treatment of Blondel's influence on de Lubac, see Russo, *Henri de Lubac*.

17. Blondel's doctoral dissertation has been called "the boldest exercise in Christian thought of modern times" (Milbank, *Theology and Social Theory*, 217).

18. De Lubac, *Brief Catechesis on Nature and Grace*, 37–38.

commentators.[19] With *Surnaturel*, de Lubac made the kind of historical argument that was necessary if there was any hope of convincing the professional theologians. His scholarly work on this issue was completed with the twin publications in 1965 of *Augustinisme et théologie moderne* and *Le Mystère du Surnaturel*.[20] In these works, he traced the development of the idea of "pure nature" in order to show that the dualistic perspective emerged long after the time of Thomas Aquinas and especially with the work of Thomas Cardinal Cajetan in the sixteenth century. Although he was met with a great deal of resistance after publishing *Surnaturel*, by 1965 his position was taking hold. In a letter to de Lubac, Étienne Gilson remarked, "*Le Mystère du Surnaturel*, which I have just thoroughly enjoyed reading from cover to cover, is absolutely perfect. I really have the impression, not that the question is closed, because people always have to muddle things up, but that it ought to be."[21]

19. Bernardi, "Maurice Blondel and the Renewal of the Nature-Grace Relationship," 822–45.

20. The publication of *Surnaturel* brought de Lubac a great deal of trouble from neoscholastic theologians. It was the publication of this book, perhaps more than any other factor, which led to his years of forced silence mentioned at the beginning of chapter 2 of this work. Indeed it was believed widely that the 1950 encyclical *Humani Generis* condemned de Lubac's position in *Surnaturel*. However, de Lubac argues that the encyclical actually vindicated his position. He has explained that "as for the Encyclical, it was . . . very different from what some had anticipated: it even caused in them some disappointments that I need not explain here. 'Disappointment' is, moreover, an understatement: as one good, very learned theologian recorded at the time, it was a 'boomerang' for them. (The details of this story would be very picturesque.) In what concerns me, one can, if one wishes, pick out two illusions in *Humani generis*. . . . The second illusion relates to the supernatural: far from containing any blame or any reservation in my regard, it borrows a phrase from me to express the true doctrine, and it is not by chance that it avoids any mention of the famous "pure nature" that a number of highly placed theologians were accusing me of misunderstanding and which they wanted to have canonized. . . . Quite the contrary of a reproach, I have never had to make, either in writing or even orally, either in public or in private, the least particular act of submission or retraction on any point" (translated and cited in de Lubac, "Mystery of the Supernatural," 281). Still, despite de Lubac's insistence that he was not the target of Pius XII's encyclical, many contemporary observers believe that he was. In 1980, de Lubac published one more book on the nature/grace issue. This last work focused more on the theological and existential dimensions of the issue than on the commentarial history. See de Lubac, *Brief Catechesis on Nature and Grace*.

21. Gilson and de Lubac, *Letters of Étienne Gilson to Henri de Lubac*, 91. Denys Turner has initiated a new discussion on the interpretation of Thomas Aquinas regarding reason and faith. Although Turner does not engage de Lubac's exegesis of Aquinas directly and does not suggest that de Lubac's genealogical work was mistaken, he does

Despite Gilson's confidence in de Lubac's thesis, the debate over nature and grace continues to this day.[22] Although a thorough treatment of the controversy is far beyond the scope of this book, I will outline some of the most important dimensions of de Lubac's position, and especially those that are most obviously relevant to the nature and task of theology, which was always a central concern for de Lubac.

De Lubac's Historical Thesis

One of de Lubac's primary contentions in *Surnaturel* was that the patristic and medieval Fathers affirmed consistently and unfailingly that persons are created in the image of God with an innate natural desire to be transformed by the vision of his glory. According to de Lubac, all creation was, for the Fathers, ordered to a supernatural end in the triune God. He

---

challenge a number of contemporary thinkers, such as Fergus Kerr and John Milbank, who have drawn conclusions from de Lubac's work regarding the relationship between faith and reason. In particular, Turner challenges the idea that reason unaided by faith is incapable, according to Aquinas, of achieving the knowledge of God. In the end, Turner simply redefines *reason* theologically, in order to suggest that reason, properly conceived, can know God. Moreover, Turner does not reject the claim that such knowledge retains an apophatic dimension. See Turner, *Faith, Reason, and the Existence of God*.

22. As mentioned previously, de Lubac's *Surnaturel* became the central focus in the debate between *la nouvelle théologie* and the neoscholastics in the 1940s and 1950s. Among the many critics of de Lubac's book, some of the more important names included Guy de Broglie, Leopold Malevez, Charles Boyer, Jacques de Blic, Marie-Michel Labourdette, and Réginald Garigou-Lagrange. Phillip P. Donnelly offered regular English-language summaries of the debate, as it raged, in the pages of the American journal *Theological Studies*. See especially Donnelly, "Current Theology: On the Development of Dogma and the Supernatural," 471–91; "Discussion on the Supernatural Order," 213–49; "Surnaturel of H. de Lubac," 554–60; "Gratuity of the Beatific Vision and the Possibility of a Natural Destiny," 374–404. Another helpful overview of the early debate can be found in Duffy, *Graced Horizon*, chapters 1–3. Although the position of de Lubac seemed to have triumphed by the 1960s, the debate has returned in recent decades and is once again receiving considerable attention. For recent critical engagements of de Lubac's position, see "Surnaturel, Une Controverse au Coeur du Thomisme au XXe Siècle," 1; Feingold, *Natural Desire*. Feingold's book, occasioned by John Milbank's total dismissal of it, was the focus of a book symposium featured in *Nova et Vetera*, English Edition 5 (2007). Perhaps the most notorious recent work seeking to defend de Lubac's early position on nature and grace is found in Milbank, *Suspended Middle*. The way we understand the relationship between nature and grace has important implications for the way we understand the relationship between faith and reason. For an excellent collection of essays inspired by John Paul II's *Fides et Ratio* and very pertinent to this issue, see Griffiths and Hütter, *Reason and the Reasons of Faith*.

claims that it was only in the sixteenth century, with the work of Cajetan, that the traditional view began to wane. From the time of Cajetan and beyond, the Thomist commentators claimed that there are two distinct ends, one natural and the other supernatural, to which humans can be ordered. This *duplex ordo*[23] allowed theologians to posit that human nature is fully capable of attaining the natural end, while the supernatural end is achievable only by the extrinsic *superadditum* of God's grace.[24] Cajetan's contribution to the idea of "pure nature" emerged from his interpretation of St. Thomas's teaching concerning the natural desire for the beatific vision. Cajetan insisted that when St. Thomas spoke of a natural desire to see God, he was thinking as a theologian of the desire that comes in response to a supernatural destiny that is revealed by God.[25] De Lubac writes:

> In fact, the theory of pure nature was born and developed in an intellectual milieu in which the notion of finality had been diminished. What this theory presupposed at its beginning, although not always explicitly, was that, before the grace of baptism or some other such substitute grace, all men, in our same world—if

23. Important is that the neoscholastics are no longer speaking here, as Aquinas had, of two different orders with the same ultimate end. Rather, their *duplex ordo* entails two distinct orders, each having its own distinct end—one natural and the other supernatural. They fail to see that the order of creation has its ultimate end in God through the *analogia entis*. Indeed, it seems that both the neoscholastics and de Lubac may have been guilty of conceiving the relationship between nature and grace in exclusively univocal terms, when for Aquinas the relationship was often conceived in analogical terms. For a helpful essay, see Staley, "Happiness," 215–34.

24. De Lubac acknowledges that Thomas Aquinas entertained the hypothetical "possibility that God could have created another man, like Adam, without granting him the supernatural 'gifts of justice, completeness, immortality, and with none of the 'grace freely given,'" though Adam was of course created with these gifts. However, whereas such a state was only hypothetical for Thomas, by the sixteenth century it had become far more meaningful and consequential. Indeed, whereas Thomas Aquinas acknowledged that Adam was created with the divine gift of original justice and ordered to the vision of God as his last end, by the time we get to the sixteenth century, theologians such as "Molina gradually accustom . . . us to the idea that the normal last end of man, his essential end, that which now belongs fundamentally to his nature and directs its whole activity, is not the vision of God but some 'natural beatitude' of an inferior order" (de Lubac, *Augustinianism and Modern Theology*, 226).

25. Ibid., 114.

one disregards original sin and its consequences—were in the state of pure nature.[26]

Although Cajetan was widely criticized in his own time for this interpretation, there was a growing need in sixteenth-century theology to overcome the naturalistic teachings of Michael Baius (1513–1589) and Cornelius Jansen (1510–1576) in defense of a supernatural gratuity.[27] De Lubac explains in *The Mystery of the Supernatural* that "one of the chief motives that have led modern theology to develop its hypothesis of 'pure nature' to such an extent that it has become the basis of all speculation about man's last end has been the anxiety to establish . . . the supernatural as being a totally free gift."[28] Fergus Kerr suggests, moreover, that "Cajetan needed a distinction between human nature as such and human nature as called to union with God in Christ, partly, no doubt, to maintain the rights of (Aristotelian) philosophy over against (Lutheran) theology,[29] but mainly to defend the order of creation over against what seemed obliteration by Protestant exaltation of the dispensation of grace."[30]

As it turned out, a dualistic ontology placing persons in a state of "pure nature" separated from the supernatural realm of God proved convenient for a variety of reasons. It allowed theologians to maintain, simultaneously, that humanity is created with (1) a natural end in accordance with its own abilities and (2) an extrinsic, supernatural end that can be achieved only by the grace of God.[31] This simple move was intended to safeguard God's supernatural gratuity from a naturalistic philosophy that rejected any notion that humans could be constituted by a natural desire for something yet not naturally equipped to attain it. In other words, the Scholastic theologians feared that ascribing to human nature a "supernatural end" would be to suggest that God is somehow obligated to grant

26. De Lubac, "Mystery of the Supernatural," 296. Cf. de Lubac, *Augustinianism and Modern Theology*, 224.

27. De Lubac, *Augustinianism and Modern Theology*, 1–86. Baius and Jansenius both tended to disregard the gratuity of the supernatural order, claiming that the vision of God is the natural end of human nature.

28. De Lubac, *Mystery of the Supernatural*, 53.

29. De Lubac actually suggests that Cajetan's interpretation was worked out before the problem of Luther and was therefore not a response to Lutheranism. See de Lubac, *Augustinianism and Modern Theology*, 214.

30. Kerr, "French Theology," 114.

31. De Lubac, *Mystery of the Supernatural*, 68–69.

the beatific vision. Accordingly, the sixteenth-century Thomists insisted that there is only one end intrinsic to human nature—a natural end. The beatific vision, on the other hand, is a supernatural end added to human nature as a kind of bonus.

According to de Lubac, Francisco Suarez, following Cajetan, became an important proponent of the theory of pure nature in the late sixteenth and early seventeenth centuries. Unlike Cajetan, however, Suarez seemed to realize that the theory's dependence upon the work of St. Thomas was questionable. De Lubac suggests that "Suarez . . . had no illusions regarding its [the theory of pure nature's] antiquity. . . . He strained his ingenuity to discover proof of it in St. Thomas by the use of interpretive exegesis, but only to find himself bound to declare modestly: 'It is the common assertion of theologians, I think, although they suppose it more than they dispute it.'"[32] De Lubac summarizes Suarez's position, arguing that he

> starts from the idea that man, being a natural being must normally have an end within the limits of his nature, since according to a principle of Aristotle all natural beings must have an end proportionate to them. 'It is necessary that every natural substance have some co-natural final end toward which it might strive.' The end of a natural being is always in strict proportion to its means. For Suarez this is an absolute principle, and its application to the case of man is no less absolute, no less undeniable. By virtue of his creation man is therefore made for an essentially natural beatitude. If we suppose that in fact he is called to some higher end, strictly speaking this could only be super-added. . . . It is therefore contradictory to envisage an end which would be, according to the maxim adopted by Soto, Bellarmine and Toletus, 'natural with respect to appetite, supernatural with respect to attainment.'"[33]

Soon after the time of Suarez, de Lubac explains, the idea of "pure nature" was almost universally affirmed. Even though there remained many different Catholic schools of thought, there was "an alliance in this particular field, thus disposing . . . of the Baianist question, so that they could contend with greater ease on another field. . . . The controversy on the mode and efficacy of grace and predestination."[34]

---

32. De Lubac, *Augustinianism and Modern Theology*, 158.

33. Ibid., 158–59. For a contemporary demonstration of the theory of pure nature, see Garrigou-Lagrange, *Beatitude*, 127–291.

34. De Lubac, *Augustinianism and Modern Theology*, 183.

De Lubac's Ontological Thesis

When de Lubac challenged the neo-Thomist doctrine of "pure nature" in the middle of the twentieth century, his primary concern was not, as it had been for Cajetan, with preserving a sense of supernatural gratuity, although this did remain an important and fundamental part of his doctrine. Rather, he believed that the neoscholastic dualism needed to be challenged in order to preserve the dignity of creation, and humankind in particular, against the nihilism of atheist humanism.

In *Surnaturel*, de Lubac railed against the perhaps-unintended consequences of the theory of pure nature,[35] saying that it allowed for an extrinsic and "timid theology . . . , which separates dogma from thought and the supernatural from nature."[36] He challenged the dualistic perspective because he believed it allowed for a conception of human nature—moral and intellectual—as fully autonomous and "self-sufficient."[37] "It seems to me" he writes, "that this line of thinking leads to a natural morality pure and simple, which must tend to be a morality without religion—or at least with only a natural religion."[38] He goes on to ask, "is there any real difference between such a hypothesis and the ideal of 'rational sufficiency'?"[39]

In de Lubac's mind, the neo-Thomists taught that humans, by the powers of natural reason and natural moral law, could achieve a well-ordered society within which justice could be maintained and a "natural" beatitude could be attained. Thus, he believed that this dualism provided

35. Famously, paragraph 26 of Pius XII's 1950 encyclical, *Humani Generis*, condemned theologians who "destroy the gratuity of the supernatural order, since God, they say, cannot create intellectual beings without ordering and calling them to the beatific vision." Many people believe that this statement was aimed at de Lubac, and it may have been. However, de Lubac never denied the possibility of a "hypothetical" state of pure nature as found in Thomas Aquinas. Thus he is careful in both *The Mystery of the Supernatural* and *Augustinianism and Modern Theology* to clarify Thomas's teaching on this point, and he acknowledges its importance in clarifying the integrity of human nature as such. Indeed de Lubac suggests that "such a solution must have satisfied [St. Thomas] the more in that in it he was uniting both the Augustinian teaching on the primitive state and Aristotle's principles on the human composite" (ibid., 220). He also concedes that the theory of pure nature as it was conceived in the sixteenth century had a measure of success in defending the gratuity of the supernatural order. See de Lubac, *Mystery of the Supernatural*, 53–54.

36. De Lubac, *Surnaturel*, 437 (my translation).

37. De Lubac, *Mystery of the Supernatural*, 47–48.

38. Ibid., 47.

39. Ibid., 48.

the foundation for a "purely natural philosophy" and a self-sufficient social order.[40] Because this dualistic perspective allowed for the development of natural (separated) philosophy, de Lubac felt that it justified, at least in part, modern secularism. Likewise, he found in the *duplex ordo*, which affirmed the possibility of a self-sufficient social order, the justification for Catholic support of secular fascist political movements like Action Française and the Nazi-controlled Vichy regime.[41]

Intrinsic Desire for a Supernatural End

Against the proponents of a pure-nature theory, de Lubac argued that humans have a "supernatural finality" imprinted on their nature even before sanctifying grace is given.[42] Not only is there no actually existing state of pure nature,[43] but concrete human nature or "historic nature" (human nature as it actually exists rather than as hypothetically conceived) is incomprehensible apart from its fulfillment and completion in God.[44]

40. Ibid., 37. For more on the insufficiency of natural reason, see de Lubac, "On Christian Philosophy." Cf. Henrici, "On Mystery in Philosophy." Another commentator suggests that "two results of the *duplex ordo* which de Lubac found unacceptable were the separation of philosophy from theology and the separation of politics from the supernatural" (Gotcher, "Henri de Lubac and Communion," 113).

41. After the Germans defeated the French army in 1940, France was divided into two parts, with the south governed by Germany and the North governed by a puppet government led by a former military hero, Marshal Pétain, and whose power was centered in the town of Vichy. For more on the complicity of the Vichy regime in relation to the Holocaust, see Marrus and Paxton, *Vichy France and the Jews.*

42. This supernatural finality is the "natural desire for the supernatural," or the supernatural end of human nature. De Lubac, *Surnaturel*, 487, my translation. For a thorough description of de Lubac's position here, see Feingold, *Natural Desire*, 489–504.

43. Again, de Lubac did not deny that God could have "hypothetically" created humans with a purely natural end, not ordered to the beatific vision. Rather, he believed that the commentators had made too much of this hypothetical state of pure nature, so he wanted to return the discussion of nature and grace back to real or historical human nature—human nature as we actually experience it. See de Lubac, "Mystery of the Supernatural," 291–92.

44. It may have been helpful for de Lubac to distinguish between proximate and ultimate ends for humankind. For a critique of de Lubac (but more important, of John Milbank) along these lines, see Long, "On the Loss, and the Recovery," 134–55. Within the order of creation, there is a certain integrity, and even an end proportionate to human nature, though humankind is directed to God as its ultimate and perfect end. Perhaps current interest in the *analogia entis* and its relationship to the *analogia fidei* may prove fruitful in finally moving beyond the nature/grace debate. Indeed, if we may subsume

According to de Lubac, this is the true teaching of St. Thomas, who "held that finality is something intrinsic, affecting the depths of the being."[45] Because the desire for the vision of God is intrinsic to concrete human nature, there can be no "natural end" for humankind within the order of creation that falls short of the supernatural revelation of God in Jesus Christ.[46]

From de Lubac's perspective, the neoscholastic interpretation of the *duplex ordo* ignores the profound consequences of sin on human nature

---

the order of creation within the order of grace, then clear "distinctions" between natural and supernatural ends disappear. We should not assume, however, that any of this would have been surprising to de Lubac. Indeed, he was far ahead of these recent debates when he pointed out that the tradition affirmed "a certain number of successive 'states' in the unfolding of the history of salvation, from the creation of human nature in Adam until its fulfillment in glory. The first of these states was that of 'human nature well created' . . . 'according to the established order' . . . [the] state of nature created, instituted, whole . . . .'" Then came the "'state of sin,' or the 'state after the fall,' or 'state of present nature shamefully spoiled by mutability,' 'state of corruption' and 'state of lapsed nature.' There then came, in the third . . . position . . . , the [state] 'of repaired nature,' which could itself be divided into 'state of grace' and 'state of glory' (or 'of eternal punishment')." (de Lubac, *Augustinianism and Modern Theology*, 221–22). De Lubac believes that the neo-Thomists went wrong by conceiving of these states as "static" when earlier theologians (and de Lubac always places Thomas Aquinas in the context of a broader tradition) considered them part of a continuum.

45. De Lubac, *Mystery of the Supernatural*, 71.

46. For several contemporary scholars, de Lubac goes somewhat astray here, in that he seems to suggest too great a continuity between the natural and the supernatural. The consequence of this exaggerated continuity is that the integrity of the natural order, or the "order of creation," is undermined so that all there is in the end is the supernatural. The central question becomes, did Christ come to perfect nature or to redeem it? Did Christ come in order to fully develop something latent within human nature, or did Christ come in order to save and redeem a fallen creation? See Hütter, "Desiderium Naturale Visionis Dei," 84. It is perhaps noteworthy that in his last explicit treatment of the nature/grace issue, de Lubac, without wholly abandoning the language of continuity, began to place more emphasis on the role of "conversion" in the movement of humans from fallen nature to supernatural grace. He writes, "Consequently the call of grace is no longer an invitation to a simple 'elevation,' not even a 'transforming' one (to use the traditional words); in a more radical fashion it is a summons to a 'total upheaval,' to a 'conversion' (of the 'heart,' i.e., of all one's being). Faith . . . restores our being 'by overturning it completely.'" He also begins to speak of the "dissimilarity . . . between two orders of being," the fallen order of creation and the order of "divine grace" (de Lubac, *Brief Catechesis on Nature and Grace*, 119). Hütter, I should point out, never mentions de Lubac's later treatment of the issue in the *Brief Catechesis* in his own essay mentioned above. For a discussion of the inconsistencies between de Lubac's earlier and later positions, see Wood, "Nature-Grace Problematic," 389–403. See also Wood, *Spiritual Exegesis and the Church*, 71–128.

and on human reason in particular.[47] He suggests that because of original sin, the human intellect is itself limited and insufficient. Indeed, humans cannot understand themselves, much less God, without the grace of supernatural revelation.[48] This is why he affirms: "the revelation of God is also the revelation of man" to himself.[49] This is the basis of his discussion in *Catholicism*, which maintains that the Church's primary role in society is to offer the world a vision of its own true self, healed and transformed in the image of Christ.[50] He suggests that

47. De Lubac, *Mystery of the Supernatural*, 48. Cf. de Lubac, *Brief Catechesis on Nature and Grace*, 128–48.

48. One recent critic of de Lubac's position argues precisely the opposite, namely, that unless we are able to comprehend nature, then we cannot hope to understand and affirm the supernatural. See Cessario, "Duplex Ordo Cognitionis," 332. "If human nature is unintelligible," asks Cessario, "what possible sense can be given to the doctrine of the incarnation of the Word?" Cessario provides an excellent example of what de Lubac calls extrinsicism. For Cessario, the incarnation of the Word is not an "illuminating mystery" enabling us to see all reality more clearly, but rather an extrinsic, supernatural revelation, which natural human reason has the capacity to recognize as such. For a helpful review and critique of Cessario and several other contemporary Catholic scholars who affirm that we can know "human nature absolutely without the illumination of revelation," see Long, "Way of Aquinas," 339–56.

49. De Lubac, *Brief Catechesis on Nature and Grace*, 131.

50. Steven A. Long suggests that de Lubac's early treatment of the relationship between nature and grace presents a problem for Nicene and Chalcedonian Christology because "a teaching that renders human nature to be a vacuole or pure nought lacking proportionate created integrity and unknowable apart from the beatific vision seems to make the doctrine of Nicea unintelligible. For *what* is assumed in the Word is defined in precision from the datum of its assumption. One does not say, "The Person of the Word assumed the nature that is defined by its being assumed by the Person of the Word"—for that would render the hypostatic union a necessary function of finite human nature" ("On the Loss and the Recovery," 151). This seems to be a legitimate critique of de Lubac's early perspective, which tended toward too great a continuity between human nature and divine grace. However Romanus Cessario's similar critique falls short. Cessario's concern is with the relationship between reason and faith when he asks, "what is it that the Second Person of the Trinity assumed if not human nature? And if human nature is unintelligible in its own right, what possible sense can be given to the doctrine of the incarnation of the Word? If being is unintelligible, then the revelation of God—who is perfect being—will be perfectly unintelligible" ("Duplex Ordo Cognitioni," 328). Cessario suggests that our understanding of divine revelation is impossible without the prior understanding of human nature unaided by revelation. In response to this suggestion, I would offer this statement from a contemporary proponent of de Lubac's position: "grace's interpretation of what is natural is the anterior condition for nature's interpretation of what is 'graced' or indeed compatible with the order of grace. Of course, the sense of this priority must be properly understood. Certainly it is possible to have some knowledge of the integrity

Nothing is more superficial than the charge made against her [the Church] of losing sight of immediate realities, of neglecting man's urgent needs, by speaking to him always of the hereafter. For in truth the hereafter is far nearer than the future, far nearer than what we call the present. It is the Eternal found at the heart of all temporal development which gives it life and direction. It is the authentic Present without which the present itself is like dust which slips through our hands. If modern men are so absent from each other, it is primarily because they are absent from themselves, since they have abandoned this Eternal which alone establishes them in being and enables them to communicate with one another.[51]

The Church as the body of Christ is thus the medium of God's transcendent and supernatural grace through which humanity is revealed to itself, and redeemed.[52] De Lubac maintains that humankind, and all of nature, is created incapable of reaching its ultimate end, of discovering itself in God, apart from the supernatural grace of God, which redeems and thereby perfects nature.

Obediential Potency

As mentioned above, Cajetan's pure-nature theory was motivated by his desire to protect a supernatural gratuity against the claims of Baius and others who posited that within human nature, there are sufficient

---

of nature directly through experience, and thus both 'before' and as distinct from the order of grace. The point is simply that this knowledge will in any case be of a grace-related nature (of always-already concretely ordered, positively or negatively, consciously or unconsciously, to the God of Jesus Christ) and thus not of a 'pure nature,' whether one is aware of this relation (or ordering) or not" (Schindler, "Christology, Public Theology, and Thomism," 252–53).

51. De Lubac, *Catholicism*, 362.

52. He writes that "by revealing the Father and by being revealed by him, Christ completes the revelation of man to himself. By taking possession of man, by seizing hold of him and by penetrating to the very depths of his being Christ makes man go deep down within himself, there to discover in a flash regions hitherto unsuspected. It is through Christ that the person reaches maturity, that man emerges definitively from the universe, and becomes conscious of his own being. Henceforth, even before that triumphant exclamation: *Agnosce, O Christiane, dignitatemtuam* [a footnote translates this: Recognize, O Christian, your dignity], it will be possible to praise the dignity of man: *dignitatem conditionis humanae* [another footnote translates this: "the dignity of the human condition"]" (ibid., 339–40).

resources to achieve the beatific vision. The Scholastics thought that to admit, as de Lubac did, a positive "natural desire" for the beatific vision was to admit a "natural ability" to attain it.[53] Rather than affirm a "natural desire" for a supernatural end within human nature, the neo-Thomists referred to the Thomistic phrase "obediential potency" to explain how persons are created with the capacity to receive supernatural grace even though they are positively oriented only toward a natural end. Réginald Garrigou-Lagrange defines obediential potency (here translated as "obediential power") as follows:

> There is in any subject a passive power which is not natural, since it does not affirm an order to a natural agent, but is a passive power that affirms an order to a supernatural agent which it obeys so as to receive from it whatever it may wish to confer. . . . Therefore the obediential power, by its formal reason, is not a positive ordination of the nature of the human soul or its faculties toward a supernatural object, and signifies nothing more than a simple

53. The problem here is that "Thomas teaches that 'the natural *movement* of the will is the principle of all things that we will. But the will's natural inclination is directed towards what is in keeping with its nature (*ST I*, q. 62, a. 2, emphasis added in Long [see below]) . . . Hence the will cannot be moved toward something beyond its nature such as supernatural beatitude without extrinsic supernatural assistance—about which last he states that 'this is what we call the assistance of grace'" (Long, "On the Loss, and the Recovery," 145–46). Thus, if there is a natural desire in humans for supernatural beatitude, then humankind must somehow be in possession of the supernatural in order to will it. In other words, humans are incapable of willing or desiring that which is wholly beyond human nature and thus inaccessible to human volitional and intellectual powers. How can we desire in any meaningful way that which we neither know nor are capable of conceiving? It seems to me that this is another legitimate criticism of de Lubac's position and that de Lubac would have benefited by acknowledging more explicitly the distinction between proximate and ultimate ends. From Long's perspective, although humans naturally desire a natural end in proportion with human nature, the fall from grace (sin) "does not put man into a state of 'pure nature' but rather does harm to nature" (ibid., 152). Thus, although humans are naturally ordered to an end in proportion to their human nature, human nature remains frustrated and incapable of achieving even a proximate, natural beatitude without being made to participate in the transcendent order of salvation. So, in the real world, with which de Lubac was exclusively concerned, there is only one end for humankind, and that is a supernatural end. Because of sin, we have no end other than the revelation of God in Jesus Christ. Although it seems to me that Long has a legitimate critique of de Lubac, he has not shown that de Lubac's criticisms of the commentarial tradition were off base. I am still convinced that Cajetan, Suarez, and the tradition that followed them tended to conceive of pure nature in a too-static fashion, and that they tended to draw problematic conclusions in relation to the nature of theological science, natural reason, moral law, and secular government.

non-aversion, or capacity, to receive whatever God may will. However, by reason of its subject and materially, it is completely identified with the essence of the soul and its faculties, whether passive or active, which can be elevated to the order of grace. . . . Thus, these gifts of grace are, at one and the same time, completely gratuitous, in no sense due to us, and perfectly becoming to our nature, with a fitness which is not, however, natural but supernatural, at once most sublime, most profound, and gratuitous.[54]

For Garrigou-Lagrange and other neoscholastics, humans are not naturally inclined toward a supernatural end. Rather, humans are naturally oriented toward a natural end, though as we read in the above quotation, they have within them a capacity that is merely a "non-aversion" toward an extrinsic supernatural end offered according to God's grace. Anything stronger than a nonaversion, according to the neoscholastics, would suggest that God is compelled to grant the beatific vision.   *ability*

While de Lubac agrees that obediential potency is a "passive aptitude," he has no problem ascribing to human nature a *longing* to accompany this aptitude.[55] Indeed, he writes that the "natural 'capacity,' to which

54. Garrigou-Lagrange, *Grace*, 307–9. For a more recent treatment of obediential potency, see Long, "Man's Natural End," 211–37.

55. It seems to me that de Lubac is right here. Because sin has harmed nature and rendered inaccessible a natural beatitude in proportion to human nature, humankind will remain frustrated, incomplete, and unfulfilled without the satisfaction brought by supernatural beatitude. Thus, while it may not be correct to say that humans have an intrinsic, natural desire for supernatural beatitude, it is correct to say that humans have an intrinsic, natural desire for natural beatitude, which can only be satisfied by the grace of supernatural beatitude. In this way, de Lubac is right to say that only (saving) grace completes and perfects nature. This also means that de Lubac is correct when he suggests that "the 'desire to see God' cannot be permanently frustrated without an essential suffering" (de Lubac, *Mystery of the Supernatural*, 54). Cf., "Within *this* order, surely nature if deprived of grace would be vain" (Long, "Man's Natural End," 229). Still, Milbank seems to be wide of the mark when he writes: "the gift of deification is guaranteed by no contrast, not even with Creation, never mind nature. How could it be, since like the Creation, it is a gift to a gift, which, in this spiritual instance, the gift then gives to itself in order to sustain its only nature? How could it be guaranteed by contrast, since the gift of deification is so much in excess of Creation that it entirely includes it? In the ultimate experience of the supernatural which orients it, namely the beatific vision, our entire being is transfigured by the divine light. Here we become the reception of this light and there is no longer any additional 'natural' recipient of this reception, Milbank, *Suspended Middle*, 46–47. Milbank insists that there can be no "contrast" between nature and grace (only continuity) because he, like the early de Lubac, does not consider the distinction between proximate and ultimate ends. However, we can affirm a natural end in proportion with human nature, as my statement above should make clear, and simultaneously

the natural 'longing' corresponds, is not a 'faculty;' it is no more than a 'passive aptitude.'[56] In his early works on nature and grace, de Lubac seeks to show that for Aquinas, and Augustine before him, human nature has only one end, the supernatural, and he does not believe that a natural desire necessarily implies a natural ability to attain the beatific vision. He writes:

> If therefore the desire is truly a "natural inclination," it is not by that fact a 'sufficient' or "proportionate" inclination; it does not desire its object "sufficiently"; or, in other words, as in the case of free will left to itself, so this desire is unable to strive 'suitably' or 'efficaciously;' to put it yet another way, it is not the source of any "sufficient activity" which would make it, however minimally, of itself "a certain inchoative possession."[57]

---

affirm that causation in the order of deification is not merely extrinsic; it also comes from the natural thirst (the first gift), which only supernatural beatitude (the gift to a gift) satisfies. D. Stephen Long provides a very helpful insight when he focuses the issue on Christology, where it belongs. He suggests that "we can intend God, not because we can make such inferences in general, but rather because in this unique relationship of the two natures we can 'see' under the aspect of the human what is invisible, the aspect of the divine" (Long, "Way of Aquinas," 350).

56. De Lubac, *Mystery of the Supernatural*, 85.

57. Ibid., 86. Steven A. Long describes obediential potency, suggesting, "The similitude of the stained-glass window illumined by the sun's rays well bespeaks the character of the doctrine of obediential potency as applied to the relation of nature and grace. The stained-glass window, were it cognizant, could not 'know what it was missing' were it never to irradiate its bright colors under the influence of the sun. It would be a window, still, and function as part of the structure—though it would, in a given respect, not be fulfilled. It would be what it is, not fail to be part of the whole structure of which it would form an integral part, nor lack its own participation in the good of the whole as a specific perfection. Yet its nature stands properly revealed only under the extrinsic causality of the sun's illumination: seeing it so illumined, we know what stained glass truly is for" (Long, "Man's Natural End," 236). What I find especially interesting about Long's analogy is that it so successfully refutes John Milbank's contention that neo-Thomist accounts place "nature and grace . . . spatially outside each other (on an extrinsicist model)" so that nature encounters the gift of grace somewhat like a "brick wall that we might inadvertently run into" (Milbank, *Suspended Middle*, 46). Indeed, in Long's analogy, the stained-glass window is created (the first gift) by God though it only discovers its deepest and ultimate purpose as it is made to participate in the divine light (the second gift). Long's analogy is not perfect, however, since human nature, unlike the stained-glass window, as it exists in the context of a fallen creation, is cognizant of the fact that it is missing something. The stained-glass window does not suffer the consequences of a nature harmed by sin with no hope of satisfaction apart from the light of the Son. In other words, even if we concede that the concept of obediential potency is preferable to "intrinsic desire for supernatural beatitude," we must remember that the first gift creates a natural desire that continues to

There is thus a natural and inherent "desire" in humans that remains unsatisfied without the vision of God, but "it is sanctifying grace, with its train of theological virtues, which must order the subject to his last end; at least, it alone can order him "sufficiently" or "perfectly" or "directly.""[58]

God's Uncompelled Grace

In light of the above discussion, it is clear that, for de Lubac, one can affirm a natural desire or longing for God within human nature while also claiming that human nature is incapable of attaining the beatific vision apart from God's grace. De Lubac summarizes the thesis of his historical studies on nature and grace when he writes that

> all tradition, in effect—taking the word in its widest sense—passing from St. Irenaeus, by way of St. Augustine and St. Bonaventure, without distinction of school, presents us with the two affirmations at once, not in opposition but as a totality: man cannot live except by the vision of God—and that vision of God depends totally on God's good pleasure. One has no right to weaken either, even in order to grasp the other more firmly.[59]

De Lubac believed that the neoscholastic tradition, following Cajetan and Suarez, had fallen short because it did not affirm both sides of the paradox. The Thomist commentators weakened the claim that "man cannot live except by the vision of God," and this led to an extrinsic theology and an exiled church, and de Lubac's persistent work on the relationship between nature and grace was motivated by his desire to see the Church reengage the world with the gospel. It is not insignificant that one of his fiercest critics was the famous Dominican theologian cited above, Réginald Garrigou-Lagrange (1877–1964). According to Fergus Kerr,

> Garrigou-Lagrange was among the first to attack *Surnaturel*. Although remaining in his university post in Rome during the war, he did not conceal his support for the Vichy regime nor his longstanding sympathies with *Action française*. He was a close associate of the Vichy ambassador to the Vatican, who assured his government in a notorious dispatch that the Holy See had no ob-

---

"long" for satisfaction, which comes only as a second gift.

58. Ibid., 85.

59. Ibid., 179.

jections to the Vichy anti-Jewish legislation, even providing supporting citations from Aquinas which de Lubac at least believed
to have been contributed by "Thomists."[60]

It was precisely this kind of Catholic complacency in the face of social and political evil that de Lubac hoped to challenge.[61] He envisioned
a Church fully engaged with the world around it. Thus, toward the end
of *The Mystery of the Supernatural*, he states that in the absence of a dualistic perspective, "'the beatific vision' is no longer the contemplation of
a spectacle, but an intimate participation in the vision the Son has of the
Father in the bosom of the Trinity."[62] For de Lubac and other proponents
of *nouvelle théologie*, theology itself is a participation in the wisdom of the
triune God. The fact that neoscholastic theology had come to resemble
museum work (divorced from the concerns of everyday life and lacking
a deep connection to spiritual exegesis) was good evidence, for de Lubac,
that nature and grace had been torn apart and needed to be fastened back
together by a return to a more authentic *sacra doctrina*.

60. Kerr, "French Theology," 112. Another commentator explains that "Garrigou-
Lagrange . . . had long supported the *Action française*, and his defense of Vichy had reached
the point of accusing anyone who supported de Gaulle of mortal sin" (Komonchak,
"Theology and Culture at Mid-Century," 601). For his own reflections on Catholicism
and Anti-Semitism during the Second World War, see de Lubac, *Christian Resistance to
Anti-Semitism*.

61. Regarding his initial attempt to make the historical argument in *Surnaturel*, de
Lubac writes of the neoscholastic opposition: "they happened to perceive, better perhaps
than I had, what was at stake in the dispute. This is because I believe I showed, particularly in the second part, the composition of which is rather strict, that since various
schools of modern Scholasticism had abandoned the traditional systematic (and already
a bit compromised) synthesis in the work of Saint Thomas, they could only wear themselves out in sterile combats, each being both right and wrong, against the others, while
withdrawing from living thought into an artificial world, leaving the field open to all ups
and downs of a 'separated philosophy.' The work thus constituted a sort of attempt to
reestablish contact between Catholic theology and contemporary thought, or at least to
eliminate one basic obstacle to that contact . . . not with a view to any 'adaptation' whatsoever to that thought, but rather with a view to engaging in dialogue with it—which, as
always when it is a question of serious ideas, could only be a confrontation, a combat" (de
Lubac, *At the Service of the Church*, 36).

62. Lubac, *Mystery of the Supernatural*, 228.

Spiritual Exegesis as Sacra Doctrina

Although de Lubac never entered into a debate with his neo-Thomist opponents over the nature of *sacra doctrina* in the *Summa Theologiae*, others did. Marie Dominique Chenu, for example, wrote several essays and books focused exclusively on this controversial issue. As early as 1935, he wrote an essay arguing that theology, unlike other human sciences, requires the gift of faith in order to proceed. Faith, according to Chenu, is among other things "an infused light; it is a mystical grace which will further develop under the impulse of the gifts of the Holy Spirit . . . faith is a sharing in the knowledge of God."[63] Moreover, Chenu argued that to call an abstract system of "given" metaphysical truth statements theological knowledge (as Labourdette seemed to do) is a distortion of an authentic *sacra doctrina*.[64] According to Chenu, theology, or *sacra doctrina*, is not "a humanly organized speculative system of abstract concepts," but "the knowledge which God has of himself and of things in their contingency." "Theology" Chenu tells us, "is the knowledge of the knowledge of God . . . it is wisdom," or a sharing in the wisdom of God.[65]

Although a number of recent commentators have challenged and corrected Chenu on several important points, including his understanding of *scientiae* in Aristotle and his failure to see that the *Summa Theologiae* is structured around the divine economy of sacred Scripture, his emphasis on *sacra doctrina* as "a sharing in God's wisdom" is widely held by Thomists. Brian Shanley, for example, explains, "the formal object of *sacra doctrina* is the intelligibility of the world as spoken by God. *Sacra doctrina* is a sharing in God's unified view of the whole."[66] Similarly, John Jenkins writes, "the subject of Sacred Doctrine is God and all other things insofar as they are related to God."[67] Jenkins writes further: "we participate in God's *scientia*" of sacred doctrine "not only in knowing

---

63. Chenu, "Eyes of Faith," 9–13. Cf., Levering, *Participatory Biblical Exegesis*, 73.

64. Chenu, "What Is Theology?" 34. Levering adds that *sacra doctrina* entails God's teaching. It is literally God's instruction of us. "In other words, encountering God teaching in and through scripture goes beyond the mere reception of abstract knowledge. God, teaching in and through Scripture, renews and transforms the entire person by directing the person to relationship with God" (Levering, *Participatory Biblical Exegesis*, 73).

65. Ibid.

66. Shanley, "*Sacra Doctrina* and the Theology of Disclosure," 177.

67. Jenkins, *Knowledge and Faith in Thomas Aquinas*, 54.

what God knows but in knowing in the way that God knows it."[68] Rudi
A. te Velde suggests that "being a *scientia*, sacred doctrine cannot be re-
stricted to factual revelation in Scripture; rather, it considers the whole of
reality under the aspect of the intelligibility which things have when seen
in the light of God's revelation."[69] Matthew Levering says that Aquinas
"understands theology as wisdom, that is, a participation in Christ's sacred instruction in divine Wisdom."[70]

As is evident in Levering's statement, Thomas Aquinas considered
theology a kind of divine pedagogy through which persons can, by grace,
attain to the knowledge of God by participating in God's own knowledge
of himself and of the world. I would suggest that de Lubac, although he
did not engage directly in the debate over the nature of *sacra doctrina* in
the *Summa Theologiae*, was motivated by a desire to refashion Catholic
theology in the twentieth century so that it once again served as a divine
pedagogy.

Consider these statements from his commentary on Vatican II's *Dei
Verbum*, which could be considered one of the most important fruits of
de Lubac's work on spiritual exegesis:

> To reflect in Christ or, as one says, "to do theology," does not only
> mean to "organize truths," to systematize them or draw new con-
> clusions from the revealed "premises;" it is more to "demonstrate
> the explanatory power" of the truths of faith in relation to the
> changing context of the world. It is to strive to understand the
> world and man, his nature, his destiny and his history, in the most
> diverse situations, in the light of those same truths. It is to attempt
> to see all things in the mystery of Christ. For the mystery of Christ
> is an illuminating mystery, and in considering it in this way, one
> really deepens it without removing its mysterious character. Thus,
> the enterprise of a "theology of history" must not be considered as
> a merely marginal phenomenon; every theologian must be, more
> or less, a "theologian of history." In no way does all of this mean,
> however, that history as such is the medium of revelation or salva-
> tion: on the contrary. Whether it is a matter of secular history or
> the history of the Church: by themselves, historical events bring
> us no increase in supernatural revelation. They remain always
> "ambiguous" and come "in anticipation," and it is they that must

68. Ibid., 74.

69. Velde, "Understanding the *Scientia* of Faith," 68.

70. Levering, *Scripture and Metaphysics*, 4.

be illuminated for us by the light that comes from the Gospel (my translation).[71]

For de Lubac, the theological task, which involves illuminating all things in the mystery of Christ, is necessarily an exegetical task: "Theological science," he suggests, "and the explication of Scripture cannot but be one and the same thing" since "knowledge of the faith [amounts] to knowledge of Scripture."[72] This explains his sustained efforts to retrieve the participatory ontology and philosophy of history that undergirded patristic and medieval exegesis. De Lubac was attracted to the way that spiritual exegesis entailed an engagement with the world through its fourfold method, which served to illumine all things in the mystery of Christ. Indeed, the methods of spiritual exegesis served to stretch Scripture so that it was able to incorporate, continually, the unfolding of history into its christocentric plot.

PATRISTIC AND MEDIEVAL EXEGESIS

De Lubac's Critique of Scientific Exegesis

According to de Lubac, spiritual exegesis facilitated the Church's continuing engagement in history—guiding it with a thoroughly christological vision of reality. Thus, his voluminous work on spiritual exegesis, like his work in the areas of ecclesiology and ontology, was intended to help the church reengage the world with the gospel. As with the relationship between nature and grace, the work of Maurice Blondel was influential.[73] In his doctoral dissertation, *L'Action* (1893), Blondel began his critique of the modern sciences and their positivist spirit, which sought total knowledge of reality through empirical investigation. According to Blondel, the kind of scientific knowledge that could be gained through the examination of

71. De Lubac, *La Révélation Divine*, 100–101.

72. De Lubac, *Medieval Exegesis*, vol. 1, 27–28. In chapters 6 and 7, I will argue that de Lubac's work on spiritual exegesis was intended to help reconstitute a properly Thomistic *scientia* of *sacra doctrina*, and I will conclude by offering several suggestions as to how contemporary scholars can appropriate de Lubac's work for the church today.

73. For more on Blondel's influence on de Lubac's critique of scientific exegesis, see D'Ambrosio, "Henri de Lubac and the Recovery of the Traditional Hermeneutic," 262–65.

physical or historical "facts" was insufficient for a true understanding of historical reality and human existence in particular.[74]

In a series of essays published in 1904 titled *Histoire et dogme: Les lacunes philosohiques de l'exégèse moderne,* Blondel took his more-general critique of scientific knowledge and applied it to biblical exegesis.[75] Writing at the time of the Catholic modernist controversy, he suggested that two dangers confront biblical exegetes. The first danger is "extrinsicism" and the other is "historicism."[76] Extrinsicism, according to Blondel, characterizes the neoscholastic tendency to treat theology as an abstract system of interrelated propositions given by divine revelation: "The logical procedure of an exegete nourished on such thoughts," he tells us, "is therefore to take the texts literally and to subject any critical study to the sovereign demand of a dogmatic ideology: the ageless facts are without local colour, vanish as the result of a sort of perpetual docetism." The biblical exegete given to extrinsicism has no need of historical investigation because his ahistorical truth "is guaranteed *en bloc*, not by its content, but by the external seal of the divine: why bother to verify the details?"[77]

In contrast to extrinsicism we have the danger of "historicism," whose object is a kind of "scientific history" made up of "abstractions."[78] The historicist approach is focused only upon the phenomena of history—the observable outer events or "historical facts." Moreover, these facts

> will be given the role of reality itself; and an ontology, purely phenomenological in character, will be extracted from a methodology and a phenomenology. A sort of dialectical evolutionism is deduced from this scientific determinism which claims to have

74. Blondel, *L'action,* 78, 438–39.

75. All citations will come from the English translation, Blondel, *Letter on Apologetics, and History and Dogma*

76. "*Extrinsicism* and *historicism* offer two answers—each in their way incomplete, but equally dangerous to faith" (ibid., 225). The modernist controversy was a struggle between Catholic scholars who felt that the Church should embrace the historical-critical methods of modern biblical scholars and those who opposed them. Blondel's critique of "historicism" is directed at modernists such as Alfred Loisy. His critique of "extrinsicism" is directed at the neoscholastics, who tended to oppose modernism. For a recent series of essays on the modernist controversy, including an essay on Blondel and Loisy, see Jodock, *Catholicism Contending with Modernity.*

77. Blondel, *Letter on Apologetics, and History and Dogma,* 229.

78. Ibid., 239.

penetrated the spiritual secret of the living chain of souls because
it has verified the external joints of the links which are no more
than its corpse.[79]

Whereas extrinsicism has no need of historical investigation because
it has received the truth *en bloc* as a revelation from God, the historicist
tends to reduce revelation to the discoveries of scientific history. Blondel
writes that "it should never be supposed therefore that history by itself
can know a fact which would be no more than a fact, and that would be
the whole fact: each link in the chain, and the chain as a whole, involve
the psychological and moral problems implied by the least action or tes-
timony. . . . Real history is composed of human lives; and human life is
metaphysics in act."[80]

Contra the extrinsicists, Blondel believes that biblical interpreters
must be concerned with history, but not exclusively with the "critical history" of the historicists, which goes no deeper than the observable facts.[81]
In contrast to an exclusive embrace of either of these options, Blondel
suggests that biblical exegesis must be concerned in the end with "real
history"—with the spiritual dynamism that animates and motivates humankind within history.

When de Lubac critiques scientific exegesis, he echoes Blondel, suggesting that the problem of the limitations of critical exegesis

> is the problem of the relation of history as science to history as re-
> ality, and it is at the same time the problem of history and dogma
> or, as one would have said of old . . . the problem of history and al-
> legory. This problem cannot be reduced to the question of know-
> ing what literal sense ought to be recognized in this or that text,
> as it could sometimes seem to be. It is of a much more general
> and fundamental order. And one recognizes it as much regarding
> the Gospel as regarding Prophecy, as regards all spiritual history.
> How should we understand the reticence of criticism? Does it re-
> ally deny, and in this case has it the right to deny, all that which
> the scientific examination of texts does not permit it to affirm? Do

79. Ibid., 240.

80. Ibid., 237.

81. It is important that Blondel does not discount the relevance and importance of
critical history. He believes, simply, that critical history is limited and must recognize
its inability to penetrate the depths of human experience. He writes that although "the
historian has, as it were, a word to say in everything concerning man, there is nothing on
which he has the last word" (ibid., 236).

other methods exist which will permit, under certain conditions, anything more to be affirmed?[82]

It is important to note that like Blondel, de Lubac believed scientific exegesis had much to offer.[83] However, he wanted to be sure that the proponents of scientific exegesis were aware of their own presuppositions, and that they understood the limits of their science. In the preface to the first volume of *Medieval Exegesis* (1959), de Lubac affirms that proponents of the modern exegetical methods

> should be applauded, inasmuch as they felt "the pressing need to undertake the research that is always being propelled further along in its course by the most rigorous of modern techniques." And, in their right and proper place, these techniques may, without undue pride, be construed as an instance of enormous progress. The key phrase here is "in their right and proper place." Without this proviso, there can be no real progress. And the Ancients can still help us to situate this right and proper place within the context of a whole picture that gives it its true measure and significance. The Ancients do not have an explanation for everything, as many have the tendency to suppose. This is because they lived in a precritical age. Nevertheless, "beyond the methods that have become strange to us," we often find "a profoundly thought out theology" in their work.[84]

The Importance of Spiritual Exegesis

Following his highly controversial work on nature and grace, de Lubac endeavored to explain and recommend the "spiritual exegesis" of the church fathers.[85] Once the philosophical divide between nature and grace

82. D'Ambrosio, "Henri de Lubac and the Recovery of the Traditional Hermeneutic," 266. See also de Lubac, *Exégèse Médiévale*, 366. The above quotation is Marcellino D'Ambrosio's translation of de Lubac and comes from the third volume of de Lubac's four-volume series on medieval exegesis. Throughout this work, I use English translations of de Lubac's works whenever possible and offer my own translations whenever I quote passages that are yet untranslated.

83. For more on de Lubac's affirmation and critique of modern scientific exegesis, see D'Ambrosio, "Henri de Lubac and the Critique of Scientific Exegesis."

84. De Lubac, *Medieval Exegesis*, vol. 1, xx.

85. Susan Wood has pointed out that for de Lubac the relationship between the literal and allegorical senses of Scripture is analogous to the relationship between nature and

had been bridged, he turned his attention toward enabling the Church to actually practice *sacra doctrina*—and thus engage culture through a more intentional participation in the divine economy.[86] For de Lubac, although it is the Eucharist that "makes the Church," this making or this immersion in God's divine economy is facilitated through spiritual exegesis. Indeed, de Lubac gives Scripture priority over the Eucharist when he suggests that "for, on the one hand, the [sacramental] 'Body', as real as it may be, is not the Divinity itself; as its name indicates, it always remains the symbol of some more spiritual reality, while, on the other hand, the 'Word' is, in its pure essence, that very reality: for the Son of God, God himself, is 'Word'"[87]

For de Lubac, spiritual exegesis enabled the Church to move beyond the external facts of biblical history in order to "plunge into" the history of salvation through the same Spirit that animated it. The genius of the ancient Christian exegete is that "he discovers in ancient documents [biblical texts] the wellsprings for his own prayer."[88] Commenting on de Lubac's understanding of spiritual exegesis, Von Balthasar explains that "the theory of the senses of Scripture is not a curiosity of the history of theology but an instrument for seeking out the most profound articulations of salvation history."[89] Indeed spiritual exegesis enables the church to perceive its own history as "animated by the Spirit," and it facilitates the

---

grace. Just as in *A Brief Catechesis on Nature and Grace*, the natural order is converted and transformed in the supernatural order, so in de Lubac's work on spiritual exegesis the literal sense is converted and transformed by the allegorical sense. This is also to say that the Old Testament is converted and transformed by the New. See Wood, *Spiritual Exegesis*, 119, n. 148.

86. I do not mean to oversimplify de Lubac's career by suggesting a clear, linear progression, without regular diversions, from his ecclesiological work, to his ontological work, and then to his exegetical work. On the contrary, de Lubac touched on various issues at different times throughout his career. However, his major works on ecclesiology and grace do seem to have prepared the way for his major efforts on patristic and medieval exegesis. I also want to emphasize the organic relationship between the historical/ontological and the historical/exegetical works. The exegetical works offer a "method," for lack of a better word, through which a participatory ontology can guide the Church's engagement with secular culture.

87. De Lubac, *History and Spirit*, 418. In chapters 5 and 6, I will suggest that the proponents of Radical Orthodoxy, and John Milbank in particular, have paid too little attention to the priority of spiritual exegesis in de Lubac's thought.

88. De Lubac, *Scripture in the Tradition*, 25.

89. Balthasar, *Theology of Henri de Lubac*, 76.

church's continued incorporation into this history of salvation. De Lubac explains that

> The Christian mystery, because of the magnificent providential Economy which embraces both Testaments and links them together, has not been handed down to us as a collection of timeless definitions, unrelated to any historical situation and demanding only to be clothed, according to our fancy, with biblical images as with just so many illustrations. The intimate links between the two Testaments are quite of another kind. Within the very consciousness of Jesus—if we cast a human glance into that sanctuary—the Old Testament was seen as the matrix of the New or as the instrument of its creation. This meant something much more than extrinsic preparation. Even the categories used by Jesus to tell us about himself are ancient biblical categories. Jesus causes them to burst forth or, if you prefer, sublimates them and unifies them by making them converge upon himself. . . . Thus, "biblical images," and the concrete facts behind them, furnish the thread, both historical and noetic, from which is woven the Christian mystery in all its newness and transcendence.[90]

For de Lubac, the spiritual interpretation of Scripture is constitutive for the Church. Without a spiritual understanding of Scripture, the Church cannot comprehend the nature of its own salvation.[91] Indeed, he suggests, "the entire process of spiritual understanding is, in its principle, identical to the process of conversion. It is its luminous aspect. *Intellectus spiritualis credentem salvum facit* (Spiritual understanding saves the believer)."[92] Again, "theological science and the explication of Scripture cannot but be one and the same thing" since "knowledge of the faith [amounts] to knowledge of Scripture."[93]

The Fourfold Interpretation of Scripture

Beginning in 1950 with his great defense of Origen, *Histoire et Esprit*, and culminating in his four-volume *Exégèse Médiévale* (1959–1964),

90. De Lubac, *Scripture in the Tradition*, 7–8.

91. "All the basic biblical themes: Covenant, Election, People of God, Word, Messiah, Kingdom, Day of the Lord, and so forth, enter into the Christian idea of salvation" (ibid., 9).

92. Ibid., 21.

93. De Lubac, *Medieval Exegesis*, vol. 1, 27–28.

de Lubac illustrates the methods and implications of spiritual exegesis practiced by the patristic and medieval Fathers. The ancient quadripartite interpretation of Scripture recognizes the literal, allegorical, tropological, and anagogical senses. In a paper presented to the Faculté de théologie de Toulouse in 1948, de Lubac recalls an old Latin saying: "Littera gesta docet, quid credas allegoria, Moralis quid agas, quo tendas anagogia." Translated, this means that "the letter teaches us what took place, the allegory what to believe, the moral what to do, the anagogy what goal to strive for."[94] What de Lubac found so appealing in the ancient hermeneutic, with its four senses, was precisely a divine pedagogy, or a *sacra doctrina*, which guides readers through the biblical text and ever deeper into a participatory knowledge of God in Christ. For de Lubac, theological science is superficial and inauthentic unless it does in fact lead to true knowledge of God, which must be participatory, since God is not an object to be known extrinsically.[95]

Briefly stated, the literal sense offers insight into the people and events of biblical history, while the allegorical shows that those persons and events were but shadows of a more complete and perfect reality—Christ and his body, the Church. The tropological sense guides our incorporation into Christ and his Church in order to share in Christ's goodness and perfection. Each of these senses "leads to the other as its end" until we come to anagogy, which shows us that the experience of time was but a preparation for eternity.[96]

Although de Lubac did not advocate a strict return to the exegetical methods enumerated above, he was convinced that contemporary exegetes could learn a great deal from the Fathers, and that they should attempt to retrieve the "spirit" of their exegetical practice, and consequently read Scripture as the Word of God incarnate in human history. Indeed, all of the fourfold senses serve to illuminate the spiritual mean-

94. De Lubac, "On an Old Distich," 109. For more on the Latin formula, See de Lubac, *Medieval Exegesis*, vol. 1, 1–14.

95. Matthew Levering suggests that for both Augustine and Aquinas, Scripture was "transformative *sacra doctrina*" since "the words of Scripture continually point beyond themselves toward the encounter with their divine source; the transformative power of the words is known in their ability to direct the reader or hearer to the divine Teacher" (Levering, *Participatory Biblical Exegesis*, 71).

96. De Lubac, *Medieval Exegesis*, vol. 2, 203. I will return to a much more comprehensive treatment of the fourfold method and its centrality in de Lubac's *ressourcement* project in chapter 6.

ing of history from a christocentric perspective. It is partly through this illumination that the Church is united with God in the incarnate Christ. Citing a statement from *Catholicism* again, we see that, according to de Lubac,

> God acts in history and reveals himself through history. Or rather, God inserts himself in history and so bestows on it a "religious consecration" which compels us to treat it with due respect. As a consequence historical realities possess a profound sense and are to be understood in a spiritual manner. . . . The Bible, which contains the revelation of salvation, contains too, in its own way, the history of the world. In order to understand it, it is not enough to take note of the factual details it recounts, but there must be an awareness of its concern for universality. . . . It was in this way that the Bible was read by the Fathers of the Church. . . . If salvation is social in its essence it follows that history is the necessary interpreter between God and man.[97]

Spiritual exegesis, which de Lubac equates with conversion, facilitates the Church's engagement with culture, first, by enabling it to understand the spirit that guided biblical history (the literal and allegorical senses) and, second, by enabling it to engage history in that same spirit (the tropological sense) as it continually interprets the world in light of the final consummation of all things in Christ (the anagogical sense). Spiritual exegesis is not, primarily, a speculative, academic exercise. Rather, it is social and political to the core since it mediates the Church's ongoing historical engagement with culture. For de Lubac, nature and all of history finds its completion and fulfillment only in God yet remains incapable of ascending to God without supernatural grace. Apart from the God who redeems creation from within, and without a vision of this telos revealed through God's incarnate and transcendent Word, which is mediated to the Church and the world through Scripture, individuals and entire civilizations fall into dissolution.[98]

---

97. De Lubac, *Catholicism*, 165.

98. I will have a great deal more to say about the role of spiritual exegesis in the Church's engagement with culture in chapter 6.

Conclusion

The preceding chapters have shown that de Lubac's major works on ecclesiology, ontology, and exegesis are related to one another organically. De Lubac was motivated by his dissatisfaction with the Church's complacency in the face of the crises of twentieth-century Europe. He felt that the Church had become exiled from the pressing concerns of everyday life, and that this exile was, at least in part, the consequence of a dualism created and perpetuated by theologians and biblical scholars. With his early works on ecclesiology, namely, *Catholicism* and *Corpus Mysticum*, de Lubac offered a vision of the Church participating with Christ in the divine economy, and described an important historical transformation that served to obscure this vision. A participatory ontology such as the one envisioned by de Lubac means that there can be no partition between the natural and the supernatural. In the end, nature and history are transformed and completed by God's supernatural grace. De Lubac argued in his works on nature and grace that the Church's great tradition is consistent in affirming that grace completes and perfects nature.

After demonstrating that the Fathers did not concur with neoscholasticism's dualistic ontology, de Lubac focused his energies on spiritual exegesis and wrote more pages on this issue than on any other during his long career.[99] The great achievement of his work is that it illustrates how spiritual exegesis enables the Church to perceive its own history as animated by the Spirit, and at the same time facilitates the Church's ongoing incorporation of itself and the world into the divine economy—of time into eternity.

Chapter 6 delves much deeper into de Lubac's work on spiritual exegesis. In the meantime, however, chapter 5 offers a slight detour, as I consider the thought of several other twentieth-century theologians who affirmed, like de Lubac, that scientific exegesis provides an inadequate hermeneutic to guide the Church in its engagement with culture. Namely, the next chapter focuses on two major "schools of thought"—postliberalism and Radical Orthodoxy—in order to examine their respective approaches to hermeneutics and culture, before considering the continuing importance of de Lubac's work in this area.

---

99. D'Ambrosio, "Henri de Lubac and the Critique of Scientific Exegesis," 366.

CHAPTER 5

Postliberalism and Radical Orthodoxy: In Search of a Participatory Christological Hermeneutic

Henri de Lubac had several goals in mind when he wrote his first major work on the history of exegesis, *Histoire et Esprit* (1950). First, he intended to rescue Origen from the widespread belief that his allegorical interpretation of Scripture flouted "the truth of history," i.e., that it was heavily indebted to Hellenistic allegorists like Philo, who tended to treat Old Testament texts from an ahistorical and abstract perspective.[1] Against this widespread criticism, de Lubac argued that Origen clearly affirmed and appreciated the history told in the Old Testament.[2] Moreover, according to de Lubac, Origen's allegorical interpretation was fundamentally different from that of Philo since its primary objective was to "grasp the spirit in the history or to undertake the passage from history to spirit."[3] Origen's interpretive method was focused on the Spirit that, he believed, animated Old Testament history, pointing it towards its christological fulfillment.[4]

As mentioned in the previous chapter, de Lubac, following Blondel, was critical of "scientific exegesis" that treated only the "external facts" of history without ever considering the "real history," or the spirit within

---

1. The first chapter of *History and Spirit*, which is titled "The Case against Origen," offers a review of the many scholarly works that have criticized Origen in this way. See ibid., 15–50. For a concise treatment of the difference between Christian and Hellenistic allegory, see de Lubac, "Hellenistic Allegory and Christian Allegory."

2. De Lubac, *History and Spirit*, 103–18.

3. De Lubac explains further that "very far from eliminating or scorning history, Origen is content to maintain it intact and to defend it, so to speak, in its raw state. He seeks to 'understand' it, as he himself says to us. He seeks the 'truth' of it" (ibid., 317).

4. The word *christotelic* has been used recently to highlight the teleological character of the Old Testament witness, which seems always to anticipate Christ. See Enns, *Inspiration and Incarnation*.

history that inspired the texts. Accordingly, de Lubac hoped that in addition to rescuing Origen from misunderstanding, his own work in the history of exegesis would inspire a new synthesis in biblical scholarship uniting the scientific methods with a more traditional appreciation for the dynamic, spiritual reality that the words of the text point to as signs.[5] During the time that de Lubac was writing his multivolume *Exégèse Médiévale*, he explained in a report to the Academy of France that

> In *Histoire et Esprit*, it is the central idea of the ancient interpretation of Scripture that I tried to bring out by taking as the center of perspective its most brilliant representative, Origen. In so doing, I hoped to make a contribution, on the one hand, to the current research into the philosophy or the theology of history and, on the other, to the synthesis that is also being sought today within Christianity between exegesis, properly so-called, dogmatic theology and spirituality. It is a continuation of this study, this time adopting the early Latin Middle Ages as the center of perspective, that is occupying me at this time.[6]

Despite his hopes, de Lubac's work in the history of ancient exegesis has not yet led to a new synthesis between biblical exegesis, dogmatic theology, and spirituality. In general, scholars were convinced by his defense of Origen against claims that he had disregarded history in the manner of Greek allegorists, but few professional biblical scholars have embraced the idea of an exegetical *ressourcement*.[7] This is not to say, however, that other scholars have not also been dissatisfied with the overly scientific character of biblical scholarship. Indeed, some of de Lubac's fiercest critics agreed that contemporary biblical scholarship was suffering from a

---

5. One commentator suggests that "de Lubac's investigation into the history of ancient Christian exegesis was, then, clearly intended to make a contribution towards a synthesis between the traditional hermeneutical wisdom of the Church and contemporary exegetical science. Yet . . . he did not himself attempt to write a blueprint for their active collaboration in the practical work of exegesis. Leaving that delicate task to others, de Lubac instead limited himself rather modestly to clearing away false oppositions between these two perspectives and attempting somewhat to clarify the issues involved historically and theologically" (D'Ambrosio, "Henri de Lubac and the Recovery of the Traditional Hermeneutic," 291).

6. De Lubac, *At the Service of the Church*, 93.

7. For a summary of the reception of de Lubac's work on ancient exegesis, see D'Ambrosio, "Henri de Lubac and the Recovery of the Traditional Hermeneutic," 239–42. Despite the skepticism of academics, de Lubac's recovery of spiritual exegesis did have a very significant influence on *Dei Verbum*.

"spiritual bankruptcy," though they did not find in de Lubac's work a solution to the problem.[8] However, beginning in the nineteen seventies, and especially with the work of Hans Frei, a new critique of scientific exegesis emerged and began to have a significant influence on biblical and theological scholarship.

The present chapter will offer a survey and critique of the movement commonly referred to as postliberalism, and specifically the approach to biblical interpretation found in the work of postliberal theologians Hans Frei and George Lindbeck. Postliberalism is among the most important theological movements of the late twentieth century, and it represents a genuine advancement beyond the overly scientific, historical-critical approach to the Bible that de Lubac found lacking. After a brief survey of select works, I will place Frei and Lindbeck into conversation with several of their contemporary critics in order to suggest a number of areas where modifications are needed. Finally I offer a brief analysis and critique of John Milbank's approach to hermeneutics and to the Radical Orthodoxy movement that he has helped spearhead.

HANS FREI AND THE RETURN TO NARRATIVE

Much like Blondel and de Lubac before him, Hans Frei believed that modern biblical scholarship had gone astray in its interpretive practices. In his groundbreaking book, *The Eclipse of Biblical Narrative* (1974), Frei offered a historical study of modern biblical interpretation, focused primarily on the eighteenth and nineteenth centuries. In the course of his study, Frei noted two negative tendencies that emerged around the eighteenth century. On the one hand was a tendency to look for the meaning of biblical texts in abstract and eternal truths about God and humans, rather than in the storied world rendered in the narrative.[9] The other tendency, according to Frei, is to regard biblical texts as records of

8. One critic of de Lubac's work writes that "the spiritual bankruptcy of scientific interpretation must be noted as a fact which can be neither explained or defended" (McKenzie, "Significance of the Old Testament for Christian Faith," 104).

9. Frei acknowledges that the universal truths referenced in the text could be taken either as "dogma (as with the neo-scholastics) or general religious ideas (meaning as ideal reference) (as with the liberals)" (Frei, *Eclipse of Biblical Narrative*, 101). It is interesting to note that although Frei focuses on liberalizing theologians such as Schleiermacher as representative of this tendency, de Lubac's (and Blondel's) critique of neoscholastic "extrinsicism" is very similar.

historical events that can be verified using the tools of historical-critical scholarship.[10]

According to Frei, both of the above-mentioned tendencies are errant because they attempt to locate the meaning of the biblical text outside the overall narrative of the Bible—in either an ideal or a historical referent.[11] However, whereas de Lubac looked to the interpretive practices of the patristic and medieval eras (spiritual or allegorical interpretation with its fourfold method) for the basis of a new synthesis capable of overcoming the limitations of modern biblical scholarship, Frei looked to the figural approach of the Reformers.

THE RECOVERY OF REALISTIC NARRATIVE

In *The Eclipse of Biblical Narrative*, Frei tells us that for the Reformers and their predecessors, Scripture was authoritative and cohesive in its depiction of history and doctrine. It was not an option for Luther or Calvin to separate the literal or figural meanings of a text from the historical events depicted there. To the precritical mind, the storied world of the Bible was "real." It was the real history of God and humanity, and it was a history that could be entered into.[12]

According to Frei, the precritical world understood its own history as continuous with the history depicted in Scripture. This history began when God created the heavens and the earth, the creatures living on the

10. De Lubac's critique of "historicism" was focused on the same tendency. Here again it is important to note that both liberalizing theologians and protofundamentalists sought to substantiate their preferred interpretations through historical argumentation—either in support of biblical claims (as with biblical creationists) or against (as with the nineteenth- and twentieth-century attempts to discover the historical Jesus). For more on Frei's critique of these two tendencies, see Placher, introduction, to *Theology and Narrative*, 7–8.

11. Frei suggests that these tendencies are a direct result of a misguided apologetics that views truth and meaning in abstracted and foundational terms: "Individual words appeared to be the basic units of meaning. Meaning itself was thought of as a kind of unvarying subsistent medium in which words flourish or, to change the figure, a kind of conveyor belt onto which words are dropped for transportation to their proper reference or destiny" (Frei, *Eclipse*, 109).

12. "The text fitly rendered what it talked about in two ways for Calvin. It was in the first place a proper (literal or figurative) rather than allegorical depiction of the world or reality it narrated. But in the second place it rendered reality itself to the reader, making the reality accessible to him through its narrative web. He could therefore both comprehend it and shape his life in accordance with it" (ibid., 24).

earth, and humans to rule over the earth. It continued as the first humans fell from grace, and the history of salvation began to unfold. This history involved a consistent interaction between humans and God as a people were chosen, covenants were made and broken, and grace was continually poured out. In the Christian Scriptures, the center of this history is Jesus. For the Reformers and those who had come before them, the history depicted in the Old Testament flows smoothly into the New Testament and then into the church. This is the history of God's redemptive activity, and to become a Christian is to join God (through the incarnation of Christ that continues in the church) in this history that provides the witness according to which all history is ultimately judged.[13]

In Frei's outlook, the precritical view of Scripture as a "realistic story," in which the literal sense of the text is identical with the historical references made there, has important implications for biblical interpretation. For Luther and Calvin, biblical interpretation was a matter of making sense of their world in light of the "real" world depicted in the "realistic narrative" of the Bible. The process of making sense of the present world was natural to the precritical mind because it involved an extension of the typological or figural sense of Scripture.[14] As mentioned above, typology allowed the Reformers and their predecessors to view the Bible as a cohesive and extended historical narrative. Important events in the Old Testament, events like the crossing of the Jordan River, were types or figures of New Testament events such as the baptism of Jesus in the Jordan River. In the same way, this figuration continues into the present. Thus, the ongoing baptism of believers is prefigured by both the original entry of the Israelites into the Promised Land and the inauguration of

13. "Long before a minor modern school of thought made the biblical 'history of salvation' a special spiritual and historical sequence for historiographical and theological inquiry, Christian preachers and theological commentators, Augustine the most notable among them, had envisioned the real world as formed by the sequence told by the biblical stories. That temporal world covered the span of ages from creation to the final consummation to come, and included the governance of man's natural environment and of that secondary environment which we often think of as provided for man by himself and call 'history' or 'culture'" (ibid., 1).

14. A major influence on Frei's thought, Eric Auerbach, explains that "figural interpretation establishes a connection between two events or persons in such a way that the first signifies not only itself but also the second, while the second involves or fulfills the first. The two poles of a figure are separated in time, but both, being real events or persons, are within temporality. They are both contained in the flowing stream which is historical life" (Auerbach, *Mimesis*, 73).

God's promised reign on earth in the baptism of Jesus. The realistic narrative of Scripture gives meaning to our contemporary experience, and our history is prefigured by the history of God's redemptive activity in the life of Israel and in Jesus.

According to Frei, however, the direction of biblical interpretation changed after the seventeenth century, as scholars began to locate the meaning and significance of the text in either abstract universal truths or historical events.[15] For those locating the text's significance in abstract, universal truths, history was relatively unimportant. However, for historical-critical scholars, the religious significance or "meaning" of a story, like the postexodus entry into Palestine, became dependent upon the historicity of the events in question. If an event was historically suspect, then the meaning was suspect, and figural interpretation was often lost.[16]

One of the primary concerns of *The Eclipse of Biblical Narrative* was that biblical scholars after the late eighteenth century consistently failed to appreciate the significance of the realistic, narrative character of Scripture.[17] According to Frei, this failure had a negative influence upon

15. "It is no exaggeration to say that all across the theological spectrum the great reversal had taken place; interpretation was a matter of fitting the biblical story into another world with another story rather than incorporating the world into the biblical story" (Frei, *Eclipse*, 130). Frei, like de Lubac before him, believes that things began to go astray in the seventeenth century and only got worse. He suggests that the method of "modern biblical-historical criticism and its slightly younger cousin, historical-critical theology. . . owes much to the seventeenth century, for instance to Spinoza's reflections in the first twelve chapters of the *Tractatus theologico-politicus*, to the conviction of the Socinians that the veracity of Scripture would and should be attested by independent rational judgment rather than dogmatic authority, and to the pioneering critical exegesis of men like Hugo Grotius and Richard Simon. But there is no doubt that as concerted practice, building into a continuing tradition and literature, it started in the second half of the eighteenth century, chiefly among German scholars" (Frei, *Eclipse*, 17).

16. "If the religious truths the Bible communicated were completely dependent for their meaning on the historical events through which they had originally come into currency, the Bible was of course at once an indispensable source of factual information and of religious truth. Moreover, its being the latter depended entirely on its also being the former. But if the religious meaning of the Bible (including the history-like) narratives did not depend logically on its connection with these stories and events, it was certainly factually dispensable; history in that case made no difference to religion" (Frei, *Eclipse*, 118).

17. Robert Jenson remarks that "any reader of pre-Enlightenment writings is struck by the way in which the stretch of time is experienced as continuity. . . . In the eighteenth century, the intellectual policy of "critique" broke this continuity and transformed experience of the stretch of time into experience of separation. The space of time ceased to

biblical scholarship and theology. He claims that "a realistic or history-like (though not necessarily historical) element is a feature, as obvious as it is important, of many of the biblical narratives that went into the making of Christian belief." The fact that much of the Bible is depicted as realistic narrative cannot be ignored if Scripture is to be interpreted properly. [18]

Though Frei's *Eclipse of Biblical Narrative* has been highly influential, its aims were fairly modest, since it was intended simply to point out an important characteristic of Scripture that was being overlooked. [19] However, Frei did not recommend a return to the precritical assumption that the literal sense of the realistic narrative always describes real history. Frei accepted many of the conclusions of historical-critical scholars, but like de Lubac, he contended that these modern exegetical methods are limited in their ability to disclose the real meaning of biblical texts. Interestingly, Frei admits that

> in order to recognize the realistic narrative feature as a significant element in its own right . . . one would have . . . to distinguish sharply between literal sense and historical reference. And then one would have . . . to allow the literal sense to stand as the meaning, even if one believed that the story does not refer historically. [20]

In other words, there can be no going back to the days when the realistic narrative and the history were unified, since the many insights of historical-critical investigation cannot be ignored. [21] However, this presents Frei and others with a problem of the relationship between biblical story and history, since the Christian faith presupposes that the God of Israel acts in history to redeem his chosen people and the world. Indeed, if the proper interpretation of Scripture requires choosing a story over and against history, then biblical redemption is a mere fiction. Although

be the space in which we live together and became distance, despite which we struggle toward each other" (Jenson, "On the Problems of Scriptural Authority," 245–46).

18. Frei, *Eclipse*, 10.

19. Ibid.

20. Ibid., 11.

21. In an unpublished address given at a Yale Divinity School symposium, Frei talked about the need for a "post-critical naiveté"—a phrase that he attributes to Karl Barth, though he acknowledges the similarities of this phrase with Paul Ricoeur's "second naiveté" (Frei, "History, Salvation-History, and Typology," 83).

Frei never addresses the relationship between story and history in *The Eclipse of Biblical Narrative*, he does elsewhere.

THE IDENTITY OF JESUS: WHERE STORY AND HISTORY CONVERGE

Frei's suggestion in *The Eclipse of Biblical Narrative* appears to be that exegetes must ignore the lack of historical reference in order to appreciate the "realistic narrative," or "historylike" quality, of a large portion of Scripture. His concern is that the typological dimension of Scripture is only comprehensible if the stories are interpreted as historylike. In the absence of a typological reading, the story has no ability to incorporate "extra-biblical thought, experience, and reality into the one real world detailed and made accessible by the biblical story."[22]

The problem with Frei's recommendation in *The Eclipse of Biblical Narrative* is that it has never been the ultimate goal of Christian redemption to draw people into a fictional story. Rather, redemption involves, as the Reformers rightly understood, a historical reality. To be redeemed is to be incorporated as a recipient of grace into God's *history* of salvation, so the matter of historicity cannot be put aside for the sake of proper interpretation.

What we learn in *The Identity of Jesus Christ* (1975) is that Frei's insistence that interpreters take seriously the literal sense of biblical stories even when historical reference is in doubt does not preclude the reality of a true history of salvation. On the contrary, what we can deduce from Frei's argument is that the essence of salvation history is best communicated in a fictionlike, narrative form. He makes this point clear in his discussion of the identity of Jesus as depicted in the gospels. He explains:

> With regard to the Gospels, we are actually in a fortunate position that so much of what we know about Jesus, beginning at the crucial initiatory point of the climactic, unbroken sequence, is more nearly fictional than historical in narration. Yet the story is about an individual who lived; and, by common agreement, it is within the passion-resurrection sequence that we come closest to historical events in his life (specifically in the trial and crucifixion). But also, in that most nearly biographical sequence, the form of the narration is more nearly like that of fiction. The main

22. Frei, *Eclipse*, 3.

example of that fact is the direct inside understanding of the person of Jesus provided by the scene in the Garden of Gethsemane. Surely one would not want to call this description biographical. It is not even pertinent to the story to ask how this sequence can be historical, if Jesus was alone there and his disciples were sleeping some distance away. It is precisely the fiction-like quality of the whole narrative, from upper room to resurrection appearances, that serves to bring the identity of Jesus sharply before us and to make him accessible to us.[23]

Frei argues cogently that fiction writers are often better able to provide insight into the essence of a person's identity than are biographer-historians, because writers of fiction offer insight into a character's inner thoughts.[24] For this reason, he suggests that we should be grateful that the gospel writers chose to give us insight into the identity of Jesus, a real person, through fictionlike narratives such as the one portraying Jesus's inner struggle in the Garden of Gethsemane.[25] We should therefore be wary of historical-critical attempts to uncover the identity of Jesus through his sayings, or by using any method that ignores the literal sense of the gospel narratives—particularly those parts describing Jesus's passion and resurrection. The identity of Jesus, according to Frei, is best communicated in the most fictionlike portions of the gospel narrative.

Importantly, Frei does not urge interpreters to concentrate on the realistic narrative over and against history. Rather, he argues that the best way to understand and enter into God's redemptive activity in history is through the story.

The nature of salvation history is such that it cannot be grasped through the kind of presentation that would be characteristic of a historical biography or through some other kind of events' chronicle. This is because at the center of salvation history is a person—Jesus; and as mentioned above, Frei contends that personal identities are best communicated in the form of narrative. George Lindbeck, much like his friend

23. Frei, *Identity of Jesus Christ*, 144–45.

24. "But also, in that most nearly biographical sequence, the form of the narration is more nearly like that of fiction. It is precisely the fiction-like quality of the whole narrative, from upper room to resurrection appearances, that serves to bring the identity of Jesus sharply before us and to make him accessible to us" (ibid., 145).

25. The gospels resemble fiction in the way that their authors arranged freely the characters, events, settings, and the like in the service of the overall plot.

and colleague Hans Frei, emphasizes the importance of story in relation to identity formation. He explains that the gospel stories

> identify and characterize a particular person as the summation of Israel's history and as the unsurpassable and irreplaceable clue to who and what the God of Israel and the universe is. They interpret the Hebrew Bible in terms of Christological anticipation, preparations, and promissory types. Jesus' story fulfills and transforms the overall biblical narratives of creation, election, and redemption, and thereby specifies the meanings of such concepts and images as Messiaship, Suffering Servanthood, Logos, and divine Sonship. He is the subject, everything else is predication. Some New Testament writings may not clearly exhibit this pattern . . . but insofar as they are treated as parts of a narrationally and christologically unified cannon, they are submitted to the same hermeneutical rule.[26]

Just as the personal identity of Jesus is best communicated through realistic narrative, so are the communal identities of Israel and the church. Lindbeck suggests that "the church is fundamentally identified and characterized by its story. Images such as 'body of Christ,' or the traditional marks of 'unity, holiness, catholicity, apostolicity,' cannot be first defined and then used to specify what is and what is not the church. The story is logically prior."[27] In other words, it is the story that identifies and defines the characteristics that the church, henceforth, must attempt to embody.

Biblical scholars have made similar arguments about the relationship between Old Testament stories, even stories that may not refer historically, and the communal identity of Israel. For example, according to Joseph Blenkinsopp, the historicity of the exodus event, as depicted in the Old Testament, is highly suspicious. For one thing, "we have no knowledge of an Israelite sojourn in Egypt or an exodus from Egypt apart from the biblical record."[28] In addition, the logistical impossibility of sustaining six hundred thousand men, plus women and children, in the desert for generations is problematic from Blenkinsopp's perspective.

Blenkinsopp explains that after the period of Babylonian captivity, the Jews had to struggle for survival. As a part of this struggle, "the new commonwealth . . . had to shape an identity and therefore construct a past

26. Lindbeck, "Story-Shaped Church," 164.

27. Ibid., 165.

28. Blenkinsopp, "Memory, Tradition, and the Construction of the Past," 80.

by a selective incorporation of memories on which their own self-understanding could be patterned. The results of these efforts are inscribed in the Hebrew Bible and especially in the Pentateuch."[29] Gerhard Lohfink explains that "the Exodus texts became a *figura*, an enduring figure to support memory, the original image for all generations. In this very way and only in this way, [the Jews] were enabled to summarize within themselves all Israel's later exodus experiences."[30]

What these scholars are suggesting is that in the case of the Old Testament, the past may have been narratively constructed in order to make sense of Israel's present and future. The gospels were arguably written for the same purpose—to make sense of the present and future of the growing Christian community, whose sacramental identity was inseparable from the historical person of Jesus. With regard to both the Old and New Testaments, there is an unbreakable bond between story and history, since the stories serve to communicate and preserve the identity of either a person or people with whom God dwells in history. In both the Old and New Testaments, story communicates what Blondel and de Lubac might call, "real" or "dynamic" history, and what Frei would call historical identity. Moreover, according to Frei and Lindbeck, the identity of Jesus provides the hermeneutical key for understanding the identity of both Israel and the church. Lindbeck explains:

> the relation of Israel's history to that of the church in the New Testament is not one of shadow to reality, or promise to fulfillment, or type to antitype. Rather, the kingdom already present in Christ alone is the antitype, and both Israel and the church are types. The people of God existing in both the old and new ages are typologically related to Jesus Christ, and through Christ, Israel is prototypical for the church in much the same way that the exodus story, for example, is seen as prototypical for all later Israelite history.[31]

From this perspective, the baptism of Jesus is not dependent for its meaning on the historical reliability of the book of Joshua. Rather, the story of the original entry into the Promised Land gains its significance from Jesus's baptism as told in narrative form in the gospels. The center

29. Ibid.

30. Lohfink, *Does God Need the Church?* 68.

31. Lindbeck, "Story-Shaped Church," 166.

of the history of salvation is the life, death, and resurrection of Jesus. Because of Jesus, the past, present, and future are redeemed, and believers are able, through grace, to join in God's redemptive history. According to Frei and Lindbeck, the function of realistic narrative in the gospels is to communicate the identity of the crucified and resurrected Jesus, who stands as the center and hermeneutic principle that gives meaning to all the rest of salvation history. [32]

Interestingly, the narrative theology of Frei and Lindbeck appears to be grounded in a philosophy of history that has much in common with de Lubac's. Namely, Frei and Lindbeck argue that biblical stories, even though they may at times be only "historylike," offer profound insight into the true historical identity of a person or a people. We recall that de Lubac defended Origen's allegorical method because rather than ignoring history, it was focused on grasping the "truth" of history, i.e., the subject anticipated in all of biblical history—Christ. [33]

SCRIPTURE ABSORBS THE WORLD

Hans Frei and George Lindbeck assert that the biblical narrative constitutes a kind of complete world or semiotic system with Jesus at the center, giving meaning to all that comes before and after him. [34] Frei holds that biblical interpretation should incorporate "extra-biblical thought, experience, and reality into the one real world detailed and made accessible by the biblical story." [35] Lindbeck considers religions, including the Christian religion, "as a kind of cultural and/or linguistic framework . . . that shapes the entirety of life and thought." [36] For both thinkers, the cultural and linguistic world found in the stories of the Bible should "absorb" and thus shape and transform the world outside Scripture. [37] The narrative world of

32. According to Frei, "however impossible it may be to grasp the nature of the resurrection, it remains inconceivable that it should not have taken place" (Frei, *Identity of Jesus Christ*, 145). This is because, according to Frei, the identity of Jesus as depicted in the passion and resurrection narrative holds the overall story of the Old and New Testaments together in such a way that without it, everything else would fall apart as meaningless.

33. De Lubac, *History and Spirit*, 317.

34. Frei, *Identity of Jesus Christ*, 59. Also Lindbeck, "The Story Shaped Church," 174.

35. Frei, *Eclipse*, 3.

36. Lindbeck, *Nature of Doctrine*, 33.

37. This complex and far from self-evident theme, found throughout the writings

Scripture should serve as a lens through which Christians "construe and construct reality."[38] Lindbeck explains:

> Until recently, most people in traditionally Christian countries lived in the linguistic and imaginative world of the Bible. It was not the only world in which they dwelt. In most periods of Christendom, the poorly catechized masses lived also in a world of hobgoblins, fairies, necromancy, and superstition; in the educated classes, everyone, not least devout Christians, had their imaginations shaped by pagan classics of the Greeks and Romans. . . . Yet the text above all texts was the Bible. . . . Thus all of experience, including sacred texts from other religions, such as the classics of Greece and Rome, was absorbed into the scriptural framework. It is more than a metaphor, it is a literal description to say that Christendom dwelt imaginatively in the biblical world.[39]

However, as Frei's study in *The Eclipse of Biblical Narrative* has argued, modern interpreters have tended increasingly to construe and construct reality through secular lenses and to approach Scripture not in search of reality but in behalf of a misguided apologetics striving to provide evidence of the Bible's credibility in relation to some other reality. Lindbeck suggests that biblical interpreters, instead of redescribing "reality within the scriptural framework," are too often "translating Scripture into extrascriptural categories."[40] The danger in this correlationist approach, according to Lindbeck, is that it encourages Christians on all sides of the political spectrum to "accommodate to the prevailing culture rather than shape it."[41] In other words, when Scripture no longer provides Christians with an endless source of imagination through which to construe and construct reality, Christian culture atrophies and perhaps disappears completely. This, according to Lindbeck, is exactly what has happened in the West, since the biblical text has increasingly been studied "as an object . . . dissociated from its use as a language with which to construe the universe."[42]

---

of both Frei and Lindbeck, will provide the basis for a critical analysis of postliberalism below.

38. Lindbeck, "Church's Mission to a Postmodern Culture," 39–40.

39. Ibid., 38, 41–42.

40. Lindbeck, *Nature of Doctrine*, 118.

41. Lindbeck, "Scripture, Consensus, and Community," 87.

42. Lindbeck, "Church's Mission to a Postmodern Culture," 44.

According to Lindbeck, modern approaches to biblical interpretation have led to "a loss of both biblical literacy and biblical imagination."[43]
Moreover, this loss is cause for grave concern, since it also entails a loss of
a common language and a common rationality—both of which may be
necessary for the survival of Western civilization.[44] Lindbeck explains that
"if imagination is basic to thought (as some modern cognitive psycholo-
gists, not to mention ancient Aristotelians, affirm), then the weakening of
the biblical substructure of our culture's communal imagination may dry
up the wellsprings of western humanistic creativity in general."[45] The result is that "we try to deal with apocalyptic threats of atomic and ecologi-
cal disaster in the thin and feeble idioms of utilitarianism or therapeutic
welfare. . . . The culture of Christians as well as of non-Christians has
been de-Christianized, and the language of public discourse has become
dangerously feeble. . . . We have, in other words, no common language in
which to discuss the common weal."[46]

The loss of a common language has also, of course, become a problem for the church, which "has become a communicative basket case"
where "genuine argument is impossible, and neither agreements nor disagreements can be probed at any depth."[47] To a certain extent, Lindbeck
affirms that the "the waning of cultural Christianity might be good for
the churches," since it could force them to return to the wellsprings of
Scripture and tradition without which they cannot survive.[48] However, he
worries that "traditionally Christian lands when stripped of their historic
faith are worse than others. They become unworkable or demonic," he
suggests, and "there is no reason to suppose that what happened in Nazi
Germany cannot happen in liberal democracies, though the devils will
no doubt be disguised very differently."[49]

43. Ibid.

44. Lindbeck suggests that "without a shared imaginative and conceptual vocabulary
and syntax, societies cannot be held together by communication, but only by brute force
(which is always inefficient, and likely to be a harbinger of anarchy). But if this is so,
then the biblical cultural contribution, which is at the heart of the canonical heritage
of Western countries, is indispensable to their welfare, and its evisceration bespeaks an
illness which may be terminal" (ibid., 50).

45. Ibid., 47.

46. Ibid., 47–48.

47. Ibid., 49.

48. Lindbeck, "Confession and Community," 494.

49. Ibid.

Accordingly, Lindbeck believes that the church must renew itself, not for its own sake but for the sake of the world. And this renewal depends above all, he suggests, "on the spread of proficiency in premodern yet postcritical Bible reading."[50] He explains that

> Biblical literacy, though not sufficient, is indispensable. This literacy does not consist of historical, critical knowledge about the Bible. Nor does it consist of theological accounts, couched in non-biblical language, of the Bible's teachings and meanings. Rather, it is the patterns and details of its sagas, its images and symbols, its syntax and grammar, which need to be internalized if one is to imagine and think scripturally.[51]

Lindbeck and Frei both describe this process of scriptural imagination and cultural engagement as "intratextual theology." According to Lindbeck, "intratextual theology redescribes reality within the scriptural framework rather than translating Scripture into extrascriptural categories."[52] Frei uses similar language when he explains that

> The direction in the flow of intratextual interpretation is that of absorbing the extratextual universe into the text, rather than the reverse (extratextual) direction. The literal sense is the paradigmatic form of such intratextual interpretation in the Christian community's use of its Scripture: The literal ascription to Jesus of Nazareth of the stories connected with him is of such far-reaching import that it serves not only as focus for inner-canonical typology but reshapes extratextual language in its manifold descriptive uses into a typological relation to these stories.[53]

For Frei and Lindbeck, if the church hopes to engage culture faithfully, it must first learn how to inhabit the world via a scriptural imagination.

A Critique of the Narrative Approach

One of the obvious differences between the postliberal approach and the allegorical approach of the Fathers is that Frei and Lindbeck, following the Reformers, make figures or types a part of the literal sense while patristic

---

50. Lindbeck, "Confession and Community," 494.

51. Lindbeck, "Church's Mission to a Postmodern Culture," 51–52.

52. Lindbeck, *Nature of Doctrine*, 118.

53. Frei, "'Literal Reading' of Biblical Narrative," 147.

and medieval commentators tend to affirm multiple, though inseparable, senses.[54] Indeed, Frei is critical of the tendency of patristic commentators, who, he believes, too often attach "a temporally free-floating meaning pattern to any temporal occasion whatever, without any intrinsic connection between [a] sensuous time-bound picture and the meaning represented by it."[55] In contrast to patristic and medieval allegory, Frei prefers the figural reading of the Reformers, and especially Calvin, whose "sense of figural interpretation remained firmly rooted in the order of temporal sequence and the depiction of temporal occurrences, the links between which can be established only by narration and under the conviction of the primacy of the literal, grammatical sense."[56] For Frei, it is precisely this narratively rendered temporal sequence, associated with the literal sense of Scripture, that enables the Bible to be read as a world unto itself with a beginning, middle, and end—a world capable of "absorbing" other worlds. However, I argue below that the literal sense of Scripture, as conceived by Frei and Lindbeck, ultimately becomes a static, ahistorical world incapable of the kind of absorption that they advocate.[57]

54. Ibid.

55. Frei, *Eclipse*, 29. Frei's criticisms here are representative of a widespread scholarly distrust of allegory. Frei was, perhaps, unacquainted with de Lubac's writings on patristic and medieval exegesis. Although de Lubac was very willing to acknowledge the excesses of the ancient approach, he would not have agreed with such a general condemnation.

56. Ibid., 31. It is important to note, once again, that de Lubac was also well aware and critical of the excesses of patristic and medieval allegory. De Lubac in no way advocated a simple return to the ancient methods. Rather, he wanted them to be understood and appreciated so that a new synthesis between biblical exegesis, dogmatic theology, and spirituality could be pursued. Regarding the four-fold sense, de Lubac asks, would we "propose returning to it as a guide for today's exegesis and theology? No one would seriously dream of that" (de Lubac, "On an Old Distich," 124).

57. De Lubac was involved in a long-running debate with his friend, Jean Daniélou, regarding the differences between allegorical and figural/typological readings of scripture. While Daniélou argued for the superiority of figural reading, de Lubac held that allegory (or something like it) was indispensable for a sufficiently Christological reading of scripture. Whereas typology connects two figures within a temporal succession, allegory "establishes the relationship of the figure to the truth, of the letter to the spirit, of the old to the new. It shows how what was written after having taken place τυπικῶς must be understood and lived πνευματικῶς" (de Lubac, "Typology and Allegorization," 129–64). Elsewhere he has written that "'typology' . . . has the virtue of doing away, at least in intention, with all the old straw in the grain of Christian exegesis, something which could not be accomplished by the word 'allegory' alone. But it has the drawback of referring solely to a result, without alluding to the spirit or basic thrust of the process which produces the result. Its connotations may be too narrow, for, strictly speaking, it

THE EMERGENCE OF NEW INTERPRETIVE METHODS

Unlike de Lubac's multivolume study of patristic and medieval exegesis, many of the insights of theologians like Hans Frei and George Lindbeck have been embraced by biblical scholars, and they have helped inspire new, widely practiced exegetical methods.[58] Indeed, one of Frei's greatest achievements may have been his success in convincing biblical scholars, not only that historical-critical methods too often miss the literal or plain sense of Scripture, but also that the full meaning of the text is incomprehensible apart from this plain sense. Regarding Frei's insight into the limitations of historical-critical methods, Mark Alan Powell explains that

> the major limitation of all these approaches, as documented by Hans Frei in 1974, is that they fail to take seriously the narrative character of the Gospels. These books are stories about Jesus, not compilations of miscellaneous data concerning him. They are intended to be read from beginning to end, not dissected and examined to determine the relative value of individual passages. In focusing on the documentary status of these books, the historical-critical method attempted to interpret not the stories themselves but the historical circumstances behind them.[59]

The work of postliberal theologians has inspired a much greater appreciation among biblical scholars for the literal sense of the stories in Scripture.[60] In the last thirty years, there has been a dramatic shift in biblical scholarship as several new exegetical methods have emerged.[61]

---

corresponds solely to the first of the three meanings spelled out in the classical division after the literal sense, 'history.' Typology thus puts narrow limitations on its object. . . . It does not include within its scope the most properly spiritual explanations. . . . We should not place exclusive dependence upon it unless we are prepared to reduce the bold and pregnant teaching of a St. Paul to a game of figures, no matter how completely they may be authenticated" (de Lubac, *Scripture in the Tradition*, 16).

58. Notably, my first in-depth reading of *The Eclipse of Biblical Narrative* took place in a New Testament seminar led by Mikeal Parsons of Baylor University. The book was first on our list of required readings.

59. Powell, *What Is Narrative Criticism?* 2.

60. For a consideration of Frei's influence on biblical scholarship, see Lee, *Luke's Stories of Jesus.*

61. Although the work of narrative theologians, and especially Frei, has helped convince many biblical scholars of the need for a renewed focus on the "realistic narrative," it should be pointed out that Frei had very little to say about how exactly biblical scholars

Narrative criticism, for example, considers biblical stories in their entirety, focusing on issues like character, plot, intended audience, and setting. Additionally, rhetorical and social-scientific criticism have become commonplace, and both are focused on understanding the social, cultural, and linguistic world within which biblical stories were originally received, in order to gain a greater understanding of their meaning.[62] Rhetorical and social-scientific criticism are often used in the service of narrative criticism.[63] Canonical criticism is another more recent interpretive approach, and it seeks to understand the relationship of particular stories and texts in relation to the biblical canon as a whole. Taken together, all these new approaches evince a renewed enthusiasm in biblical scholarship for the narrative/literal sense of Scripture that Frei, Lindbeck, and others wanted to see restored to a place of importance. However, these new interpretive methods have not generally been accompanied by a renewed engagement with culture based upon a rediscovered biblical imagination. The temptation remains for practitioners of these methods to approach Scripture as though it constitutes a closed world that can be studied as one might study an artifact in a museum.

Does the Text Really Absorb the World?

A number of theologians, though appreciative of the contributions made by Frei and Lindbeck, have raised objections to the notion of a scriptural

---

should go about investigating this neglected dimension of Scripture. Not surprisingly, then, biblical scholars, although influenced by Frei and others, have borrowed a great deal from secular literary criticism as they have endeavored to explore the literary dimensions of the Bible. For more on this subject, see Powell, *What Is Narrative Criticism?* 1–11.

62. This is perhaps what George Lindbeck has in mind when he suggests that "there can . . . be no rejection of historical-critical biblical studies, but these become auxiliary to literary-canonical readings in which narrative (especially realistic narrative à la Erich Auerbach and Hans Frei) is primary" (Lindbeck, "Atonement and the Hermeneutics of Intratextual Social Embodiment," 239–40).

63. According to Vernon Robbins, within the gospel narratives there is an "argumentative texture" that is more easily discernible through the study of ancient rhetoric. A familiarity with the conventions of ancient rhetoric, he suggests, will illumine "the depictions of Jesus' motives, actions, speech, death, and resurrection" which are the "inner fabric of the gospels." Robbins, "Narrative in Ancient Rhetoric," 368, 372. For a group of essays focused on the complimentary nature of narrative and social-scientific criticism, see Kingsbury, *Gospel Interpretation*.

"world" capable of absorbing other worlds. The problem, according to Rowan Williams, is that "the 'world of Scripture,' so far from being a clear and readily definable territory, is an *historical* world in which meanings are discovered and recovered in action and encounter."[64] Williams objects to the idea that the biblical narrative comes to us as a given reality—a "'framework' within whose boundaries things—persons?—are to be 'inserted.'"[65] Although he agrees with Lindbeck that the church needs "to revive and preserve a scriptural imagination" in order to faithfully interpret the world outside the Bible, Williams suggests that the formation of such an imagination is more complex than narrative theologians indicate.[66] He suggests,

> We are not dealing with the 'insertion' of definable blocks of material into a well-mapped territory where homes may be found for them, but with events of re-telling or re-working traditional narrative patterns in specific human interactions; an activity in which the Christian community is itself enlarged in understanding and even in some sense evangelized.[67]

In Williams's estimation, Frei and Lindbeck oversimplify the reality of the church's engagement with culture when they suggest that the direction of biblical interpretation must move in only one direction, i.e., that the text must absorb the world and not vice versa. According to Williams, the text does not absorb the world, but as the church strives to live faithfully it continually looks to the stories of Scripture to discover its own identity and future. In other words, the church brings the Scriptures constantly into contact with the world, and the consequence of this interaction is the generation of something new and unimagined. Williams writes:

> The Church may be committed to interpreting the world in terms of its foundational narratives; but the very act of interpreting affects the narratives as well as the world, for good or ill. . . . Something happens to the Exodus story as it is absorbed into the black slave culture of America. Something still more unsettling

---

64. Williams, *On Christian Theology*, 30.

65. Ibid., 29.

66. Ibid., 30. Cf. Volf, "Theology, Meaning, and Power," 101–3.

67. Williams, *On Christian Theology*, 31.

happens to Abraham and Isaac when they have passed through
Kierkegaard's hands.[68]

Instead of calling this ecclesially enacted interaction between the
text and the world "intratextual," Williams suggests that it is "generative,"
since it provides the occasion for the church's ongoing "discovery" of the
meaning of the text "as well as a discovery of the world."[69]

The intratextual approach assumes that the meaning of the text can
be known prior to an engagement with the world outside the text. Thus,
the task of the theologian is to continually reinterpret the world outside
the text in terms of the biblical narrative. From Williams's generative perspective, the theologian does not comprehend the full meaning of the
biblical narrative until it is brought into engagement with the world. As
I argue below, the difference between Lindbeck and Williams regarding
the interaction of the church with the world leads to (or perhaps arises
from) different understandings of the nature of theology.

Is Theology Intratextual and Descriptive?

For Lindbeck and for Frei, theology is intratextual and fundamentally
a "descriptive" exercise. Lindbeck suggests that "the task of descriptive
(dogmatic or systematic) theology is to give a normative explication of
the meaning a religion has for its adherents."[70] Because, for Lindbeck and
Frei, the meaning of the Christian religion is located in the text, or in
the narrative of Scripture, the task of the theologian is "to give a normative explication of the meaning" of the biblical narrative, which must be
understood as a given reality—a block of material with definable borders.
Moreover, claiming that the theologian's task is to explicate the meaning
of Scripture is to claim that the theologian operates in a space outside the
framework of Scripture. The theologian, in Lindbeck's account, becomes
an objective observer of the text, who then describes its meaning to others.[71] According to Reinhard Hütter, Lindbeck contradicts himself at this

68. Ibid., 30.

69. Ibid., 30–31.

70. Lindbeck, *Nature of Doctrine*, 113. Cf. Frei, "Theology and the Interpretation of
Narrative," 113.

71. The most insightful analysis of Lindbeck's approach to theology that I have seen
can be found in Hütter, *Suffering Divine Things*. Hütter takes issue with Lindbeck's proposal that theology is a descriptive exercise and attempts to strengthen the intratextual

point, because in order for theology to be "intratextual," the "descriptive activity" of the theologian cannot be "abstracted from the text itself."[72] Interestingly, Lindbeck compares the theological task of explicating the meaning of the scriptural world to that of an ethnologist who explicates the meaning of the "imaginative universe" of particular cultures.[73]

In contrast to Lindbeck's proposal that theology is essentially descriptive, Rowan Williams suggests that "theology is the exploration of a parable, and so of conversion."[74] This statement is consistent with his unwillingness to view "the world of Scripture" as a "clear and readily definable territory" to be explicated by the ethnographer/theologian. A parable, argues Williams, is a story whose meaning is not clear at all. He writes that "the riddle of parables, the fact that they are seen as hopelessly enigmatic by friends and enemies, lies in making the connection with one's own transformation—that is, encountering God in the parable."[75] The task of the theologian is therefore to listen to Scripture and be prepared for "radical loss and radical novelty." The theologian, in Williams's account, must be open to the possibility of surprise when reading Scripture, and she must be open to the possibility of challenge and judgment as well:

> The inner readiness to come to judgement and to recognize the possibility of truth and meaning becomes visible and utterable in the form of discipleship, abiding in the community created by God's love. The dramatic event of Jesus' interaction with his people—set out in a series of ritual, quasi-legal disputations—is an event of judgement in that it gives the persons involved definitions, roles to adopt, points on which to stand and speak. They are invited to 'create' themselves in finding a place within this drama—an improvisation in the theatre workshop, but one that

---

approach by incorporating it into a view of theology as Trinitarian church practice. In Hütter's view, only an understanding of theology as church practice can accommodate Lindbeck's own desire for descriptive theology to serve as a constructive enterprise within the church (Hütter, *Suffering Divine Things*, 59–65).

72. Ibid., 60.

73. Lindbeck, *Nature of Doctrine*, 115. Lindbeck borrows the phrase "thick description" from Clifford Geertz and Gilbert Ryle to describe this kind of explication. For a critique of Lindbeck's embrace of "thick description," see Hütter, *Suffering Divine Things*, 60–62.

74. Williams, *On Christian Theology*, 42.

75. Ibid., 41.

purports to be about a comprehensive truth affecting one's identity and future.[76]

Williams offers "feminist exegesis as an example of disturbing scriptural reading which forces on us the 'conversion' of seeing how our own words and stories may carry sin and violence in their telling, even as they provide the resource for overcoming sin and violence."[77] Because theology necessarily entails conversion, it is characterized by "silence, watchfulness, and the expectation of the Spirit's drastic appearance in judgement, recognition, conversion, for us and for the world."[78] Moreover, and perhaps most important, Williams suggests that "the theologizing of Christological and Trinitarian faith presupposes—quite simply—living in Christ and in the Trinitarian mystery, living in the Spirit."[79]

Perhaps the most important difference between the descriptive approach and the generative approach (referring to Williams's view) to theology is that the latter is more successful than the former in situating both Scripture and the theologian interpreting Scripture within a Trinitarian framework. Williams's account of the nature of theology assumes a participatory ontology while Lindbeck's does not. It seems that in arguing for a descriptive understanding of the nature of theology, Frei and Lindbeck have limited the ability of the narrative to be expanded in order to actually "absorb the world." Even though Frei and Lindbeck criticize exegetical tendencies that find the meaning of the text in an "ahistorical" space separated from the text, the postliberal approach also becomes ahistorical in the sense that the world of the text is viewed as an enclosed, semiotic system.

Reinhard Hütter makes this point when he argues that there is a tension between Lindbeck's assertions that theology is both intratextual and descriptive. He asks, "is it not the task of a purely descriptive discipline to adhere to the concrete elements already before it?" In other words, in Hütter's estimation, it is Lindbeck's insistence that theology is descriptive that leads him to view the scriptural framework as a "static" given.[80]

---

76. Ibid., 32. For a more-developed treatment of the idea of "improvisation" as a description for Christian scriptural interaction with the world, see Wells, *Improvisation*.

77. Williams, *On Christian Theology*, 42.

78. Ibid., 43.

79. Ibid., 146.

80. John Milbank makes a similar critique when he writes that "a narrative that is

In order for theology to be intratextual (a word that Hütter is willing to embrace), the text must be dynamic and expandable in order for the theologian to operate intratextually. Hütter writes that with regard to intratextuality, "the analogy with ethnology completely collapses, since this creative and constructive aspect of theology plays a role, indeed, becomes necessary only if theologians themselves participate in the substantive configurations of language and activities of the religion in question!"[81] In Lindbeck's account, the theologian, if her work is really analogous to that of an ethnographer, does not need to be a participant in the Christian faith in order to offer a theological description of its semiotic world. In contrast, for Hütter and Williams, theology is a practice of the church that entails participation in the life of the triune God.

Does the Narrative Identify Jesus?

The narrative approach of Frei and Lindbeck also falls short of a participatory ontology in its approach to Christology. Even though they insist that the scriptural world has the capacity to absorb other worlds, Frei and Lindbeck do not approach Jesus, the hermeneutical key to all of Scripture, as an absorbing character but rather as a spectacle to behold extrinsically. In the introductory chapter of *The Identity of Jesus Christ*, Frei indicates that the book is concerned with two primary issues: the "presence and the identity of Jesus."[82] Specifically, *The Identity of Jesus Christ* is focused on clarifying the order within which Christians come to experience the presence and the identity of Jesus. In Frei's estimation, "talk about Christ's identity and presence should be in that order, rather than the reverse": identity must precede presence.[83]

---

falsely presented as a paradigm is seen as over and done with, and easy to interpret. . . . He [Lindbeck] thereby converts metanarrative realism into a new narratological foundationalism and fails to arrive at a postmodern theology" (Milbank, *Theology and Social Theory*, 385).

81. Hütter, *Suffering Divine Things*, 60. Hütter remarks further that Lindbeck's descriptive model has "an emphatically static, and thus unhistoric, formal character, something evident not least in its failure to associate theology *theologically* with its pathic and poietic elements" (ibid., 64).

82. Frei, *Identity of Jesus Christ*, 1.

83. Ibid., 5. Notably Frei makes this point in contrast to the existentialist perspective represented by figures like Bultmann, who tend to reduce Christ to the Christian's inner experience.

By "identity," Frei means the "specific uniqueness of a person, what really counts about him. . . . A person's identity is the total of all his physical and personality characteristics" and implies an "unbroken relationship between the past and present experience of the same self."[84] In other words, a person's identity can be comprehended by others only as his or her actions and intentions are illuminated through the passage of time.

As mentioned above, Frei and Lindbeck both argue that the identity of Jesus is made known through the plain sense of the biblical narrative, whose meaning is "directly accessible" to the reader. According to Frei, this narratively rendered identity provides the hermeneutical basis for dogmatic theology, since it is only proper to talk about what Jesus does (presence) if we know who Jesus is (identity). Ronald Thiemann, one of Frei's former students at Yale, suggests that

> A doctrine of revelation is an account of God's identifiability. That definition locates the doctrine within the reflection on God's identity, i.e., within the doctrine of God, rather than in prolegomena or methodological reflection. The Christian claim to revelation asserts that God is identifiable 1) within the narrative of Yahweh who raised Jesus from the dead, 2) through the narrative as the God of promise who in addressing his promise to the reader is recognized as *pro nobis* and *extra nos*, and 3) beyond the narrative as the one who, faithful to his promises, will fulfill his pledge to those whom he loves.[85]

For Thiemann, as for Frei and Lindbeck, the revelation of God's identity through the biblical narrative is a prerequisite for theological reflection, since theology is a descriptive activity.

Theologians have offered two primary criticisms of the "Yale school" regarding the identity of Jesus. First, it seems that Frei, Lindbeck, and others are simply mistaken about the ability and intent of the gospel stories to render the identity of Jesus. According to John Milbank, the first mistake made by narrative theologians is to claim that the gospels identify Jesus in the way that a character would be identified in a novel. Milbank suggests that "the gospels are not 'history-like narratives' (in the sense of a predominance of 'literal reference' over allegory in the identification of event and character), nor do they in any way approximate to the 'real-

---

84. Ibid., 37–38.
85. Thiemann, *Revelation and Theology*, 153.

ism' which is an element in some eighteenth- and nineteenth-century novels." The gospel portrayal of Jesus is nothing like the literary portrayal of a character that would be found in a novel, since "we are told nothing about his tastes, quirks and inclinations, nor (pace Frei) about his 'intentions'—Jesus speaks only of what he does and must do. During the course of the gospel accounts he undergoes no psychological development."[86]

Indeed, the Jesus portrayed in the gospels remains a mysterious and elusive figure, and the "identity" given him by the gospel writers "does not actually relate to his 'character,' but rather to his universal significance for which his particularity stands, almost, as a mere cipher."[87] In other words, Milbank thinks that the gospels tell us almost nothing about the particular personality of the man Jesus. Rather, he argues, they focus narrowly on his significance in relation to the Law and the Prophets, and on his relationship to God and humanity in general. The Jesus of the gospels, it seems, almost completely lacks the kind of personal identity that a novelist would strive to create for a central character.[88]

The second criticism of the Yale school's focus on the identity of Jesus is that it is soteriologically weak. Reinhard Hütter, commenting on the fact that intratextual theology claims to be a descriptive exercise, suggests that it "loses its unique soteriological center; soteriology slips off into form."[89] Milbank clarifies the issue somewhat when he asks:

> What difference does the mere *fact*—however astounding—of God's identifying with us through incarnation make to our lives, or even to our pictures of what God is like, what he wants for us? How can mere belief in the event of atonement be uniquely transformative for the individual? To collapse both objections into a single more positive question: how can incarnation and atonement be communicated to us *not* as mere facts, but as characterizable modes of being which *intrinsically* demand these appellations?[90]

With Frei clearly in mind, Milbank is suggesting that even if the gospels did offer a clear identity description of Jesus (though he claims

86. Milbank, *Word Made Strange*, 149.

87. Ibid.

88. For more on the nonidentifiability of Jesus in the gospels, see Ward, "Bodies: The Displaced Body of Jesus Christ," 163–81.

89. Hütter, *Suffering Divine Things*, 63–64.

90. Milbank, *Word Made Strange*, 148.

that they do not and are not meant to), this extrinsic identity description would have no saving power. For Hütter and Milbank, salvation involves participation in the economic Trinity. Accordingly, any discussion of who Jesus is or what Jesus does must focus on the way that he opens up and enables a new "mode of being" in reconciled relationship with God.

It is not enough to suggest that we can know Jesus as we might know a character in a story, extrinsically. Rather, Christians claim to be reconciled to God through incorporation into Christ's body. Thus, the knowledge or revelation of God in Christ implies, for the Christian, the gift of an insider's view of the Trinitarian economy. God's identification in Jesus can only be grasped meaningfully (soteriologically) through ontological participation in his body, the church.

RADICAL ORTHODOXY AND THE SEARCH FOR A PARTICIPATORY HERMENEUTIC

Since the narrative approach of Frei and Lindbeck fails to overcome the problem of extrinsicism, there remains in theology a need for a truly participatory biblical hermeneutic. Moreover, this hermeneutic will necessarily move beyond mere theological description and into the realm of church practice if it claims to be situated in a space interior to the Trinitarian economy. In *The Word Made Strange*, John Milbank outlines a biblical hermeneutic that, he thinks, fills this need. The key to Milbank's argument is that reality itself is fundamentally linguistic. Language is "constitutive" of reality, and this, for Milbank, has important implications for Christology and hermeneutics.[91]

Milbank on the Identity of Jesus

After critiquing Frei's treatment of the identity of Jesus, Milbank endeavors, in *The Word Made Strange*, to offer a new interpretation of the gospel portrait of Jesus that is participatory and soteriologically potent. As mentioned previously, Milbank and others argue that the gospels do not offer a clear identity description of Jesus in the way that Frei and Lindbeck suggest. Importantly, Milbank believes that this is a good thing, and that the gospels were never intended to identify Jesus precisely. He

91. Bauerschmidt, "Word Made Speculative?" 418.

suggests that when the gospels do actually focus on Jesus's identity (as in the Gospel of John), they

> abandon mimetic/digetic narrative, and resort to metaphors: Jesus is the way, the word, the truth, life, water, bread, the seed of a tree and the fully grown tree, the foundation stone of a new temple and at the same time the whole edifice. These metaphors abandon the temporal and horizontal for the spatial and vertical. They suggest that Jesus is the most comprehensive possible context: not just the space within which all transactions between time and eternity transpire, but also the beginning of all this space, the culmination of space, the growth of space and all the goings in and out within this space. Supremely, he is both word and food: the communicated meanings which emanate from our mouths and yet in this outgoing simultaneously return to them as spiritual nurture.[92]

According to Milbank, the gospels portray Jesus in a way that allows him to be interpreted not merely as a specific person but rather as the total context within which all of our lives take place. In other words, the gospels portray Jesus as a figure who is both immanent and transcendent. The gospels, according to Milbank, must "evacuate the person [Jesus] of any specifiable content," since only in this way is he capable of absorbing the world.[93] The gospel portrayal is, in Milbank's view, soteriologically potent since Jesus is narrated not as a character in a novel but as the founder of a new language and a new practice. We should read the gospels "not as the story of Jesus, but as the story of the (re)foundation of a new city, a new kind of human community, Israel-become-the-Church."[94]

Jesus functions for Milbank "as primarily the 'founder' of a practice/ state of being which is fully transferable to others."[95] He suggests that the gospels outline "the general norms of that practice" and thus enable the church to move "from one kind of discourse to another"[96]—that is, from

92. Milbank, *Word Made Strange*, 149–50.

93. Ibid., 150.

94. "The high Christologies of Colossians, the Epistles to the Corinthians and the Epistle to the Hebrews are strikingly yoked to the notion that Jesus is but the foundation of the building and the first of many sons: the *archegon*, or pioneer of salvation, such that 'he who sanctifies and those who are sanctified have all one origin' (Heb 2:10–11; Col 1:15–29; 2 Cor 3:9–11; 11:1; 2 Cor 1:3–7; 4:10–11; 5:13–14, 21; 11:7)" (ibid., 151).

95. Ibid., 157.

96. Ibid., 149.

a secular discourse of violence and power to a Christianized discourse structured by "Jesus' utter refusal of selfish power."[97] Although he admits that "there is a certain specific 'flavour' of personality binding the various incidents and metaphors" identifying Jesus, these incidents and metaphors are "formal statements about, and general instructions for, every human life. In consequence, the 'shape' of Jesus' life, his 'personhood' or 'personality,' can only be finally specified as the entire content and process of every human life, in so far as it is genuinely human life, according to the formal specifications of the gospel narratives and metaphors."[98]

Because Jesus has founded a new language and a new practice of nonviolence and charity, salvation has become a possibility, and it is up to the church, through a "non-identical repetition" of Jesus's universal identity, to enact a "structured transformation" of the world.[99] Russell Reno suggests that, for Milbank, "the absence of a savior in the text creates the need for us to construct a savior in and through our own interpretive practice."[100] However, it would be more accurate to say that for Milbank, the salvific language patterns and practices formalized in the text by the ambiguous character, Jesus, *enable* the church's ongoing characterization of the savior through its own interpretive practice. Interestingly, Milbank claims that he is advancing a "high Christology," since the human Jesus has been "evacuated" of all but a proper name, thus leaving only God.[101] This contention is built upon his assertion that the primary narrative of the human Jesus has been absorbed into the metanarrative

---

97. Ibid., 153.

98. Milbank suggests that his approach to Christology, "from the context of ecclesiology actually allows a full retrieval of the Chalcedonian position," which affirms that Jesus is both fully human and fully divine (ibid., 156). I will argue below, however, that in the end, Milbank's approach doesn't do justice to the "fully human" side of the Chalcedonian equation.

99. Ibid., 152.

100. Reno, "Radical Orthodoxy Project," 40.

101. "And yet, the effect of implying that a person situated within the world is also, in himself (like God) our total situation, or that which is always transcendentally presupposed, is to evacuate that person of any particular, specifiable content. It is to ensure that Jesus who is in all places, because he is in all places, never in fact appears. Thus, for reasons belonging to the logic of discourse, it is indeed true that incarnation cannot be by the absorbing of divinity into humanity, but only by the assumption of humanity into divinity" (Milbank, *Word Made Strange*, 150).

of God's redemption, which encompasses all of Scripture from creation to consummation.[102]

Radical Orthodoxy's Pursuit of a Christianized Ontology

Milbank argues that it is better to approach Christology through ecclesiology, since in its ongoing engagement with the world, the church renarrates and re-realizes Christ, and this "must be God himself."[103] This process of "renarration" is, in Milbank's view, a kind of ontological extension through which the world is made to participate in the life of God.[104] How exactly is this "renarration" to take place? At this point, Milbank's project becomes complicated. One might expect him to turn with enthusiasm toward a more participatory approach to biblical hermeneutics, but this is not the case. Rather Milbank's next major project following *The Word Made Strange* (1997) is a collaborative effort titled *Radical Orthodoxy: A New Theology* (1999).

What is perhaps most remarkable about *Radical Orthodoxy* is that it represents an attempt to move beyond prolegomena and into a direct engagement with the secular world. Milbank and his coeditors, Catherine Pickstock and Graham Ward, explain that their interest is in "recovering and extending a fully Christianized ontology and practical philosophy consonant with authentic Christian doctrine."[105] In other words, *Radical Orthodoxy* is the beginning of an attempted "renarration," through which the world outside of the metanarrative can be made to participate in the life of God, as Jesus Christ is "re-realized" in long-abandoned places:

102. Ibid., 146.

103. Ibid., 156–57. Cf. Milbank, *Theology and Social Theory*, 386–87.

104. Milbank, et al., *Radical Orthodoxy*, 2–3.

105. Ibid., 2. One might ask what exactly the editors of *Radical Orthodoxy* mean when they use the phrase "fully Christianized ontology." Specifically, how exactly are the essays contained in the *Radical Orthodoxy* book capable of "extending a fully Christianized ontology"? It seems that Milbank and the others believe that when they combat secular social theories of economics, art, the body, friendship, and the like, and expose the nihilism upon which those theories are grounded, they have opened a space within which the church can offer a renarration of Christ. This renarration, we are led to believe, entails ontological participation in a space once uninhabited by the church—thus the extension of a "fully Christianized ontology." I will argue below that the proponents of radical orthodoxy fail to explain how exactly the theological speculation contained in their works actually enables the church to inhabit these long-abandoned places.

The central theological framework of radical orthodoxy is 'participation' as developed by Plato and reworked by Christianity, because any alternative configuration perforce reserves a territory independent of God. The latter can lead only to nihilism (though in different guises). Participation, however, refuses any reserve of created territory, while allowing finite things their own integrity. . . . Every discipline must be framed by a theological perspective; otherwise these disciplines will define a zone apart from God, grounded literally in nothing.[106]

For the editors of *Radical Orthodoxy*, the process of renarrating and re-realizing Christ, which is also the process of "recovering and extending a fully Christianized ontology," involves framing the various disciplines within a theological perspective.[107] In his *Theology and Social Theory* (1991), Milbank argued that modern social thought presupposes overwhelmingly an ontology of violence. From the nominalists of the thirteenth century and passing through figures like Kant, Malebranche, Machiavelli, Hegel, Marx, and modern liberation theologians, social theorists have assumed that the maintenance of society depends upon the use of power and violence. This ontology of violence, which has its own ethics and its own interpretation of history, is, in Milbank's view, the fabric that holds the secular social and political world together. In order to engage and overcome the secular, therefore, Milbank argues that Christians must offer a "counter-history," a "counter-ethics," and a "coun-

---

106. Ibid., 3.

107. I do not mean to imply here that Milbank's earlier works provide the only foundational influences for the Radical Orthodoxy project. Clearly, Ward, Pickstock, and the other contributors to the project have been influenced by a great many thinkers. However, insofar as Milbank is a coauthor of the introductory essay of the initial volume, I can assume that, at least for Milbank's part, the project is consistent with and builds upon his earlier works. I should also mention here that Milbank, Ward, and Pickstock dispute the idea that Radical Orthodoxy constitutes a theological "movement" or "school of thought." Pickstock, for example describes it as a "loose tendency." See Pickstock, "Reply to David Ford and Guy Collins." Ward describes Radical Orthodoxy as a "theological sensibility." He also mentions that "participation" is one of the "more fundamental" themes of Radical Orthodoxy and that it has been the motivating influence on his "continuing engagement with analogy and allegory; Catherine Pickstock's continuing engagement with Plato; John Milbank's long engagement with the ontologies of Nyssa, Augustine, and Aquinas, and the more general interest in metaphysics" (Ward, "In the Economy of the Divine," 118). My own engagement with Radical Orthodoxy will focus primarily on the editors' shared interest in participation.

ter-ontology"[108] in order to expose the nihilistic ontology undergirding modern social theory as mythological, and offer the Christian alternative of an ontology of "harmonic peace" in its place.[109]

It seems obvious that, at least for Milbank's part, the Radical Orthodoxy project, with its emphasis on a participatory ontology, is a continuation of the "strategy" proposed in *Theology and Social Theory*.[110] Indeed, this ontology is the main thrust of the Radical Orthodoxy project, and the initial volume in the Routledge series contains essays on topics as diverse as desire, language, friendship, music, the city, and knowledge. This strategy of offering a counterontology has continued as the contributors to the original volume, along with others, have published books and articles providing a theological perspective on issues where "secularism has invested heavily—aesthetics, politics, sex, the body, personhood, visibility, space," economics, and more.[111]

For Milbank and Ward, it is the vagueness and openness of the scriptural identity of God in Jesus that enables the church to identify itself with Christ as it engages in the "speculative task of ontology and theology."[112] This "speculation" has so far consisted of an ambitious scholarly effort to expose the nihilism inherent in all disciplines not framed theologically. The movement, Radical Orthodoxy, "refuses any reserve of created territory" to secular thought; so sex, science, art, music, friendship, and all other dimensions of human existence can and should be exposed for their nihilism when conceived autonomously and then brought under the umbrella of a Christian ontology.[113]

When Milbank and the others claim that theologians can recover and extend a "fully Christianised ontology" by exposing secularism's nihilism, they are assuming a reciprocal relationship between theory and practice. They are assuming, in other words, that a Christianized ontology theoretically conceived can free the church to inhabit (liturgi-

---

108. Milbank, *Theology and Social Theory*, 381.

109. "Christianity . . . recognizes no original violence. It construes the infinite not as chaos, but as harmonic peace which is yet beyond the circumscribing power of any totalizing reason" (ibid., 5).

110. Milbank refers to his proposed "counter-ontology" as a "strategy" (ibid., 279).

111. Milbank, et al., *Radical Orthodoxy*, 1.

112. Milbank, *Theology and Social Theory*, 385; Milbank, *Word Made Strange*, 145–68; Ward, "Bodies," 163–81.

113. Milbank, et al., *Radical Orthodoxy*, 3.

cally) those regions where secularism once reigned. James Smith defends Radical Orthodoxy's theoretical bent by suggesting that while a modern materialist ontology would potentially inhibit the Church's imagination and practices, Radical Orthodoxy's "participatory ontology undoes the ontological atomism of ontologies of immanence; as such it also counters the social atomism of secular modernity by generating an alternative account of sociality rooted in participation."[114]

Milbank is unapologetic in his insistence that the church needs a "social theory" to combat secularism, but he insists, "there can only be a distinguishable Christian social theory because there is also a distinguishable Christian mode of action, a definite practice. The theory explicates this practice."[115] Graham Ward offers a more complete account of Radical Orthodoxy's relationship to ecclesial practice when he writes that

> Christians are called upon, by Christ in the Gospel of Matthew most directly, to read the signs of the times. The Church is situated in an eschatological and soteriological management of time, established in its teachings on the Trinity and the relationship of the Triune God to Creation. Reading the signs of the times *is* the Church's participation in that management; Christians live in Christ and live pneumatologically through the practices of encountering, negotiating and interpreting the world around them. Those Christic and Pneumatic practices of everyday life are part of the in-gathering of all things into the Godhead. They draw creation's attention, not only to its radical contingency, but also, in and through that contingency, to its giftedness and its maintenance in grace.[116] (italics original)

In other words, the proponents of Radical Orthodoxy consider their speculative/theoretical work a participatory endeavor, and they acknowledge that their work must accompany a true Christian "mode of action, a definite practice."[117]

114. Smith, *Introducing Radical Orthodoxy*, 232.
115. Milbank, *Theology and Social Theory*, 380.
116. Ward, "Radical Orthodoxy and/as Cultural Politics," 103.
117. Milbank, *Theology and Social Theory*, 380.

For and Against Radical Orthodoxy

When *Radical Orthodoxy: A New Theology* was first published, it received considerable attention from within the academy and even some mention in popular magazines.[118] While the project has received its fair share of scholarly criticism, many of the responses have been generally appreciative. According to Milbank, although the contributors to the original volume were primarily Anglican (in addition to a few Catholics), the project has found "many surprising sympathizers amongst Baptists, Methodists, Mennonites, Nazarenes, and others."[119] Radical Orthodoxy's success in garnering attention is likely due to the fact that its proponents have drawn together several themes of considerable contemporary interest, uniting them in a coherent and constructive project.[120]

Among the themes united in the Radical Orthodoxy project are an unrelenting critique of modernity and secular autonomy, an emphasis on the cultural and linguistic contextualization of all knowledge, an energetic engagement with Christianity's great tradition (Augustine and Aquinas especially), an ecumenical spirit, and a commitment to remain both catholic and evangelical. With these foci in view, it is easy to see why Radical Orthodoxy has wide appeal, and I count myself among its sympathizers. However, to sympathize with a project such as this is to hope that it has a future, and that there is thus more work to be done. In the following pages, I discuss several important areas where clarifications and/or modifications are needed.

Does a Counterontology Atone?

One of the most common criticisms of the Radical Orthodoxy project has been that it exaggerates the role of theological speculation in influencing Christian practice. As mentioned above, Radical Orthodoxy aims to undermine secular ontologies of violence and offer in their place a

118. Attention from sources outside of academia have included Biema, "God as a Postmodern: Radical Orthodoxy"; and Tolson, "Academia's Getting Its Religion Back." For a comprehensive scholarly bibliography, see Smith, *Introducing Radical Orthodoxy*, 263–77.

119. Milbank, "Programme of Radical Orthodoxy," 36.

120. The Radical Orthodoxy project has of course been advanced by the fact that Routledge Press has published a series of recent books under its name.

Christian ontology of harmonic peace. This counterontology will, in Milbank's view, have the effect of freeing the church to "embody" those regions of culture where secularism formerly reigned:

> In elaborating the metanarrative of a counter-historical interruption of history, one elaborates also a distinctive practice, a counter-ethics, embodying a social ontology, an account of duty and virtue, and an ineffable element of aesthetic 'idiom', which cannot be fully dealt with in the style of theoretical theology. However, the developing idiom is also an allegorical representation of an idea, a speculation, which practice itself both promotes and presupposes as 'setting'.[121]

In suggesting that the "idea" is promoted and presupposed as the "setting" for Christian practice, Milbank reveals his platonic disposition and sheds light on the logic of the Radical Orthodoxy project. Christian practice needs an ideal to serve as its telos; Radical Orthodoxy aims to supply it.

Although speculation can be and always has been an important part of Christian practice (and a participatory practice at that), it seems that Milbank has overstated drastically the soteriological function of theological speculation. Frederick Bauerschmidt suggests that, with regard to Milbank's Trinitarian ontology,

> We have a case here of the philosophical tail wagging the theological dog. . . . While Milbank posits an oscillation between the "formally distinguished moments" of narrative and of speculative conceptualization . . . , it is the former that usually seems to receive short shrift . . . one must at least note that at times Milbank's commitments to certain philosophical positions regarding language push him in directions that seem to run counter to the stories and practices of the church.[122]

Interestingly, Milbank offers a justification for his theoretical and speculative disposition in the introduction to *The Word Made Strange*. It will be instructive to quote him at length here:

> Today, theology is tragically too important. For all the current talk of a theology that would reflect on practice, the truth is that we remain uncertain as to where today to locate true Christian

121. Milbank, *Theology and Social Theory*, 422–23.
122. Bauerschmidt, "Word Made Speculative?" 429.

practice. . . . The theologian feels almost that the entire ecclesial task falls on his own head: in the meagre mode of reflective words he must seek to imagine what a true practical repetition would be like. Or at least he must hope that his merely theoretical continuation of the tradition will open up a space for wider transformation. In the past, practice already 'made strange', already felt again the authentic shock of divine word by performing it anew, with variation. The theologian could articulate this and add her own further twists that might contribute to renewed vision. Yet today it can feel as if it is the theologian alone . . . who must perform this task of redeeming estrangement; the theologian alone who must perpetuate that original making strange which has the divine assumption of human flesh. . . . No: the only chance lies in the composing of a new theoretical music.[123]

The preceding statements should arouse empathy from those who, like Milbank, long for a church community where the Word of God dwells in recognizable, habitual, and consequential practices. However, these statements should also be a bit alarming for those who worship (or have worshiped) in churches "where true Christian practice" does indeed take place—making ontological inroads even in those spaces where secular social theorists claim sovereignty. Perhaps Milbank's confession should be interpreted as an indictment of the communities within which he worships, but surely he is wrong if he means to suggest that we now live in an age where "true Christian practice" cannot be found.

Despite Milbank's claim that speculation *presupposes* Christian practice, the more familiar one becomes with Radical Orthodoxy, the more one gets the impression that Christian practice is in bondage without theological speculation in the style of Radical Orthodoxy.[124] However, Milbank and the others have failed to explain how, exactly, the church is to go about embodying the space supposedly opened up through the work of speculative theology. Although the many books and essays published in the Radical Orthodoxy Series are excellent in their own right, it is hard to see how they achieve anything more than a deconstruction of secular social theory. How, for example, might D. Stephen Long's excellent work

123. Milbank, *Word Made Strange*, 1.

124. In the following chapter, I will argue that, for de Lubac, the "idea" is promoted or produced through spiritual exegesis. It seems to me that Milbank, at least, has neglected this fundamental step in his efforts to construct a speculative ontology intended to offer a "setting" for Christian practice.

titled the *Divine Economy*[125] actually enable the church to instantiate new economic practices and thus extend a Christianized ontology? In other words, if Long's work has opened up a space, how exactly does the church go about inhabiting this space? How can Long's work on economic theory lead to anything more than the kind of lament expressed by Milbank in the introduction to *The Word Made Strange*? What I am suggesting is that Milbank's speculative ontology is incapable of providing the kind of linguistic, christological mediation of Christian practice that he desires.

It is interesting that Radical Orthodoxy has thus far paid little attention to the ways in which Christian spiritual exegesis can and does in fact enable the church to inhabit new spaces by generating the "idea" (the "aesthetic idiom"[126]) that serves as a setting for the church's ongoing embodiment. In failing to do so, Milbank and the others seem to endorse a kind of dualism where the speculative idea necessarily presupposes and somehow enables the practice and the embodiment.[127] In order to overcome this impression, the proponents of Radical Orthodoxy need to focus more attention on the roles played by the Word and the sacraments in generating the conceptual setting (social ontology) that the church embodies.

Rowan Williams's approach, which views Christian social engagement as an "improvisation" within the biblical drama, could be helpful here. What Radical Orthodoxy lacks thus far is an entry point for Christian practice. Radical Orthodoxy deconstructs secular social theory but makes no concrete suggestions as to how Christians are to inhabit the space created by the deconstruction. Williams, in contrast to Milbank, casts the problem in terms of identity transformation. Modern people live in a radically secular world and derive their identities from this world. However, the biblical drama offers an invitation to identity transformation, or to use Milbank's terminology, a new "mode of being." Williams suggests that when persons encounter Jesus through the biblical drama, they find themselves in an "event of judgement" where they are given

> roles to adopt, points on which to stand and speak. They are invited to create themselves in finding a place within this drama—an

125. Long, *Divine Economy*.

126. Milbank, *Theology and Social Theory*, 423.

127. For a similar critique, see Wannenwetsch, "Political Worship of the Church," 274–75.

> improvisation in the theatre workshop, but one that purports to
> be about a comprehensive truth affecting one's identity and future.
> . . . The scope of Jesus' work is the world—so, we must assume, the
> declaration of a newly discovered identity in encounter with Jesus
> represents a change for at least some.[128]

For Williams, the biblical drama (and particularly the gospels) necessarily mediates the christological "mode of being" or "the space" that
individuals and the community as a whole embody. There is thus, for
Williams, no thought of an "ontological extension" without the christological mediation of Scripture. Radical Orthodoxy will do well to attend
more closely to the constitutive role of scripture in the church's engagement with the world.

Is the Word Made Speculative?

The recommendation above may be difficult to accomplish, however,
unless Milbank is willing to reconsider his approach to Christology. As
mentioned previously, Milbank finds Frei's stress on the identity of Jesus
problematic. He suggests that a narratively rendered identity description
of Jesus is simply nonexistent in the gospel texts, and even if it were there,
it would lack the ability to effect a transformation in readers. Rather than
identify Jesus as a distinctive character, Milbank suggests that the gospels
"evacuate the person Jesus of any specifiable content" and at the same
time portray him as the founder of a new language and a new practice.
The gospels, we are told, should be read "not as the story of Jesus but as
the story of the (re)foundation of a new city, a new kind of human community, Israel-become-the-Church."[129]

There are several problems with Milbank's proposal. First, although
he claims to offer a "high Christology" in arguing that Jesus's human identity (the primary narrative) has been absorbed into his divine identity (the
metanarrative of the incarnate Logos), he has really offered a docetic, or
at least a monophysite, Christology. This is Bauerschmidt's impression as
well. He suggests that Milbank's position "certainly is a high Christology,
but Christological error moves in both directions. Therefore we must ask
whether Milbank's Christological position amounts to, if not docetism, at

128. Williams, *On Christian Theology*, 32.

129. Milbank, *Word Made Strange*, 150.

least a 'monophysite' absorption of Christ's humanity into his divinity."[130] Milbank argues that "for reasons belonging to the logic of discourse, it is indeed true that incarnation cannot be by the absorbing of divinity into humanity, but only by the assumption of humanity into divinity."

While it is perhaps objectionable to claim that Jesus's human identity is absorbed into his divine identity, in Milbank's proposal, Jesus's human identity is not just absorbed, it is "evacuated." He is explicit on this point when he says, "all that survives that is particular in this assumption is the proper name 'Jesus.'"[131] I would argue that if the human Jesus must be evacuated of all content except a proper name, then we have effectively obliterated the doctrine of the incarnation. Milbank seems to suggest that Jesus cannot be the incarnate Logos and a human being with a distinctive personality at the same time. Bauerschmidt makes the same point when he writes:

> Milbank simply fails to make his case that Jesus is not the ascriptive subject (to use Frei's term) of the gospel narratives, and his attempt to shift the subject matter of the gospels away from Jesus and on to the church burdens the church with a load it cannot bear. It is true that Jesus is not a "character" in the sense one finds in a nineteenth-century novel, and it is also true that the story of Jesus exceeds the boundaries of his human life by virtue of the resurrection. But this does not mean that the story does not remain in some determinative sense the story of Jesus. . . . It is not so much that Milbank is wrong when he claims that the gospels enshrine an "event of transformation" that is the genesis of the church; rather, he poses a false alternative when he says that one may read the gospels *either* as the story of Jesus *or* as the foundation of the pilgrim city.[132] (italics original)

---

130. Bauerschmidt, "Word Made Speculative?" 425. Monophysitism was a christological heresy that emerged in the fifth century and claimed that Christ had only one nature, the divine. For a book-length treatment of the issue see, Frend, *Rise of the Monophysite Movement*.

131. Milbank, *Word Made Strange*, 150. To be fair, Milbank places more emphasis on Jesus's "specificity" in his later work, *Being Reconciled*. However, his comments there are too sketchy to determine whether he means to provide an alternative to the proposals found in *Word Made Strange*. See Milbank, *Being Reconciled*, 103.

132. Bauerschmidt, "Word Made Speculative?" 426–27.

It seems that Milbank's Christology lies at the heart of Radical Orthodoxy's nearly exclusive focus on speculative ontology.[133] Indeed, we can see in Milbank's suggestion that Jesus is "situated within the world" and "also, in himself (like God) our total situation," a connection to his earlier remarks in *Theology and Social Theory* regarding the "idea" or "aesthetic idiom" that provides the "setting" within which church practices take place. Because Jesus's human identity is "evacuated of content," the church is able to "go on re-narrating and re-realizing Christ,"[134] and it does this through the "strategy" of producing a "counter-ontology" prescribed in *Theology and Social Theory* and enacted beginning with the initial volume of *Radical Orthodoxy*.

In other words, Milbank, perhaps unintentionally, seems to equate the incarnate Logos of the metanarrative with the "idea" or the "aesthetic idiom" produced by theological speculation. But we should ask, returning to our previous example, how has Christ been renarrated and re-realized in D. Stephen Long's *Divine Economy*? (Long, to be fair, does not profess that he has renarrated Christ.) Or how has Christ be renarrated or re-realized in any of the books or essays that compose Routledge's Radical Orthodoxy Series? How does Radical Orthodoxy's *Kulturkritik* mediate a new "mode of being" that accounts for a true ontological extension? I suggest that if we must approach Christology through ecclesiology, as Milbank recommends, then Radical Orthodoxy is rendered incompetent in its pursuit of a new mode of being.

For several reasons, Milbank's Christology will eventually fail. First, in subsuming Christology under ecclesiology, he has rendered Jesus incapable of judgment (theoretically speaking). Milbank argues, "the only thing which will really remove us from extrinsicism is the primacy of ecclesiology."[135] Milbank wants to avoid a Christology that will focus on an extrinsic identity description because such a description is soteriologically weak. He believes that salvation entails ontological "participation" in the life of the Trinity, and a Christology that enables us to gaze upon Jesus as though he were only a spectacle to behold fails to enter the realm

133. Although Graham Ward and Catherine Pickstock may dispute this claim, it should be expected, given the popularity of Milbank's work, that such an interpretation would be commonplace. Moreover, it is reasonable to suggest that, at least for Milbank, the Radical Orthodoxy project is consistent with his earlier "strategy."

134. Milbank, *Word Made Strange*, 157.

135. Milbank, *Word Made Strange*, 165.

of participation. However, Milbank fails to consider the fact that participation in Christ (which begins with baptism) is always preceded by repentance.[136] We encounter Jesus, first, as wholly (and Holy) other. Before the Jesus who is narrated in the gospels we stand judged. We are then invited to be baptized and to become participants in Christ's body.[137]

Moreover, because the church on earth exists in this time between the times, its participation in Christ will remain a story of continual repentance and baptismal immersion. Perhaps this is what Bauerschmidt means when he writes that to "shift the subject matter of the gospels away from Jesus and on to the church burdens the church with a load it cannot bear."[138] Indeed, the church stands always under the judgment of Jesus, finding itself forgiven, redeemed, and transformed into the body of Christ through its continuing acts of repentance, confession, and worship.[139]

In order to avoid making the church responsible for bearing the load that only Jesus is meant to bear, Radical Orthodoxy theologians should, as mentioned above, focus more attention on the constitutive role of the Word and the sacraments in mediating the church's participation in the life of the Trinity and engagement with the world. Milbank's proposal that Christology should be subsumed under ecclesiology should certainly be rejected. In its place, a Christology capable of reading the

136. Milbank's Christology is quite consistent with his views on the "total continuity" between nature and grace. While de Lubac, especially in his later works, placed greater emphasis on the discontinuity between the order of creation and the order of grace precisely because he recognized the difference between Jesus and fallen humanity, Milbank insists that "deification is guaranteed by *no* contrast, not even with Creation, never mind nature" (Milbank, *Suspended Middle*, 46, italics original).

137. Hans Frei discusses the importance of recognizing the *difference* between Jesus and his followers. He suggests that "the particular story of Jesus, then, is pre-empted by him and him alone. Only those refractions of it will be credible and concrete that do not seek to reiterate it completely but only in part, not from too close by but at a distance, in the figure of a disciple rather than in the cosmic, miraculous, and abysmal destiny of the original" (Frei, "Theological Reflections," 56).

138. Bauerschmidt, "Word Made Speculative?" 426.

139. Dawson, following Hans Frei, suggests that Christians should embrace and preserve the particularity and difference of Jesus's identity in relation to their own: "There is no 'sharing of identity,'" he suggests, "that could lay the groundwork for supersession; there is instead an 'identifying with' that never dissolves into a 'common identity.' Human beings are invited to 'identify with' one who, in his own unique identity, has chosen to 'identify with' them. The very possibility of the action of 'identifying with' presupposes the unsubstitutable and non interchangeable identities of the agents" (Dawson, "Figural Reading," 193).

gospels as the story of Jesus (judge and redeemer), and simultaneously as the founder of a new universal language and practice, should be affirmed so that the church's ontological participation in the life of the triune God, will be continually mediated through *this* Person and the texts that tell his story.

Conclusion

As this chapter's introduction mentioned, Henri de Lubac hoped that his work on the history of ancient exegesis would inspire not a return to the fourfold interpretive method but a new synthesis of biblical interpretation, dogmatic theology, and Christian spirituality—a synthesis capable of guiding the church in a more robust and faithful engagement with secular culture. Unfortunately, his hopes have not yet been fully realized, since the majority of biblical scholars view the allegorical method as characteristic of a prescientific age and as incapable of offering guidance in these more enlightened times.

Yet the efforts of narrative theologians such as Hans Frei and George Lindbeck have been highly influential in theology and in biblical studies, providing at least some of the inspiration for a host of new exegetical methods that attempt to avoid the twin problems that de Lubac referred to as historicism and extrinsicism. Indeed, these new interpretive methods represent a healthy new respect for the literal sense of Scripture that Frei hoped to see restored to a place of prominence.

The narrative approach associated with the Yale school has its limitations, however, and these limitations also apply in large part to contemporary biblical scholarship. Namely, narrative theologians have failed to offer an adequate account of the relationship between Scripture and the church's theological practice. Frei and Lindbeck both consider theology a descriptive discipline, and they view Scripture as an enclosed semiotic system that can be studied as an ethnologist might study a foreign culture. This account of the relationship between theology and Scripture falls short of a participatory hermeneutic, and this is problematic for a variety of philosophical and theological reasons.

John Milbank argues that a more philosophically sound hermeneutic can be found by reconsidering the "identity of Jesus." Rather than portray him as a character in a nineteenth-century novel, Milbank argues, the gospels portray Jesus as the founder of a new language and a new prac-

tice, and these provide the "situation" within which the church participates ontologically. However, Milbank's "strategy" for "extending a fully
Christianised ontology" is built upon a potentially docetic Christology
that "evacuates" Jesus's humanity, leaving only a proper name. Moreover,
the process of "extending a fully Christianised ontology" so far enacted
by Radical Orthodoxy theologians has not been mediated by biblical
interpretation. The ironic result is that when viewed as an extension of
Milbank's earlier work, Radical Orthodoxy offers a strategy for engaging and transforming culture that is dualistic and ahistorical. Scripture
does not absorb the world for Radical Orthodoxy theologians. Rather,
the "aesthetic idiom" generated by speculative theologians absorbs the
church.

In the following chapter, I argue that de Lubac's intended synthesis
is capable of capitalizing on the achievements of postliberalism while
also providing a more christologically orthodox biblical hermeneutic
to undergird the very important cultural critique of Radical Orthodoxy
theologians. In short, I argue that de Lubac's work on spiritual exegesis
can advance the work of Frei and Lindbeck while providing an important
missing element in Milbank's theological program.[140]

---

140. In a critical review of the original volume, David Ford remarked that "the editor's Introduction promises, as an alternative to the 'ploddingly exegetical' approach of
Barthianism, a collage of 'exegesis, cultural reflection and philosophy' which, at least as
regards scriptural exegesis, is not fulfilled. The absence of reference to the Old Testament
is especially striking. I find all this very disturbing, because I do not see a good theological future for the movement unless this is urgently addressed. Scripture is so intrinsic to
the traditions, practices and theologians they espouse that without it their claim to be in
continuity with these is hopelessly compromised" (Ford, "Radical Orthodoxy and the
Future of British Theology," 398). In response to Ford's remarks, Catherine Pickstock
promised that "all the editors intend that this should be remedied in the future, and wel-
come contributions along these lines" (Pickstock, "Reply to David Ford and Guy Collins,"
411). My argument here is that in order to remedy this problem, Radical Orthodoxy
either will need to state explicitly that its efforts in "extending a fully Christianised ontology" are not logically continuous with Milbank's earlier works, or Milbank will need to
revisit several important matters discussed here.

CHAPTER 6

Mystical Christology:
Spiritual Exegesis at the Center of de Lubac's Ressourcement

John Milbank has published a provocative essay in which he suggests that Henri de Lubac's struggles with the Roman Catholic hierarchy in the years before Vatican II "traumatized" him to such an extent that he lost focus and failed to bring his revolutionary theological program to its logical completion.[1] Milbank cites as evidence the well-known fact that de Lubac never completed his "theological-historical-mystical treatise on Christ," which was to be his most important work.[2] De Lubac himself admitted that he lacked the "physical, intellectual, and spiritual strength" needed to complete this work. Milbank infers from this confession that the papal encyclical *Humani Generis* and its implicit denunciation of de Lubac's thesis on nature and grace caused severe distress and limited his scholarly production to histories of dogma that tended to obscure

---

1. Milbank, "Henri de Lubac," 79. This essay was expanded to become a brief monograph. See Milbank, *Suspended Middle*.

2. Milbank, "Henri de Lubac," 79. The following words were written in 1956 and cited later in his collected memoirs: "I truly believe that for a rather long time the idea for my book on Mysticism has been my inspiration in everything; I form my judgments on the basis of it, it provides me with the means to classify my ideas in proportion to it. But I will not write this book. It is in all ways beyond my physical, intellectual, spiritual strength. I have a clear vision of how it is linked together, I can distinguish and more or less situate the problems that should be treated in it, in their nature and in their order, I see the precise direction in which the solution of each of them should be sought—but I am incapable of formulating that solution. This all is enough to allow me to rule out one by one the views that are not conformed to it, in the works I read or the theories I hear expressed, but all this does not take its final form, the only one that would allow it to exist. The center always eludes me. What I achieve on paper is only preliminary, banalities, peripheral discussions or scholarly details" (de Lubac, *At the Service of the Church*, 113).

his true theological voice.[3] Milbank suggests that de Lubac's "increasing indirection reflected both a continuing trauma after 1950 [and *Humani Generis*], and a continued need for caution, even into his old age."[4]

There may have been other issues, however, that made it difficult for de Lubac to write in his own theological voice. Milbank admits that

> the *surnaturel* thesis deconstructs the possibility of dogmatic theology as previously understood in modern times, just as it equally deconstructs the possibility of philosophical theology or even of a clearly autonomous philosophy *tout court*. . . . De Lubac elaborated a 'discourse of the supernatural' that was neither dogmatics nor philosophical theology—although he would have insisted that this was a restoration of an Augustinian 'Christian philosophy' or a Thomist *Sacra Doctrina*. This usually took the (only partially apparent) form of a historical theology. Such a form was inevitable in so far as a combination of event and sign in continuous process would seem to be the only possible ground that de Lubac's paradoxical discourse can occupy. De Lubac indeed declared that theology should be a mysticism and that mysticism was essentially a reading of signs.[5]

Still, Milbank thinks that de Lubac's theological work was unnecessarily confined to *ressourcement* projects and that this constitutes "a failure to proceed to a newly enhanced 'speculation' on the part of a thinker at once traumatized and forced to speak always with caution."[6] Elsewhere Milbank has claimed that his own theological project, with its "speculative" ontological extension, is a deliberate advancement of de Lubac's *nouvelle théologie*.[7] Milbank suggests that there is continuity between de Lubac's theological program and his own and that that his project offers

3. De Lubac's "crucial views were . . . always expressed indirectly through historical interpretations" (Milbank, "Henri de Lubac," 79).

4. Ibid., 80.

5. Ibid. De Lubac was quoting Jean Lacroix when he wrote that "the deepest thing in the spiritual history of mankind is the comprehension of the sign, and every great philosophy is a semeiology: the discovery of the world's cipher and the consequent ability to reveal its language is the object of man's basic desire. And mysticism is undoubtedly the meaning of signs before anything else" (quoted in de Lubac, *Scripture in the Tradition*, 70–71).

6. Milbank, "Henri de Lubac," 80.

7. Milbank, "Programme of Radical Orthodoxy," 35–36. See also Milbank, et al., *Radical Orthodoxy*, 2.

an advancement where de Lubac failed "to proceed to a newly enhanced speculation."

Milbank's claim that de Lubac's scholarly production was overly cautious due to the trauma of *Humani Generis* makes good sense. Indeed, de Lubac lamented, well into his old age, that his work was always focused on narrow historical themes when he might have offered guidance to a confused age by stating his own positions more directly. He writes:

> I am still haunted by the questions I have asked myself . . . concerning the choice of subjects approached in the course of my life, to the degree that these choices depended on me. Thinking of the pressing necessities of the present time, I feel some shame in having been able to offer to so many disoriented minds, as the final fruit of my work, only a study of Pico della Mirandola, whose usefulness no one would assert to be imperative.—But one cannot start our lives over again, and regrets are pointless.[8]

While it is fair to assume that de Lubac may have been overly cautious regarding his choice of subjects, Milbank's contention that he failed "to proceed to a newly enhanced speculation" is questionable, since there is no evidence to suggest that de Lubac ever intended his work to culminate in a new speculative theology like the one that Milbank has initiated in Radical Orthodoxy. Indeed, Milbank himself has acknowledged that de Lubac's great ambition was to write a mystical treatise on Christ. De Lubac regretted not that he failed to proceed to an enhanced speculative engagement with secularism in the style of Radical Orthodoxy but that he never completed his mystical Christology, which was always at the center of his thought.[9] He wrote in 1956, "for a rather long time the idea for my book on Mysticism has been my inspiration in everything; I form my judgments on the basis of it, it provides me with the means to classify my ideas in proportion to it. But I will not write this book. It is in all ways beyond my physical, intellectual, spiritual strength."[10] This book on mysticism was to be his treatise on Christ, and the statement above suggests that his major works on ecclesiology, ontology, and exegesis were inspired and guided by his mystical-christological thought. Although he

8. De Lubac, *At the Service of the Church*, 151.

9. "Milbank's admiration for de Lubac seems ultimately grounded, at least as I read his text, in his insistence that de Lubac was really the first advocate . . . of Radical Orthodoxy" (Oakes, "Paradox of Nature and Grace," 682).

10. De Lubac, *At the Service of the Church*, 113.

never completed this work, de Lubac did write an important essay on mysticism,[11] and this essay contains a number of insights into the christological assumptions that guide the major works mentioned above.

Ironically, whereas Milbank believes that his speculative ontology advances de Lubac's theological revolution, I will argue that de Lubac's mystical Christology has the potential for correcting the problems in Milbank's work, mentioned in chapter 5. Moreover, whereas Milbank contends that de Lubac's confinement to *ressourcement* projects prohibited him from bringing his revolution to completion, all the necessary components of this revolution are implicit in the historical projects that de Lubac completed. Specifically, the fundamental elements of de Lubac's mystical Christology can be extracted by examining his essay on mysticism in combination with his other major works and especially his work on spiritual exegesis.

Toward the end of chapter 5, I outlined several areas where Milbank's project needs to be redirected. I suggested that Milbank would do well to reconsider his argument in favor of the "primacy of ecclesiology" over Christology and that he should attend more closely to the way that the church's engagement with culture is necessarily mediated through biblical interpretation. This chapter illustrates how de Lubac's theological project can correct the aforementioned weaknesses in Milbank's work. In the first two sections, I examine the Christology implicit in several of de Lubac's works, including his essay entitled "Mysticism and Mystery." In the following section, I compare and contrast de Lubac's Christology with Milbank's. The third section illustrates how de Lubac's mystical Christology is mediated through the practices of spiritual exegesis as a kind of *sacra doctrina*, which guides the church's engagement with culture. In conclusion I summarize the ways that de Lubac's christological mysticism complements and corrects both postliberalism and Radical Orthodoxy.

Henri de Lubac's Mystical Christology

The word *mysticism*, like many words, needs clarification if it is to be useful. De Lubac was well aware of this problem, and he wrote "Mysticism

---

11. De Lubac, "Mysticism and Mystery," 35–70. The original, shorter version of this essay first appeared as the preface to a series of essays collected in the following work: Ravier, *La Mystique et les Mystiques*.

and Mystery" in order to among other things articulate a distinctively Christian and Catholic understanding of mysticism. First, he admits that the word "has mixed origins, and its present meaning has only fairly recently been accepted by theologians."[12] This, however, is no reason to think that the word has no usefulness. The same could be said of the words *religion* and *spirituality*, "which ordinarily no one thinks of challenging."[13] Mysticism, for de Lubac, "is to be understood as a kind of perfection attained in spiritual life, a form of actual union with the Divinity."[14] This union, however, is in no way to be construed as a kind of "essentialism" or basic spiritual experience of the divine that is common to all humans through a variety of religious traditions. De Lubac criticizes those who claim "there is only the infinite, eternal, and indefinite Essence that is absolutely pure and beyond all reach, and its transcendence must be demonstrated by the dissolution of all forms as well as by its radiance that shines through them."[15] In contrast, he suggests, "all mysticism is not 'ignorant' in the same way, nor is it 'learned' in the same way."[16] Rather mysticism, like all human knowledge and experience, "is never without an a priori." Thus, when de Lubac uses the word *mysticism*, he is speaking of a distinctively Christian way of experiencing union with the Divinity, and he insists that this union necessarily has certain characteristics.

The Distinctiveness of Christian Mysticism

According to de Lubac, Christian mysticism "can only mean the union with the tripersonal God of Christian revelation, a union realized in Jesus Christ through his grace."[17] When de Lubac speaks of mysticism, he has in mind "an 'infused' gift of 'passive' contemplation,"[18] or the vision or

12. De Lubac, "Mysticism and Mystery," 39.

13. The following comments are added in a footnote after the above statement: "Various authors, even Catholic ones, influenced more or less directly by Karl Barth (poorly understood) or by Bonhoeffer, avoid calling Christianity a religion, or even, not content to distinguish the two notions, contrast religion and faith" (ibid., 40, fn. 9).

14. Ibid., 39.

15. Ibid., 47.

16. Ibid., 45.

17. Ibid., 39.

18. Ibid. De Lubac's reference to a "passive" contemplation is likely meant to correspond logically with the idea that grace is "infused." For de Lubac, the contemplation of Christ is itself a gift of grace and does not occur on the basis of a "natural" human ability,

perspective of persons who participate in the body of Christ. He writes that Christian mysticism

> is not only a participation in the experience of Christ—albeit superior and unique—it is a participation, always deficient and the deeper it goes the more the mystic becomes aware of the deficiency, in the *reality* of Christ. Christian mysticism, then, is never pure interiority. . . . The deeper it goes, the more it involves the intentional movement that carries the mystic beyond himself in the direction of the Source who is forever filling in the gulf that separates them. . . . Mysticism is the interiority of faith by the interiorization of the mystery; but, as the mystery becomes interiorized, the mystic's faith in the mystery sends him out of himself. The ecstasy (one that is truly ontological) always prevails over the enstasis.[19]

When de Lubac speaks of mysticism, he hopes to express what St. Paul meant when he claimed to have the "mind of Christ" (1 Cor 2:13). Indeed, one of the reasons that de Lubac uses the word *mysticism* is because he believes that it communicates, accurately, the Pauline and Johannine perspectives. He describes the "Christological mysticism . . . of St. Paul," which offers us "a more complete awareness of the depths and heights of the spiritual life on earth." He goes on to suggest that "the Pauline doctrine on the union of the believer with Christ, on the presence and action of the Spirit in the Christian community, is quite clear. . . . Paul's mysticism is so conspicuous . . . that several exegetes whose systematic mentalities never hesitate to make drastic amputations have wished to remove entire chapters from even the most important of his letters."[20] The christological mysticism of St. John, de Lubac suggests, is "even more evident." "According to John," he writes, "the Christian has received divine life; he is reborn from water and the Spirit. . . . He affirms that this Life came and dwelt among men and that, by his Spirit, Life dwells in men's hearts."[21] Accordingly, we can say that, for de Lubac, *mysticism* is a word that can be used to describe the contemplative existence of those who dwell in Christ and in whom Christ dwells. Moreover, what

---

although it does fulfill a "natural" human appetite.

19. Ibid., 55–56, italics added.

20. He does not mention any names here, but a host of early twentieth-century biblical scholars could apply. Ibid., 50.

21. Ibid., 50–51.

it describes is consistent with the perspective of Pauline and Johannine literature as well as the great Christian tradition that follows.[22]

The Principal Characteristics of Christian Mysticism

Having established its distinctiveness and its theological basis in Scripture, de Lubac suggests several additional "principal characteristics" of Christian mysticism, which help to clarify his christological thought.[23] He tells us first: "it is a mysticism of likeness. 'God, who is completely present everywhere, does not dwell in everyone.' In other words, the divine image is inalienable in every human being, but the union of God is a 'union of likeness.'"[24] This suggests that having been created in the image of God, humans have no guarantee that they will be united with God, or that they will be conformed to the likeness of God. Humans always remain in a condition where their own completion and fulfillment depends upon the intervening grace of God. De Lubac suggests that mysticism is not an awareness of the "self, at the deepest part of one's being." On the contrary, persons can only ever know themselves through the "gracious intervention of God in giving the mystery,"[25] and this mystery is given in Christ. He explains:

> Christ completes the revelation of man to himself. By taking possession of man, by seizing hold of him and by penetrating to the very depths of his being Christ makes man go deep down within himself, there to discover in a flash regions hitherto unsuspected. It is through Christ that the person reaches maturity, that man emerges definitively from the universe, and becomes conscious of his own being . . . for through the Christian revelation not only is the scrutiny that man makes of himself made more searching, but his examination of all about him is at the same time made more

22. "Mysticism is not a late graft on the trunk of the Christian tree. Well before Pseudo-Denys, who has been honored (or reproached) for having been the grafter, it is possible to find incontestably mystical elements not only in the writings of Evagrius—who precedes Denys by only a little and whose doctrine is questionable—and in those of the great Cappadocians but as far back as St. Ignatius of Antioch, who lived less than a century from Christianity's origins" (ibid., 49).

23. Although I mention all of the "characteristics" that de Lubac discusses, I change the order to suit my own purposes.

24. De Lubac, "Mysticism and Mystery," 57.

25. Ibid.

comprehensive. Henceforth, the idea of human unity is born. That image of God, the image of the Word, which the incarnate Word restores and gives back to its glory, is "I myself"; it is also the other, every other. It is that aspect of me in which I coincide with every other man, it is the hallmark of our common origin and the summons to our common destiny. It is our very unity with God.[26]

This stress on "likeness" and the idea that humankind discovers itself and the world only as it is drawn, by the grace of God, toward Christ, in whose image persons are made, is the christological foundation upon which the *Surnaturel* thesis rests. Indeed, de Lubac suggests that "Christian mysticism is directed toward a goal, toward God who calls to us and beckons us to meet him at the end of the road. It presupposes a process that can never be finished, and it contains an element of eschatological hope."[27] The process of being conformed to the "likeness" of God is the process of human nature finding its completion and fulfillment in the supernatural. Humans, although they are created in the image of God, are misdirected in their search for fulfillment. Christ comes, then, as an interruption of grace through which fallen human nature is redirected toward its supernatural destination.

The second principal characteristic of Christian mysticism is that it is biblical. According to de Lubac, Christian mysticism "is essentially an understanding of the holy Books. The mystery is their meaning; mysticism is getting to know that meaning."[28] Elsewhere he writes that the "spiritual understanding" of Scripture is "identical to the process of conversion. It is its luminous aspect."[29] In equating mysticism with the meaning of Scripture, de Lubac is not limiting the content of mystical experience. Rather, he is claiming that all reality is discerned in its fullness and truth only as it is understood through the lens of Scripture. Scripture, for de Lubac, acts as a "prism" through which the christological "unity of the universe" is comprehended.[30] Christian mysticism is thus the understanding of reality in conformity with the christological perspective of Holy Scripture. Hans Urs von Balthasar captures this principle when

26. De Lubac, *Catholicism*, 339–40.

27. De Lubac, "Mysticism and Mystery," 57.

28. Ibid., 58.

29. De Lubac, *Scripture in the Tradition*, 21.

30. De Lubac, "Mysticism and Mystery," 58, fn. 74.

he writes that "to penetrate into the spirit of Scripture means, in the final analysis, to learn to recognize the inner nature of God, to appropriate to oneself God's thoughts about the world."[31]

Here, then, is the christological center of de Lubac's voluminous work on spiritual exegesis. The spiritual exegesis of Christian Scripture, as practiced by patristic and medieval theologians, serves to illumine all reality in the "light of Christ." It is through spiritual exegesis that the church comes to know the historical person of Jesus as the ascended Christ who is omnipresent, or, in Milbank's terminology, our "total context." De Lubac writes:

> The mystical or spiritual understanding of scripture and the mystical or spiritual life are, in the end, one and the same. Christian mysticism is that understanding pushed to its most fruitful phase by its four traditional dimensions—history, "allegory" or doctrine, ethics or "tropology" and anagogy—each of which is absorbed by the following one. . . . It is by submitting to historical-doctrinal facts and assimilating them that the necessary foundation for union [with God] can be found. The anagogical sense by which the spirit raises itself to God in a unique intuition has the richness of the three preceding dimensions concentrated within itself. Far from excluding them or freeing itself from them, it includes the full historical realization of salvation that is the permanent and indispensable base for mysticism, a gift of God.[32]

For de Lubac, spiritual exegesis plays a constitutive role in the church's participation in the life of the Trinity. Indeed, he affirms that the stages of history, allegory, and tropology on the way to anagogy shape Christian mysticism around an "indispensable" structure whose fabric is Christ. If one were to speak of a participation in Christ that bypasses these stages, then "there would be a fall from Christian Mysticism into natural mysticism."[33]

Another characteristic of Christian mysticism, according to de Lubac, is that it is "attached to the symbolism of spiritual marriage."[34] What this means is that the spiritual "union" of the church with Christ is

---

31. Quoted in de Lubac, *Scripture in the Tradition*, 23. What is important is that this suggests an empathic knowledge of God that does not deny God's hiddenness.

32. De Lubac, "Mysticism and Mystery," 58.

33. Ibid., 60.

34. Ibid.

"not an identification."[35] He explains that "between the human soul and its God, as in the marriage of the Church and the Lamb, there is always a union, not absorption."[36] The union between humans and God involves "mutual love," though it is God who first loves humans and not vice versa. This love, which is at the heart of the great commandment, suggests that the union results from the human desire for God, who is other. De Lubac cites John of the Cross:

> When we speak of the union of the soul with God, we are not referring to the union that already exists between God and all his creatures, but to the union of the soul with God and its transformation by his love. This transformation takes place, however, only when the soul, through love, resembles that of the Creator. That is why this union is called supernatural. It takes place when two wills, that of the soul and that of God, are in agreement, and one has nothing that repels the other. Thus, when the soul completely rejects in itself all that is repugnant or does not conform to the will of God, it is transformed into God through love.[37]

The union of love described above is, according to de Lubac, a "unity of desires," or a "mysticism of the will," such as one would find in the writings of Bernard of Clairvaux or William of St. Thierry. For these thinkers, the will was "not a mere 'faculty,' but the most profound element of being."[38] This aspect of de Lubac's Christology is central to the thesis of *Corpus Mysticum*, which stresses that the church's true nature and identity are inseparably linked to the flesh and blood of Jesus. The church discovers itself repeatedly through its eucharistic encounter with the crucified and risen Christ whose fullness always transcends the earthly *ekklesia*.

---

35. "One might fear, however, that the expression 'spiritual marriage,' which allows personal duality to survive, does not sufficiently convey the profound unity resulting from the mystical process. Such concern, however, would be unfounded since it would proceed from a false notion of unity. Surely there is a veritable unity in the image of the divine Trinity, and yet the distinction of personal Beings is not only maintained but carried to perfection" (ibid., 61).

36. Ibid., 60.

37. Quoted in ibid., 62; originally a saying of St. John of the Cross.

38. De Lubac argues that this mysticism of the will, or of desire, is based on a long biblical tradition that culminates in the Pauline imagery of the church as bride and is taken up with enthusiasm by Origen and many later commentators. See ibid., 60–61, fn. 84.

This brings us to another principal characteristic of Christian mysticism, which, according to de Lubac, "is necessarily an ecclesial mysticism, since the incarnation achieves first of all in the Church the marriage of the Word and humanity."[39] He writes, "if mystical life at its summit consists of an actual union with Divinity, such a union could be possible only through a supernatural grace whose normal setting is the Church and whose normal conditions are the life of faith and the sacraments. . . . It is only in the Church that a true mysticism can be found; outside of the Church, no mysticism."[40] Whereas *Catholicism* is concerned primarily with the church's role in mediating Christ to the world, *Corpus Mysticum* is focused on the importance of the Eucharist in mediating Christ to the church.

A final characteristic of Christian mysticism is that it is always Trinitarian. According to de Lubac the Trinitarian God

> is not the infinite One, as undifferentiated as he is unlimited, whom our spirit risks losing in some empty space. He is not the "All-Possibility" or the "place of indefinite possibilities." Neither is he the *Ungrund*, the original chasm, the obscure core of being— or nonbeing—from which persons emerged. The God whom we adore and who wants us to be united with him is not faceless: he has a superior form, an infinitely determined form." His infinity is not one of dispersion but of concentration: in him all the mystery of personal Being is condensed. Contemplation may enable man to plumb other depths and abysses, but unless they are explicitly or implicitly depths of the triune, human-divine and ecclesial life, they are either spurious or demonic.[41]

For de Lubac, Christian mysticism is necessarily a structured mysticism. Indeed, the characteristics mentioned above are patterned after the economic Trinity. Humans are created in the image of God and conformed to his likeness through grace, united with God in spiritual marriage through the Son, and participate in the life of God through the community of the Holy Spirit—the church. Christian mysticism, according to de Lubac, is not a natural capacity inherent in human nature. Rather, it is a gift of God. He suggests that "what the Catholic Church calls mysticism is only the conscious actualization of this gift of God." Moreover, Christian

39. Ibid., 62.
40. Ibid., 43.
41. Ibid., 62–63.

mysticism is not something reserved only for a few. Rather, it defines "all Christian reality."[42] Christian mysticism, in de Lubac's thought, is simply the human actualization of God's self-disclosure, which is always also the revelation of humans to themselves.

CHRISTOLOGY IN DE LUBAC AND MILBANK

I argued in chapter 4 that Hans Frei and George Lindbeck failed to articulate a participatory theological hermeneutic capable of avoiding the problem of extrinsicism. Milbank is particularly critical of Frei's claim that Jesus is clearly "identified" through the biblical narrative, because even if he were, this rendering of Jesus's identity would be nothing more than a mere "fact," having no ability to reconcile persons with God. According to Milbank, theological hermeneutics must be Trinitarian and participatory, and Christology must focus on the "force" of Jesus's identity—its ability to transform others.[43] Accordingly Milbank argues that the gospel portraits of Jesus do not render a clear identity description, and seem instead to "evacuate" Jesus of all personal and "specifiable content," to such an extent that only the proper name, Jesus, remains.[44]

Rather than a clear identity description, Milbank argues that the gospels portray Jesus as the founder of a new "mode of being." He claims that the force or soteriological potency of Jesus derives from the fact that he inaugurated a new language and a new practice of "harmonic peace," which is "fully transferable to others." Jesus's persistent identity, according to Milbank, should not be attached to "any 'subsistent' dimension within the individual," as "Chalcedonian high Christology" and "Aquinas still supposed."[45] For Milbank, a person's persistent identity "resides purely on the surface of a series of events which exhibit a certain pattern

---

42. Ibid., 63.

43. Milbank, *Word Made Strange*, 164.

44. Ibid., 150.

45. Milbank suggests that his own "'postmodern' escape from preoccupation with an 'interior' subject and its 'intentionality', allows us to retrieve a more objective understanding of 'personhood', detached from notions of physical individuality, consciousness, will and so forth—all of which were, of course, fully and purely human in Christ. So that Chalcedonian high Christology need no longer seem so embarrassing as it did for modernist theology. . . . I do not wish to disguise the fact that I am transposing Chalcedonian orthodoxy into a new idiom which only perfects it by dissolving 'substantial' notions of subjectivity which it did not always fully overcome" (ibid., 157).

and coherence."[46] Reconciliation between God and humans occurs as the church renarrates and re-realizes this "pattern and coherence," which, for Milbank, is the *totus Christus* (ontologically speaking). Accordingly, "the only thing which will really remove us from extrinsicism," Milbank claims, "is the primacy of ecclesiology."[47]

Happily, de Lubac's mystical Christology avoids the problem of extrinsicism that characterizes postliberalism, without affirming the primacy of ecclesiology over Christology as Milbank does. Indeed, de Lubac's mystical Christology entails a participatory and Trinitarian hermeneutic focused on the soteriological potency of Christ while avoiding the errors of Milbank's approach, which are discussed at the end of chapter 5. The first thing to say about de Lubac's Christology, in contrast to Milbank's, is that it does not allow the need to overcome extrinsicism to obscure the fact that Jesus is first encountered, in the gospels and in the worship of the church, as other. De Lubac's insistence that the union between humans and God be symbolized by the image of "spiritual marriage" rather than "identification" differs from Milbank's focus on Jesus's "state of being which is fully transferable to others."[48] Because there is nothing persistent about Jesus, for Milbank, that is not fully transferable to the church, there is no reason why Christology (as well as the doctrine of atonement)[49] should not be subsumed under ecclesiology. Among the various problems with Milbank's approach to Christology, the one that stands out as particularly problematic is the way that it eliminates the distance/difference between Jesus and the church and thus renders Christ incapable of judgment (theoretically speaking).[50] How is the church to worship Jesus

46. Ibid., 157.

47. Ibid., 165.

48. Ibid., 157. It is interesting how the problems inherent in Milbank's Christology might stem from his insistence that there is no "contrast" between nature and grace. Whereas de Lubac, especially in his later works, places greater emphasis on the contrast between fallen nature and the grace of redemption, Milbank insists on total continuity. See Milbank, *Suspended Middle*, 46.

49. "If Jesus' death is efficacious, not just as the offering of an enabling sign, but also as a material reality, then this is because it is the inauguration of the political practice of forgiveness; forgiveness as a mode of 'government' and social being" (Milbank, *Word Made Strange*, 161).

50. John David Dawson writes that "the body of Christ is irreducibly particular, uniquely Christ's own. How then does membership 'in' that body enhance rather than suppress the individual identities of its members? Would it not make more sense for each of us to interpret the body of Christ as a metaphor for the various meanings that we

as judge and redeemer if he is accessible only through the church's renarration of him? If Christology is subsumed under ecclesiology, as Milbank recommends, then the distance between Jesus and the church, which allows distinctions such as teacher/disciple, savior/saved, creator/created, judge/judged, and lover/beloved disappears.[51] Christianity traditionally affirms that the will of individual persons must be conformed to God's will through an encounter with God's one and only Son, Jesus, before his language and practice can be renarrated and re-realized through the church's worship and witness.

As I mentioned in chapter 5, baptism is preceded by repentance, and repentance occurs when persons recognize the unique perfection of Jesus in *contrast* to their own imperfection.[52] Accordingly, the primacy of Christology has to be maintained, and de Lubac's christological mysticism ensures that it will, with its insistence on a union symbolized by spiritual marriage rather than identification via a fully transferable pattern, as in Milbank's thought. De Lubac affirms, with the tradition and in contrast to Milbank, that Jesus's persistent personal identity (the identity that the church weds) rests in his will—in his love/desire for the Father. Consider de Lubac's prayer to Jesus:

> Jesus, I believe in You. I confess that You are God. You are for us the whole Mystery of God. What other definition of God would we seek than that given by your Apostle? And was it not in con-

---

might wish to give our own unique lives? Would not such 'Christic meaning,' precisely because it would no longer be attached to, and identified by, the actions and passions of that particular body, be sufficiently malleable to accommodate our own irreducible diversity? Conversely, if we all were to become identified by means of inclusion in Christ's body, in his person, would not our own uniqueness be superseded by Christ's? Would we not become hollow figures whose distinctiveness had given way to a single, universalizing fulfillment?" (Dawson, "Figural Reading," 192).

51. Again, Milbank's Christology is consistent with his insistence that there is no "contrast" between nature and grace. What is at stake here is the integrity of creation and the question of whether there is some contrast/disruption, or whether there is only continuity between the order of creation and the order of grace. See especially the footnotes from chapter 4 above for more on these controversial issues surrounding the relationship between nature and grace.

52. It is noteworthy, I believe, that de Lubac's later work on nature and grace, which emphasizes the *contrast* (rather than the total continuity) between fallen human nature and the grace of God in Christ, is fully consistent with his mystical thought and with his voluminous work on exegesis. This undermines Milbank's contention that de Lubac's later positions are an unfortunate capitulation to ecclesial authority. See Milbank, *Suspended Middle*, 33–47.

templating You that he found it? God is Love. The single word contains an unfathomable mystery, which I adore. But through You this mystery illumines our night already. For Love has done a great deed, and this Deed of Love, the Love made visible to our eyes, perceptible to hearts of flesh, effective and saving Love, is You Yourself! It is God made man, it is the Incarnation of God.[53]

Not only is Jesus's persistent identity here described as "Love," but it is precisely the Love of Jesus that de Lubac describes as "effective." Regarding this love he writes: "An efficacious feat: through this 'divine strength' already recognized by the Apostle Paul, he uproots us from our egotism, he opens us, takes us, makes us capable of adopting the contours of it in our turn. He eradicates the old man and implants the new man."[54]

This, of course, is quite different from Milbank's claim that the force of Jesus's identity (its efficaciousness) has nothing to do with any "interior" subsistent characteristic like the "will," but rather resides in the fully repeatable language and practice that he inaugurated. Aware that his position might be construed as rendering Jesus dispensable, Milbank explains that

The universal repeatability of Jesus is made possible *by* his specific historic occurrence, and this is never 'dispensable' in specifying the conditions of our salvation . . . because a genuine 'foundation' is not the first instance of a general phenomenon, but rather is itself the 'general', though specific, definition of that phenomenon. It follows . . . that Jesus can be talked of as uniquely a 'substitute' and 'representative', not because these attributes cannot be repeated, but precisely in so far as they can be and are.[55]

The strange thing about this statement is that it so completely contradicts Milbank's lament in the introduction to *The Word Made Strange* concerning his own difficulty in locating true Christian practice. In the quotation above, it sounds as though Jesus's "total refusal of selfish power" is something easily and "fully repeatable." The truth, of course, is that the

53. De Lubac, "Light of Christ," 218.

54. Ibid. Here again, de Lubac's perspective on grace entails much more than a simple "elevation." The grace of God, working on our human nature, leads to a disruption and a transformation that is more discontinuous than Milbank's view of the treatment of the relationship between nature and grace.

55. Milbank, *Word Made Strange*, 158.

mode of being inaugurated by Jesus in the gospels is not fully repeatable. Jesus's entire life was given over to the will of the Father, and it is precisely the union of the divine and human wills in Jesus that characterizes a new mode of being—one that can be only partially (not fully) realized in the earthly *ekklesia* through the practices of repentance, baptism, and worship.

The fact that de Lubac affirms the otherness of Jesus via the symbolism of "spiritual marriage" and locates the persistent identity of Jesus in his love of the Father does not, however, mean that his Christology is extrinsic. On the contrary, de Lubac's Christology moves from the historical narration of Jesus that is characteristic of the Synoptic Gospels toward an affirmation that Jesus is indeed the *totus Christus*, or the total context within which human life takes place.[56] De Lubac's appreciation for the "Cosmic Christ" is perhaps most evident in his works on the thought of Teilhard de Chardin.[57] He writes of de Chardin that "if it is true that he attributes to the risen Humanity of our Lord (as others also do) 'a presence in the world as vast as the very immensity of God,' can we be certain that in holding this against Teilhard our censure may not at the same time embrace St. Paul?" De Lubac writes further: "*Omnia in ipso constant*—'in him all subsist'—this sentence from the Epistle to the Colossians had long fired Teilhard's enthusiasm. Following some of his seniors, he had learnt during his years of theology to set them at the heart of Christian thought. Nor could he have felt that he was introducing any innovation when he said that, 'Christ is the term supernaturally, but also physically, assigned to the consummation of humanity.'"[58]

In the quotations above and in many other places de Lubac clearly embraces the "cosmic point of view" regarding Christ, and he explicitly states that Teilhard has done theology a great service by working to retrieve such a view.[59] Indeed, it is the cosmic Christ that de Lubac identi-

56. For more on the christological concerns of de Lubac's exegetical work, see Wood, *Spiritual Exegesis*, 71–128.

57. See the following works: de Lubac, *Teilhard de Chardin*, 35–54; *Teilhard Explained*.

58. De Lubac, *Teilhard de Chardin*, 42–43.

59. "We should, it is true, recognize at any rate that during the last few centuries this 'cosmic' aspect of Pauline teaching had become somewhat blurred in current Catholic thought. There can be no doubt that most modern theologians have devoted little attention to it. Some of the best New Testament exegetes, both Catholic and Protestant, have commented only briefly on the passages in which it is to be found. It was this lack that

fies in the mystical Christology of St. Paul and St. John. How, though, does the church progress from an encounter with the Jesus of the gospels, who "uproots us from our egotism," to the cosmic Christ, who "makes us capable of adopting the contours" of his "divine strength"? For de Lubac, spiritual exegesis enables the church to comprehend that the historical Jesus is the cosmic Christ who reigns over all of heaven and earth. In other words, in de Lubac's thought, the "extension of a fully Christianised ontology"[60] takes place as the church interprets and understands Scripture according to the Spirit through a christological mysticism that is, essentially, a *sacra doctrina*.

The Mediation of Christ in Spiritual Exegesis

For Milbank and the other editors of *Radical Orthodoxy*, secularism is engaged and overcome as "every discipline" is "framed by a theological perspective." Thus, the theologian's task is to expose the nihilism inherent in secular social thought while contrasting it with the beauty and "relative worth" of social reality conceived as a participation in God.[61] The fruit of this speculative engagement, or so it is claimed, is that "space" formerly governed by secular social theory is now opened up, and the church is freed to inhabit those places where secularism once reigned. However, it remains unclear how this speculative engagement actually enables and promotes the instantiation of new participatory practices. I argued in chapter 4 that Radical Orthodoxy has offered an interesting deconstruction of secular social theory but has failed, thus far, to show how Christians inhabit the space created by this deconstruction.

Although Milbank, Pickstock, and Ward suggest that "radical orthodoxy mingles exegesis, cultural reflection and philosophy in a complex but coherently executed *collage*,"[62] sustained biblical interpretation is relatively absent in Radical Orthodoxy's engagement with secularism.[63] This missing exegetical element is, in my view, the reason why Radical

---

Père Teilhard wished to supply: and even those readers who find themselves unable to accept what is most personal to him in his explanations, should be willing, I believe, to recognize that his attempt will prove to have been well worthwhile" (ibid., 44).

60. Milbank, et al., *Radical Orthodoxy*, 2.

61. Ibid., 3.

62. Milbank, et al., *Radical Orthodoxy*, 2; emphasis original.

63. Ford, "Radical Orthodoxy and the Future of British Theology," 398.

Orthodoxy, which intends to advance a "fully Christianized ontology," has not really moved beyond the speculative deconstruction of secular social theory. It is here that de Lubac's work on spiritual exegesis can supply the missing element in Milbank's program.

The Fourfold Method: From Jesus of Nazareth to Totus Christus

For de Lubac, as mentioned above, Jesus is necessarily mediated to the church, at least in part, through spiritual exegesis. In other words, it is through spiritual exegesis that the church moves from an encounter with the historical Jesus to a union with the cosmic Christ. In his essay on mysticism, de Lubac argues that the union of humans with God "includes the full historical realization of salvation." He holds that christological mysticism is essentially an understanding of the Scriptures that has progressed from history to allegory and then to tropology in pursuit of the eschatological vision of God (anagogy).[64]

The Literal/Historical Sense

In the second volume of *Medieval Exegesis*, de Lubac devotes a lengthy chapter to each of the four traditional senses of Scripture. With regard to the first, he explains that the Fathers use the terms *littera* and *historia* interchangeably to denote either what has been clearly spoken or what has taken place in history.[65] Both terms, according to de Lubac, are used to describe "the exterior and sensible aspect of things, as opposed to their mystic or hidden signification, which is not at all perceived by the sense but only by the understanding."[66] It is through the historical sense that we

---

64. De Lubac, "Mysticism and Mystery," 58.

65. According to de Lubac, the Fathers were well aware of the fact that the "sensible aspect of things" often entailed a metaphoric or symbolic meaning, as in the case of parables or poems. Thus, to speak of the literal sense is not to exclude certain literary genres that rely on symbolism. Also, when the Fathers spoke of the historical sense, they had no "interest in the human past for its own sake" as a nineteenth-century historian may have. Rather, the historical sense was that sense of Scripture that recognized God's involvement in human affairs, leading them towards his intended end. De Lubac writes that "our ancient exegetes did not have any idea, thanks be to God, of that 'absolutized History,' which is one of the principal idols invented by our age. On the other hand, they did have a sense of biblical history, or even of universal history" (de Lubac, 2:41–44).

66. Ibid., 42.

first "make a real contact with . . . the object of scripture: the development of the revelation of the mystery of Christ."[67] According to de Lubac

> We are obliged to believe in a whole series of facts that have really come about. God has chosen a people for himself; in this way he has intervened in the history of men: the first thing to do, then, is to know, according to the book in which the Holy Spirit has recorded it, the sequence of his interventions. Thus it will never be possible to forget history, nor to put it into question again, nor to free oneself of it or spurn it. One must endeavor to receive and preserve its testimony.[68]

The literal/historical sense of Scripture provides the signs that point to Christ. Importantly, these signs are themselves the products of God's intervention in history, i.e., through the election and gathering of a people and especially through his incarnation in Jesus of Nazareth. The historical sense provides what de Lubac refers to as the "biblical facts." He suggests that "he who neglects to study [the historical sense] is . . . like the grammarian who would believe he could neglect the alphabet."[69] Indeed, the historical sense, when considered in light of the anagogical sense, provides the fabric from which the allegorical and tropological senses are built. Without the historical sense, there would be no deeper understanding (allegory) and no participation in Christ (tropology), just as there could be no words without the letters from which they are built.

In the same way that the other senses depend upon the historical sense, the Fathers affirmed that the historical sense remains incomplete unless it is surpassed by those that come after it. Paul's famous saying in 2 Cor 3:6 ("the letter kills, but the spirit gives life") provided the basis for the ancient way of understanding the relationship between the first sense and those that follow it. According to de Lubac, "it was not the 'letter' that bothered them, but the 'mere letter', the 'mere surface of the letter', the 'property of the letter alone.'"[70] They never approached history for mere information. Rather, patristic and medieval commentators believed that history was pregnant with the Spirit of God, and that its true meaning

---

67. De Lubac, "Mysticism and Mystery," 59.

68. De Lubac, *Medieval Exegesis,* vol. 2, 44.

69. Ibid., 45.

70. Ibid., 51.

was to be found in its final end—Christ. Accordingly, to focus "merely" on the literal or historical sense was simply to miss the point.

It is interesting to note that Milbank, in his engagement with the gospels in *The Word Made Strange*, never moves beyond the literal/historical sense. He argues, contra Hans Frei, that the literal sense of the biblical narrative fails to provide a personal identity description of a character named Jesus, but he is not troubled by this fact, because, for him, such a description would have no soteriological potency. Milbank claims that "the name 'Jesus' does not indicate an identifiable 'character', but is rather the obscure and mysterious hinge which permits shifts from one kind of discourse to another."[71] Jesus saves because he inaugurates a new language and a new practice that is "fully transferable" to the church.[72] Jesus, in Milbank's account, is indispensable because he inaugurates and therefore "defines" a new mode of being in reconciled relationship to God. Jesus "persists" in history because his identity resides on the "surface of a series of events which exhibit a certain pattern and coherence," and this identity can be re-realized and renarrated by the church through a "non-identical repetition" of Jesus.[73]

In Milbank's account, the historical Jesus has become the total context within which human life takes place only because he has been depersonalized and essentially abandoned to the first century.[74] In Milbank's account, the church participates in a language and in a practice, but not

71. Milbank, *Word Made Strange*, 149.

72. It is noteworthy that in subsuming Christology under ecclesiology, Milbank loses the distinction between head and body in the *totus Christus*. Cf. Eph 5:23; Col 1:18.

73. Milbank, *Word Made Strange*, 152–65.

74. By "depersonalized," I am referring to Milbank's contention that "the effect of implying that a person situated in the world is also, in himself (like God) our total situation, or that which is always transcendentally presupposed, is to evacuate that person of any particular, specifiable content" (Milbank, *Word Made Strange*, 150). John David Dawson takes a very different approach to the gospel portrayal of Jesus's identity when he suggests that "[Jesus] moves ever closer to an identification with the one he calls 'Father', yet in doing so, becomes ever more himself, until, at the moment of resurrection, we see only the identity of Jesus in the Father's action by which he is raised. Maximal submission to the will of the Father coincides with maximal expression of individual identity" (Dawson, "Figural Reading," 192). Unlike Milbank, Dawson argues that the personal identity of Jesus is clarified, not distorted, as Jesus submits to the will of the Father. For Dawson, then, there is no need to suggest that the historical Jesus is somehow evacuated of personal content as his personal narrative is subsumed into the metanarrative. On the contrary, the person of Jesus is most fully illumined as we come to understand his place in the metanarrative.

necessarily in the divine-human person, Jesus of Nazareth. Milbank sees, like the church fathers, that the letter is limited. However, Milbank's Christology capitalizes on the letter's inability to identify Jesus, whereas the Fathers proceeded to allegory. Milbank is forced to leave Jesus behind because he, like Frei, has attempted to make too much out of the literal sense of Scripture. He has transformed the "non-interior" identity of Jesus, which "resides purely on the surface" (thus in the literal sense) into an omnipresent reality within which persons can participate.[75]

The Allegorical Sense

De Lubac, in contrast to Milbank, views allegory as the means through which the historical Jesus is transformed into the omnipresent, *totus Christus*, and tropology as the means through which the church comes to participate in Christ. Important is that Christian allegorical interpretation is, according to de Lubac, not an invention of the patristic age. Rather it was the Apostle Paul who first read the Old Testament allegorically, and he was followed by a host of other New Testament authors.[76] The allegorical sense of Scripture is simply that sense that views all the Old Testament, both its history and its words, as a signification of Christ and the church.[77] De Lubac suggests that "as Saint Paul said, Christ and the Church are just one great mystery: this is the mystery of their union. Now the whole mystery of Scripture, the whole object of *allegoria*, resides in this. This enables one to discover everywhere the 'deeper mysteries about Christ and his body.'"[78]

De Lubac points out consistently that the allegorical interpretation of Scripture is not abstract or ahistorical. He writes that "it does not exist in idea. It does not consist in any atemporal truth or object detached from speculation. This mystery is a reality in act, the realization of a Grand Design; it is therefore, in the strongest sense, even something historical,

---

75. Milbank, *Word Made Strange*, 157.

76. De Lubac, *Medieval Exegesis*, vol. 1. It is also important to note that the sacraments of baptism and Eucharist, which are instituted by Jesus in the gospels, are themselves based on allegorical interpretations of the Old Testament.

77. Consider the following statements: "allegory exists when the present sacraments of Christ and the Church are signed by means of mystical words or things. . . . All the Scripture of the Old Testament invites us to behold the mysteries of Christ and the Church" (de Lubac, *Medieval Exegesis*, vol. 2, 91).

78. Ibid., 92.

in which personal beings are engaged."[79] The allegorical sense searches for the spiritual meaning within the history told in the Old Testament.[80] De Lubac explains:

> to discover this allegory, one will not find it properly speaking in the text, but in the realities of which the text speaks; not in history as recitation, but in history as event; or if one wishes, allegory is indeed in the recitation, but one that relates a real event. "The actions speak. . . . The deeds, if you understand them, are words." Allegory is prophecy inscribed within the facts themselves: "not only in the things said, but also, God disposing all things marvelously, in the deeds themselves."[81]

As mentioned above, allegorical interpretation assumes the omnipresence of Christ. Thus, it sees Christ in things that have already happened, and it finds Christ in the unfolding of history as well.[82] De Lubac considers the ontological assumptions of allegorical interpretation as follows:

> To go into a little detail: if . . . the manna is really the figure of the Eucharist, or if the sacrifice of the paschal Lamb really prefigures the redemptive death, the reason for this is not extrinsic resemblance alone, no matter how striking this might be. There is actually an "inherent continuity" and "ontological bond" between the two facts, and this is due to the same divine will which is active in both situations and which, from stage to stage, is pursuing a single

---

79. Ibid., 93–94.

80. I should note that de Lubac does not mean to oversimplify matters by drawing a sharp distinction between literal and spiritual senses. He explains that "the antithesis which we have set out is, to be sure, a formal one. We can even admit that it is somewhat artificial. Its precise importance can be measured by what will follow. Concretely, the spiritual meaning of Scripture and the religious meaning of the Bible [the literal/historical sense] coincide at many points. The ideal is for them to continue each other and interpenetrate. They somehow need one another: the former must have a permanent basis, and the latter must not be truncated. We might express this fact by saying that, before we can undertake any spiritual interpretation of the Old Testament through the New, we must first have historically understood the New Testament through the Old" (de Lubac, *Scripture in the Tradition*, 28).

81. De Lubac, *Medieval Exegesis*, vol. 2, 86.

82. "And by the words of Christ we do not mean those only which He spake when He became man and tabernacled in the flesh; for before that time, Christ, the Word of God, was in Moses and the prophets. For without the Word of God, how could they have been able to prophesy of Christ?" (Origen, *On First Principles*, 1).

Design—the Design which is the real object of the Bible. And if St. Paul, looking back on the events which occurred in the desert and the "spiritual" rock at which the Israelites quenched their thirst, can add: "*Petra autem erat Christus*," it is because 'the event which took place in the desert was itself part of the forward movement, driven on by a force which surpasses time and for which 'a thousand years are as a day', towards the Easter event, and was destined to find in that event, its own true meaning.[83]

The allegorical sense presumes that the history of salvation described in the Old Testament was "driven by a force which surpasses time," and that this force was God. There is thus a genuine "ontological bond" between Old Testament characters and the Messiah that emerges from Mary's womb. When de Lubac suggests that allegory assumes more than an "extrinsic resemblance" between Christ and that which came before, he is critiquing biblical interpretation that sees no need to move beyond the literal/historical sense. Typology as mere extrinsic resemblance is, in de Lubac's mind, insufficient precisely because it remains on the surface of a series of events and does not assume an ontological bond in the way that allegory does.[84]

Just as the allegorical sense of Scripture finds Christ everywhere in the "pregnant past" of the Old Testament, so too does it always interpret the future through a christological lens: "The object of allegory, by relation to the facts that the Old Testament reports," writes de Lubac, "is therefore a reality to come: this is its most immediately tangible characteristic. *They foretell the things to come*."[85] Accordingly, allegorical interpretation unites

83. De Lubac, *Scripture in the Tradition*, 37. Cf. Auerbach, *Mimesis*, 73–74.

84. De Lubac, "Typology and Allegorization," 129–64. John David Dawson makes a similar point when he writes that "a person or an event is a *figura* precisely because it begins an extended divine utterance that embraces subsequent persons and events. 'Figuralness' denotes the status of things as significant—not in themselves and not in their meanings—but insofar as they are, in all their concrete reality, the enacted intention of God to signify. If Jesus is the fulfillment of Joshua, that is because both Joshua and Jesus are moments within a single divine intention to signify. Discerning that intention as a literary congruence, the figural reader makes explicit the similarities by which otherwise separate events are related to one another as moments in a single, divine utterance" (Dawson, "Figural Reading," 188). Whereas de Lubac distinguishes between typology and allegory, Dawson refers to a reading that is focused only on extrinsic resemblance as "figurative" and reading that recognizes the "ontological bond" between persons and events as "figural."

85. De Lubac, *Medieval Exegesis*, vol. 2, 94 (emphasis original).

not only sacred history but also the church's present and future in an "ontological bond" with God in Christ. De Lubac explains that just

> as history is not enough to contain the mystery, it is very true that Christian allegory is not contained by the historical dimension. To receive it totally and not to warp it, we must not restrict this reality "to come," which is the New Testament, within the bounds of the "*superficies histotriae*," the "surface of history." It overflows these boundaries. It involves another "dimension." For a mystery, in the Christian sense, is indeed a fact, but it is much more than an ordinary fact. Allegories discover for us a good deal of "*mysteria futura*," but these are also "*futura mysteria*," and the emphasis can be put in turn on the one or the other element of this pair of words. The "mystery of the dispensation" is a "dispensation of the mystery"; this is the "mystical dispensation of Christ."[86]

Allegorical interpretation finds Christ everywhere in the Old Testament, and it also enables the church to see Christ everywhere in the present and future. In other words, allegorical interpretation assumes that the meaning of scripture is inexhaustible—boundless. Allegorical interpretation is not interested in discovering ultimate truth as a "given," though it always embraces the indispensable signifying role of biblical facts. It enables the church to continually interpret reality from a christological perspective. It functions, for patristic and medieval Christians, as a christological hermeneutic through which the unfolding of reality can be continually interpreted in light of the biblical drama. De Lubac emphasizes the aesthetic role that allegory plays when he writes that

> The divinity of the Word of God incarnate is in fact the central object of allegory. It is revealed, however, only to the "eyes of the heart," to those "inner eyes," those "spiritual eyes," those "eyes of the soul," those "better eyes," that are opposed to the eyes of the flesh and which are in reality the eyes received from God, the eyes "illuminated by the Gospel" or, following a frequent expression, the "eyes of faith." For *faith has her own eyes.* Faith is the light 'that makes one see the light of the spirit in the law of the letter; it is like a lamp lit in the night, penetrating the thick cloud of all the biblical "sacraments" which surround it.[87]

---

86. Ibid., 95–96.
87. Ibid., 108.

For de Lubac, allegorical interpretation supplies the "aesthetic idiom" (to use Milbank's term) within which church practice takes place. For de Lubac, in contrast to Milbank, this aesthetic idiom, which is always mediated by Scripture, makes Christology primary. Accordingly, we can say that the allegorical interpretation of Scripture functioned, for the Fathers, as a christological *poesis* through which the church extends the reign of God on earth.[88]

The Tropological Sense

Whereas de Lubac indicates that the literal sense of Scripture must be surpassed by the spiritual or allegorical sense, the remaining senses require "no such jump."[89] Indeed, there are only two basic senses of scripture—the literal/historical and the spiritual/allegorical, so the tropological and anagogical senses should be considered subcategories within the allegorical sense. De Lubac, following "the school of Saint Victor," suggests that "in all of Scripture there are two objects to look for: the 'cognition of the truth' and the 'form of virtue': history and allegory converge on the first; tropology supplies the second."[90]

Whereas the allegorical interpretation of the literal sense of Scripture provides a kind of christological illumination, the tropological sense is concerned with Christian practices that ensue from this illumination: "The fruits of tropology," according to de Lubac, "can come only after the 'flowers of allegory.'"[91] Tropology is intimately connected to the spiritual understanding of Scripture that comes through allegorical interpretation. Accordingly, de Lubac insists that the tropological sense is not concerned with morality as a kind of natural law. Rather the tropological sense offers

88. Interestingly, Milbank makes an important departure from the Christology of *The Word Made Strange* when he assigns greater weight to the gospel portrait of Jesus in his more recent book, *The Suspended Middle*, which happens to be an analysis of de Lubac's work. He writes that "in insisting upon traditional allegory," de Lubac shows that "Christ's human nature could not exhibit the divine idiom unless the literal events of his life were doubled by an allegorical summation of all of the Old Testament and indeed all foregoing reality"(57). For discussions of the relevance of the word *poesis* to Christian theology, see the chapter titled "A Christological Poetics" in Milbank, *Word Made Strange*, 123–44. See also Hütter, *Suffering Divine Things*, 29–37.

89. Lubac, *Medieval Exegesis*, vol. 2, 127.

90. Ibid.

91. Ibid., 128.

insight into a distinctively christological approach to human action and virtue. He writes:

> If allegory develops dogma, it develops not just any morality, but Christian anthropology and the spirituality that flows from the dogma. After the *facta mystica* ["mystic deeds that have been done"] given by the allegory, both in immediate dependence and in internal dependence upon them, it indicates the *facienda mystica* ["mystic deeds that are to be done"]. After the "mystery of faith" come the 'works of faith." After the "mystical faith" comes the "moral grace." It makes us see everywhere in Scripture something that concerns us: "Look these are your affairs, brothers . . . , your affairs, I say, your affairs!"[92]

The word *tropology* comes from the Greek *tropos*, which indicates a "turn of phrase" through which some expression is turned in order to make it designate something new. The "turning" characteristic of *tropos* is captured by the Latin translation, *conversio*, which obviously means conversion. The tropological sense thus concerns the way that Scripture is "turned . . . toward us, i.e., toward our ways of behaving," leading to our conversion. De Lubac cites Robert of Melun who suggests that "*tropologia* means speech that turns (*sermo conversivus*) because (*eo quod*) it designates a deed of such a sort that it is necessary for us to be converted to it with respect to the establishment of moral edification."[93] The tropological sense is in no way an appendix to the spiritual sense. De Lubac writes that

> Tropology . . . has its own indispensable place in the concatenation of the scriptural senses. Far from being exterior and inferior to the "deeper sense" of allegory . . . it even marks, in a certain sense, a deepening of it, or even its summit: "We are nourished on history and parables; we grow by means of allegory; we are brought to perfection by morality." . . . Its procedure is essential to the full understanding of Scripture. After the "transposition of the fundamental data of the Word of God with reference to Christ," ought to come the "assimilation of these data to ourselves through his mediation."[94]

92. Ibid., 132–33.
93. Robert of Mellun, quoted in ibid., 129.
94. Ibid., 133.

The tropological sense focuses on the relevance of Scripture, christologically interpreted, for the church and for individual Christians.[95] Tropological interpretation allows Christians to "interiorize" the mystery of Christ. For example, one medieval theologian writes of Israel's liberation from Egypt that, "though those deeds were corporeally performed in Egypt, they are nevertheless being performed spiritually in us."[96] Offering another example of tropological interpretation, de Lubac paraphrases Gregory the Great, who suggests that "the tabernacle of Moses or the Temple of Solomon, which allegorically is Christ, is also by necessary consequence 'our heart.' It is 'the very mind and consciousness of the faithful.'"[97]

Through the tropological sense, persons are made to understand the relevance of Scripture for their own lives. The tropological sense enables the church, daily and in every age, to share in both the judgment and in the redemption of Israel.[98] It is thus a mediator of both repentance and liberation. According to de Lubac, the tropological sense leads the church to see that "in everything, Scripture invites us to conversion of heart. All the wars that it recounts are the wars of the Lord; all the migrations, all the travels it traces are the wanderings and travels of the soul: it is thus from one end to the other the book of spiritual combat at the same time as it is the book of departure and of mystical ascent."[99] He goes on to explain that

95. "The tropological sense therefore does not only presuppose the Mystery of the Christ, but also that of the Church, which is, as we have seen, inseparable from it. The tropological sense presupposes, or rather, expresses the mystery: for if the souls are Christian only within the Church, the reverse holds: 'it is within the souls that the Church is beautiful.' The whole life of the Christian flows from the 'mystical fecundity of the Church. Everything that the Gospel history contains, says Saint Bernard, can therefore be interpreted 'according to tropology, so that what has preceded in the head may consequently also be believed to come about morally in its body'" (ibid., 135).

96. Elmer of Canterbury, quoted in ibid., 134.

97. Ibid., 135.

98. Tropology thus entails more than the church's participation in a "fully transferable" language and practice. Tropology enables the church to recognize, because it can identify itself in Israel's idolatry, the degree to which it falls short of Christ's goodness. Tropological interpretation mediates a union with Christ involving both repentance and baptism.

99. De Lubac, *Medieval Exegesis*, vol. 2, 141. Frei worries that the kind of "interiorization" of the narrative that is represented in this quotation from de Lubac is in danger of losing its grounding in "providentially governed biblical history" (Frei, *Eclipse*, 152). De

with Abraham we abandon our home and we arrive at the oak of Mamre, where God goes to visit us. With the children of Israel we flee "the furnace of Egyptian servitude," we cross the Red Sea, we wander in the desert, our forces are refreshed by a miraculous nourishment, we enter at last into the Promised Land. With them we again collide with the surrounding peoples; with them we return from the captivity of Babylon and rebuild the temple and the city. . . . Finally, whatever page I meditate upon, I find in it a means that God offers me, right now, to restore the divine image within me. Thus, I myself become Jerusalem, the holy city; I become or become again the temple of the Lord; for me the promise is realized: "I shall dwell in their midst." God walks with me in the garden, when I read the divine Scriptures.[100]

If allegorical interpretation illumines all reality in the light of Christ, then tropological interpretation finds a place for the church, and for individuals, within the illumined space that has been created. De Lubac suggests that "Scripture first presents itself to us as a mirror," and that "in this mirror we learn to know our nature and our destiny; in it we also see the different stages through which we have passed since creation, the beautiful, and the ugly features of our internal face. It shows the truth of our being by pointing it out in its relation to the Creator."[101]

De Lubac's argument is supported by an example of tropological interpretation used earlier, in chapter 3. In a homily by an unknown medieval author, the identity and destiny of a king is illustrated allegorically. In this allegory, the king is identified with the donkey that carried Jesus into Jerusalem on Palm Sunday. The unknown author writes,

> It is true, the animal after having made its entrance into Jerusalem Judea, was returned to its owner, but the prophecy, related to the animal, remained in Judea. For of that animal, Christ had needed not the visible, but the intelligible nature; that is, not the flesh, but

---

Lubac was well aware of this danger and was thus very enthusiastic about the potential of new historical-critical methods to keep theological interpretation grounded. He believed that a genuine appreciation for the literal sense of the text was absolutely essential for the proper functioning of spiritual exegesis. See, for example, de Lubac, *Scripture in the Tradition*, 29.

100. De Lubac, *Medieval Exegesis*, vol. 2, 141.

101. Ibid., 142.

the idea. Hence, the flesh was returned, but the idea retained: *caro remissa est, ratio autem retenta est.*[102]

The point of this story is that the king's true identity and ultimate destiny are derived from his service to Christ in the temporal realm. The role of the king was conceived liturgically. Through his service to Christ in the temporal realm, the king was wedded to Christ and incorporated into the divine economy.[103]

This example shows how tropological interpretation serves the church's engagement with culture by providing Christians a means for entering into the divine drama. The king, who is the subject of the above homily, is invited to understand himself and his kingship in relation to Christ and his divine mission. Through tropological interpretation, the king's life can become an "improvisation" in this ongoing drama, as he struggles each day to discover himself in the stories of Scripture.[104]

Tropological interpretation mediates a genuine ontological extension because it serves to convert and transform persons according "to the divine likeness."[105] With the tropological sense, persons are united with the Word of God in spiritual marriage and discover themselves in this union. The tropological sense is considered the "summit" of biblical interpretation perhaps because of its "force" or soteriological potency. In contrast to Milbank's proposal in *The Word Made Strange*, tropological interpretation is potent not because it approaches Jesus as a nonidentifiable character whose language and practice are "fully transferable," but because it introduces the church, in every age and cultural context, to Jesus, the divine prophet, priest, and king who judges, challenges, and transforms.

102. Quoted in Kantorowicz, *King's Two Bodies*, 85.

103. It is interesting how in Isa 44:28—45:6, the Persian king, Cyrus, is incorporated into the divine economy unknowingly.

104. "It is the Scripture that measures us, and which scrutinizes us, and which makes the fountains of living water spring forth in us, and which ends by saying to us, not to deny it to us by showing us the unity of the first source: 'Drink the water from your vessels and from your wells,'" (de Lubac, *Medieval Exegesis*, vol. 2, 142).

105. Ibid., 141.

The Anagogical Sense

Hans Urs von Balthasar has suggested that de Lubac's theological "position moved into a suspended middle in which he could not practice any philosophy without its transcendence into theology, but also no theology without its essential inner substructure of philosophy."[106] This paradox lies at the heart of de Lubac's thesis that nature is contingent and finds its completion and fulfillment only in the supernatural grace of God. John Milbank thinks that the phrase "suspended middle" represents de Lubac's position with "great accuracy," since de Lubac focuses neither on dogmatics nor on metaphysics, insisting instead that "theology should be a mysticism and that mysticism [is] essentially a reading of signs." For de Lubac, mystical theology is "a combination of event and sign in continuous process."[107] Interestingly, (and Milbank pays too little attention to this fact) de Lubac also suggests in numerous places that "theological science and the explication of Scripture cannot but be one and the same thing."[108]

It is important to note that for de Lubac, the "suspended middle" is not a paralysis. Rather, it simply suggests, with St. Paul, that Christians are equipped not with epistemic certainty but with faith, hope, and love. Spiritual exegesis enables the church to progress in its ascent toward God through a continual formation in faith, hope, and love. Indeed, the three spiritual senses of Scripture are identified by patristic and medieval commentators with these three theological virtues. Allegory builds up faith; tropology builds up love, and anagogy builds up hope.[109] Spiritual

---

106. Balthasar, *Theology of Henri de Lubac*, 15.

107. Milbank, *Suspended Middle*, 11–12.

108. He writes further: "In its most profound and far-reaching sense this estimation of the situation remains true even to our own day. But in its stricter and more immediate sense, this idea flourished right to the eve of the thirteenth century. The vocabulary, which still remains as a witness to this state of affairs, may strike us as quite curious at first glance. But the great scholastics remained faithful to it. 'Sacred Scripture which is called theology,' says Saint Bonaventure. And similarly Saint Thomas speaks of 'Theology, which is called Sacred Scripture.' We know, too, that in the first Question of the *Summa theologica*, the two expressions 'sacred doctrine' and 'Sacred Scripture' are used alternately, as equivalents. In the previous era it had been more truly the case that the scholar was a commentator, and dogma was a kind of exegesis" (de Lubac, *Medieval Exegesis*, vol. 1, 27).

109. De Lubac, *Medieval Exegesis*, vol. 2, 181. Cf., Levering, *Participatory Biblical Exegesis*, 73.

exegesis entails a christological hermeneutic that mediates, continually, the graced ascent of nature toward the supernatural. Because it leads the church always higher in its ascent to God, anagogy unifies all of the other senses of Scripture. De Lubac writes:

> It is in traditional eschatology that the doctrine of the four senses is achieved and finds its unity. For Christianity is a fulfillment, but in this very fulfillment it is a promised hope. Mystical or doctrinal, taught or lived, true anagogy is therefore always eschatological. It stirs up the desire for eternity in us. This is also why the fourth sense is forced to be the last. No more than it could really lack the three others could it be followed by a fifth. Neither is hope ever lacking nor, in our earthly condition, is it ever surpassed even if it already encroaches upon its term.[110]

The anagogical sense of Scripture, then, is driven by the faith of allegory and the love of tropology always deeper into the mystery of Christ. De Lubac explains that "however high anagogy leads, it always leaves something to look for and always with greater fervor, because it still does not uncover the Face of God."[111] He acknowledges his debt to Augustine: "'Always seek his face, so that discovery may not bring an end to this quest, whereby love is meant, but, as love increases, let the quest for what has been discovered increase as well.'"[112] It is the anagogical sense of Scripture that continually graces nature and draws it toward its destination and completion in the triune God. The anagogical sense ensures that Christ never becomes a mere extrinsic spectacle, because his "face" remains always beyond the church's reach.

In *The Word Made Strange*, John Milbank suggests that ecclesiology should have primacy over Christology, since, among other reasons, Christ's atonement is made real only as the church makes reconciliation a reality in its own practices. He writes that "if Jesus' death is efficacious, not just as the offering of an enabling sign, but also as a material reality, then this is because it is the *inauguration* of the 'political' practice of forgiveness; forgiveness as a mode of 'government' and social being."[113] Christ's death is efficacious, in Milbank's view, only if the church con-

---

110. De Lubac, *Medieval Exegesis*, vol. 2, 197.

111. Ibid., 193.

112. Augustine, *Exposition on the Psalms*, CV, no. 3, quoted in ibid.

113. Milbank, *Word Made Strange*, 161.

tinues the "practice of forgiveness" as its own "mode of government and social being." One of the many problems with this approach is that it forgets that the church itself remains always in need of forgiveness. The church, in this time between the times, cannot perform a complete "non-identical repetition" of Jesus's atoning mode of being. Rather, the church's true nature remains always only partially realized. The church receives itself as a gift of love, and as Augustine reminds us, "as love increases, let the quest for what has been discovered increase as well."[114] In short, Milbank's ecclesiology, if it is given primacy over Christology, is cut off from eschatology. In spiritual exegesis, which de Lubac embraces, the anagogical sense ensures that the church will remain always in pursuit of the fullness of Christ.

CONCLUSION

De Lubac's theology as christological mysticism is able to both complement and correct postliberalism and Radical Orthodoxy. De Lubac's christological hermeneutic is intended to help the church engage secular culture more faithfully, and in this way its central concern is consistent with the work of Frei, Lindbeck, and Milbank. Frei and Lindbeck advocate a biblical hermeneutic that focuses on the identity of Jesus, but their approach to Christology remains extrinsic and, in the words of Reinhard Hütter, "loses its unique soteriological center."[115] Milbank, on the other hand, wants to avoid extrinsicism, but in his attempt to articulate a Christology with soteriological potency, he evacuates the human Jesus of all specifiable content except a formal name, and his speculative ontological project has thus far engaged scripture far too infrequently.

I have argued that de Lubac's mystical Christology, which is mediated by spiritual exegesis, offers a truly participatory hermeneutic while avoiding the weaknesses found in the works of Frei and Lindbeck as well as in Milbank. His Christology is not extrinsicist like that of the postliberals, yet it assigns a positive and indispensable role to the gospel depiction of Jesus, in contrast to Milbank. Whereas Milbank endeavors to articulate a Christology with soteriological potency, he assigns primacy to ecclesiology and thus renders Jesus incapable (theoretically speaking) of judg-

---

114. Augustine, *Exposition on the Book of Psalms*, 521.
115. Hütter, *Suffering Divine Things*, 64.

ment and transformation. In contrast, de Lubac's mystical Christology is mediated by spiritual exegesis and is focused upon a transformation of the will and the building up of faith, hope, and love in the church.

Consistent with the postliberal approach, de Lubac believes that biblical exegesis must mediate the church's engagement with secular culture. However, whereas Frei and Lindbeck treat the biblical text as an enclosed semiotic system that renders an extrinsic identity description of Jesus and "absorbs the world" through typological extension, de Lubac sees Scripture as a multivalent gateway into the mystery of the cosmic Christ and thus as the means through which all reality is made intelligible. For de Lubac, the ultimate end of theological science, which is inseparable from biblical exegesis, is "a many-faceted wisdom,"[116] rooted in the virtues, through which the church participates in the mission of Jesus. Theological science is, for de Lubac, a participation in the mind of Christ. It is a christological mysticism mediated by Scripture that endeavors to understand all things in relation to the divine light and to build up the church in Christ's virtues.

De Lubac's theological program is intended to show that theology is intrinsically an engagement with secular culture. Theology necessarily entails a "confrontation, a combat" with contemporary secular thought,[117] since its ultimate goal is the illumination of all reality in the light of Christ. Although de Lubac never entered into a direct engagement with all the "various modes of secular knowledge," much of his work was focused on showing that this ongoing engagement is necessarily mediated by spiritual exegesis. One might wonder, however, whether de Lubac's retrieval of patristic and medieval exegesis remains a viable alternative for twenty-first-century Christians, who are many centuries removed from precritical interpretation. Although de Lubac did not advocate a

---

116. De Lubac, *Medieval Exegesis*, vol. 1, 35.

117. De Lubac, *At the Service of the Church*, 36. Bonhoeffer suggests that Christian engagement with secularism entails a "participation in the sufferings of God in the secular life. . . . allowing oneself to be caught up into the way of Jesus Christ, into the messianic event. . . . This being caught up into the messianic sufferings of God takes a variety of forms in the New Testament. It appears in the call to discipleship, in Jesus' table-fellowship with sinners, in 'conversion' in the narrower sense of the word (e.g. Zacchaeus), in the act of the woman who was a sinner (Luke 7) . . . in the healing of the sick . . . , in Jesus' acceptance of children. . . . The only thing that is common to all these is their sharing in the suffering of God in Christ. That is their faith" (Bonhoeffer, *Letters and Papers from Prison*, 361–62).

strict return to the fourfold method, he did argue that the church needs a new "synthesis" that combines the methods of critical biblical scholarship with the theological concerns of patristic and medieval exegetes. In the concluding chapter, after providing a brief review of de Lubac's theological program, I offer several suggestions for how the church can appropriate de Lubac's mystical Christology while embracing the very legitimate contributions of critical biblical scholarship.

CHAPTER 7

Political Witness and the Future of Spiritual Exegesis

It will be helpful to recall that Henri de Lubac's theological career should be interpreted largely as an attempt to draw the Catholic Church out of its self-imposed cultural exile in order to reinvigorate its engagement with secular society. De Lubac believed that the Church's response to secularization was inadequate because its theological vision was too narrow to speak effectively to the social ills of European civilization. Faced with world wars and fascist governments, most citizens of Europe, even Catholics, did not look to the Church for guidance in social and political matters. Rather, people poured their hopes and energies into secular social and political movements like *Action française*, because the Catholic Church had in recent centuries begun to endorse a theology that separated the natural and the supernatural realms.[1] The church's mission, it seemed, was to save souls and little more. Theologians who endorsed the neoscholastic view, insisting on a purely natural end for human nature, were hard-pressed to relate their work to the concerns of secular society.

De Lubac accused neoscholasticism of extrinsicism because it presumed theology to be a separated science, concerned with the objective content of supernatural revelation, which is to be found in Scripture and in the magisterial authority of the Church as a "given." In order to disentangle the church from the constraints of theological extrinsicism and help it come out of its self-imposed exile to engage the secular world more faithfully, de Lubac focused his academic career on challenging the philosophical and theological presuppositions upon which neoscholasticism stood. His theological program focused on three controversial

1. For the complexities of the debate concerning the relationship between nature and the supernatural, see chapter 4 above, and especially the footnotes from the section on nature and grace.

themes: the social and sacramental nature of the church, the relationship between nature and grace, and biblical exegesis. In his earliest ecclesiological work, *Catholicism* (1938), de Lubac showed that the church is fundamentally social in character, since its beginning and its end are found in the fullness of Christ—"humanity as a whole" healed and redeemed.[2]

With *Corpus Mysticum* (1944), he described an important transformation in sacramental language. Whereas prior to the twelfth century, the sacramental elements were most often called *corpus mysticum* and the worshiping community was called *corpus verum*, these designations were reversed at some point during the twelfth century so that the elements became the real body of Christ while the worshiping community was called the mystical body. For de Lubac, this transformation marked the beginning of a kind of sacramental piety that looks upon the body of Christ as a mere "spectacle" to behold—a separate and extrinsic presence rather than a presence within which the church participates. This transformation in sacramental language undermined the christological mysticism that de Lubac believed characterized most Christian theology prior to the twelfth century.[3]

Whereas, in de Lubac's mind, Catholicism's movement away from a thoroughly participatory ontology began at least in the twelfth century with sacramental developments, it was the emergence of the concept of "pure nature" in the seventeenth century that solidified this transformation. Accordingly, *Surnaturel* (1946) followed *Corpus Mysticum*, as de Lubac engaged in his most direct confrontation with neoscholasticism over the relationship between nature and grace.

The next major work to follow *Surnaturel* was *Histoire et Esprit* (1950), de Lubac's defense of Origen's allegorical approach to exegesis. This was de Lubac's first major work on spiritual exegesis, though he eventually wrote more pages on this issue than on any other. In de Lubac's mind, Catholic hermeneutics had succumbed to the extrinsicism of neoscholastic theology, which saw in Scripture objective truth propositions that formed, along with magisterial teachings, the given "content" of supernatural revelation. Since he was equally unsatisfied with the increasing historicism of biblical scholars (a tendency that also treated truth as extrinsic), de Lubac sought to retrieve the philosophy of history

2. De Lubac, *Catholicism*, 25–47.

3. For a concise account of this change in sacramental piety, see ibid., 93–101.

and participatory ontology that had undergirded patristic and medieval exegesis. He hoped that his work would lead to a "new synthesis," blending theology, exegesis, and spirituality together.[4]

Interestingly, it was in 1956, not long after he had written his book on Origen, that de Lubac suggested that his intended mystical treatise on Christ served as his "inspiration in everything."[5] In other words, his major works on ecclesiology, ontology, and exegesis, all of which challenged obstacles hindering the church's engagement with secular culture, were inspired and guided by his christological thought. For de Lubac, christological mysticism, in the spirit of St. Paul, St. John, and the patristic and medieval theological tradition that followed, is fundamental in the church's engagement with the world. Jesus Christ is the supernatural grace of God that rescues and completes nature. He is the beginning and the end of the church, and through the mediation of spiritual exegesis, he illumines all reality and reveals the path through which humanity is reconciled to God: indeed he is that path. For de Lubac, the church's engagement with the world is an aspect of its participation in Christ and is necessarily mediated by the spiritual interpretation of Scripture. It is important to note that de Lubac never attempted to formulate a contemporary "method" of spiritual exegesis or "hermeneutical theory," and it is doubtful that he would have approved of such attempts.[6]

---

4. De Lubac, *At the Service of the Church*, 93.

5. Ibid., 113.

6. De Lubac was concerned with the metaphysical and ecclesiological presuppositions and implications of spiritual exegesis. In recent years, it has become much more common for theologians and biblical scholars to treat biblical exegesis as an ecclesial practice rather than as a disinterested scholarly method. See, for example, Fowl, *Engaging Scripture*. See also Johnson and Kurz, *Future of Catholic Biblical Scholarship*. In perhaps the most recent contribution to this discussion, Barry Harvey, acknowledging his indebtedness to Fowl, suggests, "all efforts to produce a general theory of meaning, also known as a general hermeneutics, are necessarily question-begging and should be avoided. Interpretation . . . should be underdetermined, that is, it should be free to use a variety of interpretive practices and results without granting epistemic priority to any of them." Harvey proposes "a theological hermeneutics grounded in the life and language of the church" (Harvey, *Can These Bones Live?* 13–14). Matthew Levering's recent work, *Participatory Biblical Exegesis*, considers the relationship between exegesis and metaphysics.

The Future of Spiritual Exegesis

Rather, he believed that the church would always have to struggle in order to interpret Scripture faithfully, and he assumed that this struggle would often lead down unexpected paths. De Lubac did believe that the church could learn a great deal from the ancients. He suggested that contemporary interpreters "must approach matters in greater depth and with greater freedom if we hope to recapture anything of the spiritual interpretation of Scripture as it existed during the first centuries of the Church. We must, above all else, reproduce a spiritual movement, often through completely different methods, while avoiding a retreat into the archaic or into slavish imitation."[7] Although he was not specific about what exactly spiritual exegesis should look like today, we can glean a few simple guiding principles from his work that are particularly relevant for the contemporary context.

Respect for the Letter

First, de Lubac's work suggests that the literal/historical sense of the text plays an indispensable and determinative role in *theological* interpretation. Although patristic and medieval exegetes insisted that the allegorical senses of Scripture must be properly grounded in the historical sense, de Lubac readily admits that their lack of historical insight "led to many abuses."[8] Indeed, early Christian interpreters tended, like many distinctively modern exegetes, to project their own cultural and theological assumptions onto the authors of Scripture. Patristic and medieval theologians were not equipped with modern historical-critical tools and knew very little, for example, about Semitic culture. The absence of a genuinely critical approach to the text led to a gradual decline away from "the historical and social character of the Christian synthesis" toward an excessively individualistic approach by the late Middle Ages. De Lubac remarks that "an exegesis which, in essence, concentrated on the interior life was, however, worlds apart from what we call today 'the end of history.' Centered as it was on the individual soul, it really could tell us no more about the triumphant Church than about the militant Church. . . .

---

7. De Lubac, *Scripture in the Tradition*, 24.
8. De Lubac, "On an Old Distich," 126.

As spiritual individualism gained ground, the great dogmatic vision became blurred."[9]

De Lubac believed that a depreciation of the historical sense during the late Middle Ages necessitated a renewed interest in the literal meaning of the text. However, when that renewal finally came, it was not employed for the same reasons as it had been in earlier times—in the service of spiritual exegesis:

> After a long life, it had eventually grown old. The problems had changed, and so had the needs of Christian thought. Once the period of intense effervescence in which it had originated had passed, mystical exegesis had furnished the apologists with a weapon, then the Doctors had drawn from it a unified vision of the divine Economy; and then the monks had found in it a method useful in their "*lectio divina.*" Now came the intellectuals who were interested in constructing a new theology with new methods, but within the continuity of the faith. With them, reason awakes from its symbolic dream. "The Age of Proof" begins. . . . It was certainly more valuable for argumentative theology to hold fast to the letter. . . . Beginning with the sixteenth century, the development was to become more pronounced. . . . the onslaught of Protestantism soon required a concentration of effort on the establishment of the literal meaning.[10]

A renewed emphasis on the literal sense finally came, but it was too often put into the service of polemics and apologetics. De Lubac suggests that, following the Protestant Reformation,

> The onslaught of rationalism and the necessity of examining the biblical accounts in the light of the documents discovered by modern scholarship again brought apologetical considerations to the fore. The problem of inerrancy received the major share of attention, and the spiritual interpretation of the sacred texts, along with the earlier method of understanding the faith, were henceforth almost completely abandoned.[11]

9. De Lubac, *Scripture in the Tradition*, 52–53.

10. Ibid., 57–58.

11. Ibid., 58. Hans Frei has made similar observations about the way that biblical interpretation was dominated by apologetic concerns during much of the modern era. See Frei, *Eclipse*, 105–64.

For de Lubac, there is nothing wrong with historical-critical approaches to biblical interpretation.[12] However, he believes that critical methods produce too little fruit in the church because they are too often employed for the wrong reasons. When the critical methods are used within the context of either extrinsicist or historicist agendas, they are used in the pursuit of an abstracted and objectified meaning rather than in pursuit of God.

What de Lubac hoped to see was a renewed emphasis on the literal/historical sense of Scripture, through critical methods, as a means of inspiring, correcting, and controlling a new and vibrant spiritual exegesis. He believed that a proper understanding of biblical "persons, events, ideas, and texts in their proper historical contexts"[13] should strengthen spiritual exegesis in a host of ways. De Lubac believed that there is a "religious meaning" inherent in all Scripture, and that scholars offer a great service by attending to it. He suggests, "we must reject too all-embracing or too automatic a practice of spiritual interpretation, so as to preserve the religious value of the Old Testament, considered both literally and in its historical situations."[14]

Attention to the historical context can strengthen spiritual exegesis precisely because it offers greater insight into the reality of Jesus. Indeed, if spiritual exegesis is to serve as a divine pedagogy, through which we come to know the historical Jesus as the *totus Christus*, then it is imperative that the church understand the gospel portrayal of Jesus to the best of its ability. Jesus of Nazareth, not just any person, is the Word incarnate, so understanding Jesus in literary and historical context is an indispensable first step in understanding what his life, death, and resurrection means for the church and the world in every age. De Lubac explains the impor-

---

12. He defends himself against charges of denigrating scientific approaches to biblical interpretation, explaining, "I have recently been accused of some sort of opposition to the acceptance of scientific exegesis in the Church and, by the same token, to the works of my colleagues and to the spirit of our Faculty. This rumor, although absurd, has become persistent, it has spread quite far, enough for me to see myself obliged to combat it. I thus find myself . . . in the most ridiculous position: that of the man who must defend himself from having denigrated the very thing of which all those who know him well know that he was always the warmest supporter" (de Lubac, *At the Service of the Church*, 311).

13. D'Ambrosio, "Henri de Lubac and the Recovery of the Traditional Hermeneutic," 256.

14. De Lubac, *Scripture in the Tradition*, 29.

tance of understanding Scripture on the literal and historical levels when
he suggests that

> Even the categories used by Jesus to tell us about himself are an-
> cient biblical categories. Jesus causes them to burst forth or, if
> you prefer, sublimates them and unifies them by making them
> converge upon himself. But he somehow needs them. . . . Thus,
> "biblical images," and the concrete facts behind them, furnish
> the thread, both historical and noetic, from which is woven the
> Christian mystery in all its newness and transcendence.[15]

Jesus was fully human, a Jew who lived during the Roman occupa-
tion of Palestine. We should expect that his actions and words, as they are
narrated in the gospels, would take on greater depth and meaning as we
become more familiar with the cultural, religious, and political context
within which he lived.

Indeed, studies like Ched Myers's *Binding the Strong Man*,[16] which
focus on the sociopolitical climate of first-century Rome and on Jesus's
radical subversion of it, offer invaluable insight into the character who,
according to Christians, now reigns over heaven and earth. According
to Meyers, the Gospel of Mark offers a portrait of Jesus as a Jew whose
entire life is an interpretation of the Old Testament, and particularly of
the prophetic tradition, which tended to emphasize the relationship between apostasy and social injustice. Meyers's investigation of Jesus within
the context of first-century Jewish and Roman culture shows how Jesus
continually subverted Roman imperial power and pronounced judgment
upon Jewish responses to it. It is quite difficult to reconcile this Jesus with
any form of temporal authority exercised through violent force.

One wonders whether the medieval church would have been as willing to ascribe a liturgical role in the divine economy to kings and princes
had they understood Jesus of Nazareth as Meyers suggests he is portrayed
in Mark's gospel.[17] Rather than suggesting, as in the allegory mentioned
in chapters 3 and 6, that medieval kings are like the donkey that carried

---

15. Ibid., 7–8.

16. Myers, *Binding the Strong Man*.

17. Although Myers's book provides an interesting early example, it should be noted
that New Testament scholarship in general, and especially study of the gospels, recognizes, increasingly, the radical social and political nature of Jesus's ministry when studied
within the social and historical context of first-century Palestine. For an excellent example by a popular contemporary author, see Wright, *Jesus and the Victory of God*.

Jesus into Jerusalem,[18] most political and military leaders would have been more accurately portrayed in an allegory as Caiaphas or Pontius Pilate.[19] This is the way that the historical/literal sense should exercise control over the spiritual senses. The more clearly we understand the historical Jesus, as portrayed in the gospels within the context of a unified canon, the more clearly we understand what it means to say that "through him all things were made" (John 1:3), and that "in him all things hold together" (Col 1:17). Jesus of Nazareth, with all his social and historical particularities, is God, and this particular God/Man created all things and now reigns over heaven and earth. If we affirm with Athanasius that, "the Word submitted to appear in a body, in order that He, as Man, might centre [human] senses on Himself, and convince them through His human acts that He Himself is not man only but also God, the Word and Wisdom of the true God,"[20] then critical biblical scholarship, aimed at comprehending the Word in context (incarnate), should be an essential first step in a revitalized spiritual exegesis serving as a divine pedagogy (*sacra doctrina*).

John David Dawson makes a similar point when he suggests that "Christianity demands respect for the letter of the spirit, respect for the grammars of difference that constitute identity. Christians choose to identify themselves with one who has already identified himself with each person."[21] For Dawson, because Christians come to know themselves in relation to Jesus, it is of utmost importance that we allow him the particularity and difference that comes with individuality and historic existence. Should we ignore the letter and fashion Jesus's identity

---

18. I am referring here to the medieval allegory quoted in Kantorowicz, *King's Two Bodies*, 85, and mentioned above, in which a king is identified with the donkey that carried Christ into Jerusalem.

19. It may not be necessary to draw a sharp, either-or distinction here. Perhaps the average medieval king could have been represented accurately by the donkey at times, and at other times by Pontius Pilate. However, it is well known that even some of the greatest medieval theologians (Bernard of Clairvaux and Thomas Aquinas) approved of the Crusades, for example, and believed that God's work was being done through them. I would suggest that a better understanding of Jesus of Nazareth in his social/historical context would have engendered a great deal more caution among ancient thinkers in relation to the use of force by Christians who claimed to be doing God's work.

20. Athanasius, *On the Incarnation*, 44.

21. Dawson, "Figural Reading," 194.

after our own, then we are thwarted in our attempt to discover ourselves in relation to him.

Accordingly, exegetical methods focused on understanding the literal sense have much to offer the church as it strives to engage the world faithfully in the Spirit of Christ. The emergence of new interpretive approaches such as literary, rhetorical, and social-scientific criticism suggest that interest in the literal/historical sense will continue and may serve the church in unforeseen yet beneficial ways.[22] Indeed, de Lubac is confident that in the future "the Bible will be enjoyed and understood anew because a healthy spiritual exegesis will once more rise on the foundations of a tested science."[23]

The Ultimate End Is God

De Lubac's work suggests a second hermeneutical principle: the church must be clear about the ultimate "end" of biblical interpretation (and of the spiritual life in general), which is nothing less than the vision of God "face-to-face" (1 Cor 13:12). This means that the church can never be satisfied with the mere surface of the letter.[24] As I mentioned in the previous chapter, the literal sense is itself incomplete and finds its fulfillment in the allegorical sense, since biblical history is a participation in the divine economy and can be understood fully only in reference to the God

---

22. Interestingly, de Lubac did not think that professional biblical scholars—trained in methods that focus on the literal and historical sense of the text—need to try to be all things at once. He believed that scholarly specialization can benefit the church, so long as there is a healthy exchange of gifts and ideas. He writes: "to sum up, learning and spirituality are not in the least incompatible. Normally, they must give each other a hand, and it is obviously desirable that they be combined in the same individual. But it is not ordained by God that the most learned will inevitably be the most believing, nor the most spiritual; nor that the century which sees the greatest progress realized in scientific exegesis will, by that fact alone, be the century with the best understanding of Holy Scripture. We need, then, both men of learning, who will make us read Scripture historically, and men of the spirit—who must be 'men of the Church'—to deepen our spiritual grasp of it. If the former deliver us from our ignorance, it is still only the latter who possess the gift of discernment which protects us from interpretations which are dangerous for the faith" (de Lubac, *Scripture in the Tradition*, 157).

23. Ibid., 71.

24. "What [ancient exegetes] wanted was not at all that one should stop short at the letter, but rather that one might discover and gather the fruit of the spirit hidden under its foliage" (de Lubac, *Medieval Exegesis*, vol. 2, 51).

who animates it.[25] The triune God, whose face is revealed most clearly to human eyes in the person of Jesus Christ, is the ultimate meaning of all Christian Scripture.[26] De Lubac gets carried away in contemplating this fact:

> Christ was the sole end of all biblical history and of all biblical reality. . . . In short, the spirit of the letter is Christ: *Spiritus ipsius literae, Christus.* The Gift of which Prophecy and the whole Law spoke prophetically is Christ. The New Testament is Christ: *Novum Testamentum, qui est Christus.* The Gospel is Christ: *Evangelium, Christus est.* The Breath of our nostrils is Christ the Lord: *Spiritus ante faciem nostrum, Christus Dominus.* . . . Jesus Christ effects the unity of Scripture because he is its end and its fullness. Everything in Scripture is related to him. And he is its unique Object. We could even say that he is the totality of its exegesis. . . . He is the Head of the body of Scripture, just as he is the Head of the body of his Church. He is the Head of all sacred understanding, just as he is the Head of all the elect. He is the complete contents of Scripture, just as he contains it all in himself. . . . Just as he is the exegesis of Scripture, Jesus Christ is also its exegete. He is really its Logos, both in the active sense and in the passive sense. . . . It is he and he alone who explains it to us, and in explaining it to us he is himself explained.[27]

Thus the "meaning" of Scripture can never be equated with or limited to an objective given, since Jesus Christ is not an object. As mentioned above, de Lubac was critical of both "extrinsicism" (as in neoscholasticism and Protestant fundamentalism) and "historicism" (as in Protestant and Catholic liberalism), because both of these interpretive tendencies treat the text as though its meaning may be grasped extrinsically.

---

25. "Linked to the mystery of the Incarnation of the Logos, history, if it is in fact mediatory, must not hold us indiscriminately. Its whole role, on the contrary, is to *pass on*. . . . Thus, in its entirety, up to its final event, history is a preparation for something else" (Lubac, *History and Spirit*, 322, italics original).

26. Interestingly, the relationship between the Old Testament and the New Testament is essentially the same as the relationship between nature and grace. The Old Testament is characterized by a kind of longing or anticipation for something (Christ) that it is incapable of articulating fully, just as humankind, in a fallen state of nature, knows it is missing something but hasn't the capacity to conceive or desire its savior without the grace of God in Christ.

27. De Lubac, *Scripture in the Tradition*, 105.

De Lubac's study of the patristic and medieval exegetical tradition illustrates that the Fathers interpreted Scripture not in search of objective knowledge as an ultimate end but in search of God. Although the complete revelation of God's face remains always a future hope, the early church believed that spiritual exegesis enables a real, spiritual union with God through the struggle to interpret and engage historical reality with the mind and will of Christ. Spiritual exegesis fortified the early church in a distinctively christological wisdom and virtue that enabled it to be a faithful witness to the reign of God on earth. The church today should strive for nothing less.

This does not mean, however, that the church should return to the fourfold method in an effort to read Christ and the church back into every word of the Old Testament. To a large extent, the church does not need to return to the fourfold method, because allegorical interpretation has already achieved its purposes.[28] Jesus of Nazareth is already transformed into the Omnipresent Christ through allegorical interpretation *within* the New Testament. Jesus himself initiates this transformation when, during the Passover meal, he commands his disciples: "take, eat, this is my body" (Matt 26:26). The author of John's gospel follows Jesus's lead when he writes, "In the beginning was the Word. . . . and the Word became flesh and lived among us" (John 1:1–14), and Paul expands the mystery when he describes the church as the "body of Christ" (1 Cor. 12:27).[29]

The early church did not invent allegorical interpretation; it merely prolonged and formalized a tradition that had begun with the authors of the Old Testament and blossomed in the imaginations of New Testament writers. Allegorical interpretation does not need to be revived today, because it continues to flourish in the liturgy, in hymns, and especially in the sacraments of baptism and Eucharist. Moreover, spiritual interpretation will inevitably continue as sermons are preached and persons are invited to "'create' themselves in finding a place within" the biblical

---

28. "Spiritual exegesis accomplished an essential part of its task a long time ago. It has made its contribution to the expression of the Christian mystery and to the building of the Church. It would be impossible to restore it today in all its fullness. As long as there is no repudiation of the achievements of spiritual exegesis, no mortal damage has been done. It should, however, be borne in mind that in the spiritual order it is an illusion to think that anything can be absolutely acquired, once and for all" (ibid., 64–65).

29. These are just a few of the many allegorical interpretations that can be found in both the Old and New Testaments.

drama.[30] Whenever a sermon is preached on the Prologue to John's gospel, the church is introduced to the mystery of the omnipresent Christ, the "Word" who was with God in the beginning, came to dwell on earth among us, and now reigns as exalted Lord. Throughout the Christian year, as pastors all over the world follow the lectionary and struggle to lead their congregations through the preached Word, the light of the omnipresent Christ shines in a multitude of human situations.[31] It is in these situations especially that the church's engagement with culture takes place. The church's ongoing struggle to discover "what the text may become (and so of what it is)," is always also "a discovery of the world."[32] The church's interpretation of Scripture necessarily mediates, to borrow a phrase from Radical Orthodoxy, the extension of a "Christianized ontology."[33]

For de Lubac it is not that the church needs to find a new hermeneutic. Rather the church must simply resist the ever-present temptation to destroy or discard the rich, symbolic interpretation of the Word that has already been gifted to us in Scripture and in the church's structured worship life. De Lubac warns against this temptation when he writes that,

> Unlike the Christian ages . . . we are victims of totalitarian "terrenness" and humanism. In their various ways, psychologists, sociologists, and metaphysicians conspire to impose such views upon us. To put it very briefly, our main temptation is to make of God a symbol for man, the objectified symbol of himself.[34]

The church must avoid historicist and extrinsicist approaches to biblical interpretation because these seek not the triune God but an idol fashioned after human likeness.[35] The revival of spiritual exegesis should above all else take the form of an earnest quest for the God who reveals himself yet can never be objectified. Although this quest begins with an effort to understand Christ as he is portrayed in the literal sense of the biblical narrative, it must also entail an attempt to interpret all real-

---

30. Williams, *On Christian Theology*, 32.

31. For his appreciation of Origen's exegetical service to the church within the context of preaching, see de Lubac, *History and Spirit*, 143–58.

32. Williams, *On Christian Theology*, 30–31.

33. Milbank et al., *Radical Orthodoxy*, 2.

34. Lubac, *Scripture in the Tradition*, 69–70.

35. The various nineteenth- and twentieth-century "quests" for the historical Jesus offer well-known examples of this temptation.

ity through a distinctively christological, biblical hermeneutic. This will mean, as Rowan Williams has suggested, a continual process of "re-telling" and "re-working" the biblical narrative in relation to a seemingly infinite number of human situations.[36] It will mean that the church always looks to Jesus of Nazareth as portrayed in the biblical drama in order to discover itself and find its way in the world.

Although his work on medieval exegesis was not well received by Catholic biblical scholars in the years just after its release,[37] the work of de Lubac and others, such as Jean Daniélou, has had a significant influence on the practices of the Catholic Church since Vatican II.[38] This is especially evident in the way that contemporary liturgies use far more Scripture than preconciliar liturgies did, continually interpreting passages from the Old and New Testaments in light of each other.[39] The abundance of biblical citations from both Old and New Testaments throughout the latest catechism is also evidence of a revival of spiritual exegesis in Catholicism. Importantly, this ecclesial revival of spiritual exegesis in liturgy and catechism constitutes a genuine revival of *sacra doctrina*. This is because, as Lewis Ayers reminds us, the "practice" of *sacra doctrina* or theology "encompasses, as part of a continuum, a number of activities, from preaching to private scholarly activities," as well as liturgy and catechesis.[40] A genuine theological revival, in other words, should bear its greatest fruit not in the academy but in the church's corporate worship life.[41]

The Politics of Spiritual Exegesis

Henri de Lubac's work suggests one final hermeneutical principle: spiritual exegesis has profound political implications for the church—political implications that should always be kept in mind. Spiritual exegesis is indeed the logic and foundation of the church's worship, and Christian

36. Williams, *On Christian Theology*, 31.

37. D'Ambrosio, "Henri de Lubac and the Recovery of the Traditional Hermeneutic," 126–40.

38. De Lubac is well known to have had a major influence on Vatican II's Dogmatic Constitution, *Dei Verbum*, which was focused on hermeneutics and the revelation of God in Scripture. See Neufeld, "In the Service of the Council," 74–105.

39. For an important and influential study, see Daniélou, *Bible and the Liturgy*.

40. Ayers, "On the Practice and Teaching of Christian Doctrine," 33.

41. Cf., Levering, *Participatory Biblical Exegesis*, 146.

worship is a fundamentally political act. It is in Christian worship, especially, that the church learns to fix its gaze on Jesus Christ, the world's Creator and everlasting king, and thus to discern and turn away from all idols that compete for her allegiance. Indeed, "every act of praise is a strong act of negation as well as affirmation."[42] De Lubac puts it this way: "Scripture . . . is itself wholly 'the book of the battles of the Lord'. . . . to recognize the one God is to declare total war on all the others."[43] He writes further:

> The Church in the world is thus the Church amid conflict, prefigured by the warrior Israel led by Yahweh to the conquests of its inheritance. Her God is the God of peace, and she herself is "a blessed vision of peace"; she desires as her members men who are gentle and peaceful, she preaches him who has made "peace through the blood of his cross", and when her message is listened to she always exercises a pacifying influence. But she has to begin by tearing us away from the false peace which was that of the world before Christ and in which we are always trying to take refuge again.[44]

According to de Lubac, it is not the responsibility of the church to redeem the world on its own. The church is not called to "forge itself" or secure its own destiny, as is often the case with liberation theology.[45] Rather, the church's primary "social role" is to "bring [the world] back to that communion which all her dogma teaches . . . and all her activity makes ready."[46] The church's primary social role is to offer the world a vision of itself, healed and transformed in the image of Christ. What this suggests is that "the Church's proper mission is not to assume the general direction of social movements any more than of intellectual ones."[47] It means that the church's mission will always transcend, and probably offer at least a relative condemnation of, the limited and disordered temporal aims of secular social and political movements.

42. Witvliet, "Opening of Worship," 12.

43. De Lubac, *Splendor of the Church*, 185.

44. Ibid., 187.

45. "By working, transforming the world, breaking out of servitude, building a just society, and assuming its destiny in history, humankind forges itself" (Gutiérrez, *Theology of Liberation*, 90).

46. De Lubac, *Catholicism*, 362.

47. Ibid.

When in its corporate worship life, the church interprets Scripture according to the Spirit, it is de facto placing itself within the context of God's redemptive work in human history. When it practices spiritual exegesis, the church acknowledges that Christ alone is the head of the body to which all Christians belong. The earthly *ekklesia* finds its place in the midst of the people of God who have been, through the ages, called out of the nations and away from their false gods in order to be gathered together in praise of the Trinity.

Through the spiritual exegesis of Scripture, the church looks to Jesus of Nazareth as portrayed in the biblical drama in order to discover itself and find its way in the world as a distinctive people under the authority of Christ the King. It is in the quest to interpret reality through the christological lens of Scripture that God discloses himself and becomes effectual in and through the church's manifold witness. As the grace of God enables the church to identify itself with Christ, seeing the world as he sees it, judging the world as he judges it, desiring for the world what he desires for it, and suffering for the world as he suffered for it, then Christians come to "know" God in an intimate, participatory way. According to de Lubac, "the beatific vision," which is the ultimate end of biblical interpretation and human life in general, is not "the contemplation of a spectacle, but an intimate participation in the vision the Son has of the Father in the bosom of the Trinity."[48]

A CONCLUDING REMARK ABOUT RADICAL ORTHODOXY

While John Milbank's Christology and approach to Scripture are problematic, there is nothing necessarily objectionable about the Radical Orthodoxy project. The problem with Radical Orthodoxy is that it does not do what Milbank, Pickstock, and Ward suggest that it does in their introduction to the volume titled *Radical Orthodoxy*. That is, Radical Orthodoxy's speculative deconstruction of secular social theory does not "extend a fully Christianized ontology." Radical Orthodoxy's *Kulturkritik* does not supply the "aesthetic idiom" that the church embodies. As Milbank seems to acknowledge in his most recent work on de Lubac, the "divine idiom" is christologically mediated through the spiritual ex-

---

48. De Lubac, *Mystery of the Supernatural*, 228.

egesis of Scripture.[49] However, Radical Orthodoxy's speculative engagement with secular thought can play an important role, and should be commended. Because secular social theorists "conspire to impose" their vision and way of life upon us, Christians must work diligently to expose the nihilism inherent in secular interpretations of reality. Although Radical Orthodoxy does not "renarrate" Christ or create, as a precursor to practice, the space that the church embodies, it can endeavor to show that the space created by secular social theorists is a dangerous illusion.

Although Radical Orthodoxy intends a vigorous engagement with secular culture, it has thus far ignored the constitutive role played by spiritual exegesis in this engagement. However, considering de Lubac's ecclesiological, ontological, and exegetical works in light of one another, we see more clearly that spiritual exegesis mediates (as a kind of divine pedagogy) our vision of Jesus as the omnipresent Christ, and our participation in the ecclesial body of Christ.

Spiritual exegesis enables us to see, recalling the opening lines of this work, that "all nature" is an "infinitely vast and diverse symbol across which the Face of God is mysteriously reflected."[50] We will do well, therefore, to follow de Lubac's example in striving to comprehend, protect, and preserve (in a way fitting for our own time) spiritual exegesis, since it resides at the heart of Christian worship and necessarily mediates a truly christological witness to the world.

49. Milbank, *Suspended Middle*, 57.

50. De Lubac, "Disappearance of the Sense of the Sacred," 231.

Bibliography

Anonymous. "La Theologie et Ses Sources: Réponse." *Reserches de Science Religieuses* 33 (1946) 385–401.

Arnal, Oscar. "Why the French Christian Democrats Were Condemned." *Church History* 49 (1980) 188–202.

Aschheim, Steven E. *The Nietzsche Legacy in Germany, 1890–1990*. Weimar and Now 2. Berkeley: University of California Press, 1992.

Athanasius. *On the Incarnation*. Crestwood, NY: St. Vladimir's Seminary Press, 1996.

Aubert, Roger. "Aspects Divers." In *Die Kirche in Der Gegenwart*, edited by Roger Augert, et al., 133–227. Freiburg, Germany: Herder, 1973.

Auerbach, Erich. *Mimesis: The Representation of Reality in Western Literature*. Princeton: Princeton University Press, 1968.

Augustine. *Exposition on the Book of Psalms*. Select Library of the Nicene and Post-Nicene Fathers, first series, second printing, 8. Peabody, MA: Hendrickson, 1995. Online: http://www.ccel.org/ccel/schaff/npnf108.html/

Ayers, Lewis. "On the Practice and Teaching of Christian Doctrine." *Gregorianum* 80 (1999) 33–94.

Balthasar, Hans Urs von. *The Theology of Henri de Lubac*. Communio Books. San Francisco: Ignatius, 1991.

Balthasar, Hans Urs von, and Georges Chantraine. *Le Cardinal Henri de Lubac, L'homme et Son Œuvre*. Collection "Le Sycomore." Série "Chrétiens aujourd'hui" 9. Paris: Lethielleux, 1983.

Bauerschmidt, Frederick Christian. "The Word Made Speculative? John Milbank's Christological Poetics." *Modern Theology* 15 (1999) 417–32.

Bernardi, Peter J. "Maurice Blondel and the Renewal of the Nature-Grace Relationship." *Communio (US)* 26 (1999) 806–45.

Biema, David van. "God as a Postmodern: Radical Orthodoxy." *Time*, December 17, 2001, 34.

Blenkinsopp, Joseph. "Memory, Tradition, and the Construction of the Past in Ancient Israel." *Biblical Theology Bulletin* 27 (1997) 76–82.

Blondel, Maurice. *L'action: Essai D'une Critique De La Vie Et D'une Science De La Pratique*. Paris: Alcan, 1893.

———. *The Letter on Apologetics, and History and Dogma*. Translated by Alexander Dru and Illtyd Trethowan. 1st ed. New York: Holt Rinehart and Winston, 1965.

Boersma, Hans. "Nature and the Supernatural in *nouvelle théologie*: The Recovery of a Sacramental Mindset." Paper presented at the annual meeting of the American Academy of Religion, San Diego, CA, November 20, 2007,

Bonhoeffer, Dietrich. *Letters and Papers from Prison*. Edited by Eberhard Bethge. Enlarged edition. New York: Touchstone, 1997.

Bosworth, William. *Catholicism and Crisis in Modern France: French Catholic Groups at the Threshold of the Fifth Republic*. Princeton: Princeton University Press, 1962.

Brown, William Eric. *The Catholic Church in South Africa*. London: Burns & Oates, 1960.

Canning, Joseph. *A History of Medieval Political Thought, 300–1450*. New York: Routledge, 1996.

Cavanaugh, William T. *Torture and Eucharist: Theology, Politics, and the Body of Christ*. Challenges in Contemporary Theology. Oxford: Blackwell, 1998.

Certeau, Michel de. *The Mystic Fable*. Volume 1, *The Sixteenth and Seventeenth Centuries*. Translated by Michael B. Smith. Religion and Postmodernism. Chicago: University of Chicago Press, 1992.

Cessario, Romanus. "Duplex Ordo Cognitionis." In *Reason and the Reasons of Faith*, edited by Paul J. Griffiths and Reinhard Hütter, 327–38. Theology for the Twenty-first Century. New York: T. & T. Clark, 2005.

Chantraine, Georges. Foreword to *At the Service of the Church: Henri de Lubac Reflects on the Circumstances That Occasioned His Writing*, 7. San Francisco: Communio, 1993.

Chenu, Marie-Dominique. "The Eyes of Faith." In *Faith and Theology*, 8–14. Translated by Denis Hickey. New York: Macmillan, 1968.

———. *Is Theology a Science?* 1st edition. Translated by A. H. N. Green-Armytage. Twentieth-Century Encyclopedia of Catholicism, vol. 2, sec. 1, Knowledge and Faith. New York: Hawthorn, 1959.

———. *Nature, Man and Society in the Twelfth Century: Essays on New Theological Perspectives in the Latin West*. Medieval Academy Reprints for Teaching 37. Toronto: University of Toronto Press, in association with the Medieval Academy of America, 1997.

———. "What Is Theology?" In *Faith and Theology*, 15–35. Translated by Denis Hickey. New York: Macmillan, 1968.

Connolly, James M. *The Voices of France: A Survey of Contemporary Theology in France*. New York: Macmillan, 1961.

Cornwell, John. *Hitler's Pope: The Secret History of Pius XII*. New York: Viking, 1999.

D'Ambrosio, Marcellino G. "Henri de Lubac and the Critique of Scientific Exegesis." *Communio (US)* 19 (1992) 365–88.

———. "Henri de Lubac and the Recovery of the Traditional Hermeneutic." PhD diss., Catholic University of America, 1991.

Daley, Brian. "The Nouvelle Théologie and the Patristic Revival: Sources, Symbols and the Science of Theology." *International Journal of Systematic Theology* 7 (2005) 362–82.

Daly, Gabriel. *Transcendence and Immanence: A Study in Catholic Modernism and Integralism*. Oxford: Clarendon, 1980.

Daniélou, Jean. *The Bible and the Liturgy*. University of Notre Dame Liturgical Studies 3. Notre Dame: University of Notre Dame Press, 1956.

———. "Les Orientations Présentes de la Pensée Religieuse." *Études* 249 (1946) 5–21.

———. *The Salvation of the Nations*. Notre Dame: University of Notre Dame Press, 1962.

Dawson, John David. "Figural Reading and the Fashioning of Christian Identity in Boyarin, Auerbach and Frei." *Modern Theology* 14 (1998) 181–96.

Donnelly, Philip J. "Current Theology: On the Development of Dogma and the Supernatural." *Theological Studies* 8 (1947) 471–91.

———. "Discussion on the Supernatural Order." *Theological Studies* 9 (1948) 213–49.

———. "The Gratuity of the Beatific Vision and the Possibility of a Natural Destiny." *Theological Studies* 11 (1950) 374–404.

———. "The *Surnaturel* of H. de Lubac." *Theological Studies* 9 (1948) 554–60.

Doyle, William. *The Ancien Régime*. Studies in European History. Atlantic Highlands, NJ: Humanities, 1986.

Duffy, Eamon. *The Stripping of the Altars: Traditional Religion in England, c.1400–c.1580*. New Haven: Yale University Press, 1992.

Duffy, Stephen. *The Graced Horizon: Nature and Grace in Modern Catholic Thought*. Theology and Life 37. Collegeville, MN: Liturgical, 1992.

Enns, Peter. *Inspiration and Incarnation: Evangelicals and the Problem of the Old Testament*. Grand Rapids: Baker Academic, 2005.

Feingold, Lawrence. *The Natural Desire to See God according to St. Thomas Aquinas and His Interpreters*. Dissertationes. Series Theologica 3. Roma: Apollinare Studi, 2001.

Figgis, John Neville. *The Political Aspects of St. Augustine's "City of God."* London: Longmans, 1921.

Fitzpatrick, P. J. "Neoscholasticism." In *The Cambridge History of Later Medieval Philosophy: From the Rediscovery of Aristotle to the Disintegration of Scholasticism, 1100–1600*, edited by Norman Kretzmann et al., 838–51. Cambridge: Cambridge University Press, 1982.

Ford, David. "Radical Orthodoxy and the Future of British Theology." *Scottish Journal of Theology* 54 (2001) 385–404.

Fourier, Francois Marie Charles. *Le Nouveau Monde Industriel Sociétaire*. 2 vols. Paris: Bossange, 1829–1830.

Fowl, Stephen. *Engaging Scripture: A Model for Theological Interpretation*. Challenges in Contemporary Theology. Oxford: Blackwell, 1998.

Frei, Hans W. *The Eclipse of Biblical Narrative: A Study in Eighteenth and Nineteenth Century Hermeneutics*. New Haven: Yale University Press, 1974.

———. "History, Salvation-History, and Typology." In *Hans Frei: Unpublished Pieces*, edited by Michael Higton, 76–88. New Haven: Yale Divinity School Archives, 1998–2004. Online: http://www.library.yale.edu/div/Freitranscripts/Frei06-Typology.pdf

———. *The Identity of Jesus Christ: The Hermeneutical Bases of Dogmatic Theology*. Philadelphia: Fortress, 1975.

———. "The 'Literal Reading' of Biblical Narrative in the Christian Tradition: Does It Stretch or Will It Break?" In *Theology and Narrative: Selected Essays*, edited by Hans W. Frei et al., 117–52. New York: Oxford University Press, 1993.

———. "Theological Reflections on the Accounts of Jesus' Death and Resurrection." In *Theology and Narrative: Selected Essays*, edited by Hans W. Frei et al., 45–93. New York: Oxford University Press, 1993.

———. "Theology and the Interpretation of Narrative: Some Hermeneutical Considerations." In *Theology and Narrative: Selected Essays*, edited by Hans W. Frei et al., 94–116. New York: Oxford University Press, 1993.

Frend, W. H. C. *The Rise of the Monophysite Movement: Chapters in the History of the Church in the Fifth and Sixth Centuries*. Cambridge: Cambridge University Press, 1972.

Garrigou-Lagrange, Réginald. *Beatitude: A Commentary on St. Thomas' Theological Summa, 1a, IIae, Qq. 1–54*. Translated by Patrick Cummuns. St. Louis: Herder, 1956.

———. *Grace: Commentary on the Summa Theologica of St. Thomas, Ia, IIae, Q. 109–114*. Translated by the Dominican Nuns, Corpus Christi Monastery, Menlo Park, California. St. Louis: Herder, 1952.

———. "La Nouvelle Théologie, où Va-T-Elle?" *Angelicum* (1946) 126–45.

Gilson, Étienne, et al. *Recent Philosophy: Hegel to the Present*. A History of Philosophy 4. New York: Random House, 1966.

Gilson, Étienne, and Henri de Lubac. *Letters of Étienne Gilson to Henri de Lubac*. Translated by Mary Emily Hamilton. San Francisco: Ignatius, 1988.

Glover, Jonathan. *Humanity: A Moral History of the Twentieth Century*. New Haven: Yale University Press, 2000.

Golomb, Jacob, and Robert Wistrich, editors. *Nietzsche, Godfather of Fascism? On the Uses and Abuses of a Philosophy*. Princeton: Princeton University Press, 2002.

Gotcher, Robert F. "Henri de Lubac and Communion: The Significance of His Theology of the Supernatural for an Interpretation of *Gaudium et Spes*." PhD diss., Marquette University, 2002.

Goubert, Pierre. *The Ancien Régime: French Society, 1600–1750*. New York: Harper and Row, 1974.

Greenstock, David L. "Thomism and the New Theology." *Thomist* 13 (1950) 567–96.

Griffiths, Paul J., and Reinhard Hütter, editors. *Reason and the Reasons of Faith*. Theology for the Twenty-first Century. New York: T. & T. Clark International, 2005.

Grumett, David. *De Lubac: A Guide for the Perplexed*. With a foreword by Avery Cardinal Dulles. London: T. & T. Clark, 2007.

———. "Yves de Montcheuil: Action, Justice and the Kingdom in Spiritual Resistance to Nazism." *Theological Studies* 68 (2007) 618–41.

Gutiérrez, Gustavo. *A Theology of Liberation: History, Politics, and Salvation*. Maryknoll, NY: Orbis, 1988.

Harvey, Barry. *Can These Bones Live?: A Catholic Baptist Engagement with Ecclesiology, Hermeneutics, and Social Theory*. Grand Rapids: Brazos, 2008.

Hennesey, James. "Leo XIII's Thomistic Revival: A Political and Philosophical Event." *The Journal of Religion* 58 (1978) 185–97.

Henrici, Peter. "On Mystery in Philosophy." *Communio (US)* 19 (1992) 354–64.

Hobsbawm, E. J. *The Age of Revolution: Europe 1789–1848*. New York: New American Library, 1962.

Holland, Joe. *Modern Catholic Social Teaching: The Popes Confront the Industrial Age, 1740–1958.* New York: Paulist, 2003.

Hütter, Reinhard. "Desiderium Naturale Visionis Dei—Est autem Duplex Hominis Beatitudo sive Felicitas: Some Observations About Lawrence Feingold's and John Milbank's Recent Interventions in the Debate over the Natural Desire to See God." *Nova et Vetera* 5 (2007) 81–132.

———. *Suffering Divine Things: Theology as Church Practice.* Grand Rapids: Eerdmans, 2000.

Jenkins, John I. *Knowledge and Faith in Thomas Aquinas.* Cambridge: Cambridge University Press, 1997.

Jenson, Robert W. "How the World Lost Its Story." *First Things* 36 (1993) 19–24.

———. "On the Problems of Scriptural Authority." *Interpretation* 31 (1977) 237–50.

Jodock, Darrell, editor. *Catholicism Contending with Modernity: Roman Catholic Modernism and Anti-Modernism in Historical Context.* Cambridge: Cambridge University Press, 2000.

Johnson, Luke Timothy, and William S. Kurz. *The Future of Catholic Biblical Scholarship: A Constructive Conversation.* Grand Rapids: Eerdmans, 2002.

Kantorowicz, Ernst Hartwig. *The King's Two Bodies: A Study in Mediaeval Political Theology.* Princeton: Princeton University Press, 1957.

Kaufmann, Walter Arnold. *Nietzsche: Philosopher, Psychologist, Antichrist.* Princeton: Princeton University Press, 1950.

Kerr, Fergus. "French Theology: Yves Congar and Henri De Lubac." In *The Modern Theologians: An Introduction to Christian Theology in the Twentieth Century,* edited by David F. Ford, 105–17. Oxford: Blackwell, 1997.

———. *Twentieth-Century Catholic Theologians: From Neoscholasticism to Nuptial Mysticism.* Malden, MA: Blackwell, 2007.

Kingsbury, Jack Dean, editor. *Gospel Interpretation: Narrative-Critical & Social-Scientific Approaches.* Harrisburg, PA: Trinity, 1997.

Komonchak, Joseph. "The Ecclesial and Cultural Roles of Theology." *Catholic Theological Society of America: Proceedings* 40 (1985) 15–32.

———. "The Enlightenment and the Construction of Roman Catholicism." *Annual of the Catholic Commission on Intellectual and Cultural Affairs* (1985) 31–59.

———. "Theology and Culture at Mid-Century: The Example of Henri De Lubac." *Theological Studies* 51 (1990) 579–602.

Körner, Bernhard. "Henri Lubac and Fundamental Theology." *Communio* 23 (1996) 710–24.

Labourdette, Marie-Michel. "La Thélogie et Ses Sources." *Revue Thomiste* 46 (1946) 353–71.

Lacroix, Jean. *The Meaning of Modern Atheism.* Translated and introduced by Garret Barden. New York: Macmillan, 1965.

Ladner, Gerhart B. "Aspects of Medieval Thought." *Review of Politics* 9 (1947) 403–22.

Lee, David. *Luke's Stories of Jesus: Theological Reading of Gospel Narrative and the Legacy of Hans Frei.* Journal for the Study of the New Testament Supplement Series 185. Sheffield: Sheffield Academic, 1999.

Leo XIII, Pope. *Aeterni Patris.* In *The Papal Encyclicals,* compiled by Claudia Carlen, 2:17–27. 5 vols. Wilmington, NC: McGrath, 1981.

———. *Inscrutabili Dei Consilio*. In *The Papal Encyclicals*, compiled by Claudia Carlen, 2:5–10. 5 vols. Wilmington, NC: McGrath, 1981.

———. *Quod Apostolici Muneris*. In *The Papal Encyclicals*, compiled by Claudia Carlen, 2: 6–11. 5 vols. Wilmington, NC: McGrath, 1981.

———. *Rerum Novarum*. In *The Papal Encyclicals*, compiled by Claudia Carlen, 2:241–61. 5 vols. Wilmington, NC: McGrath, 1981.

Levering, Matthew Webb. *Participatory Biblical Exegesis: A Theology of Biblical Interpretation*. Reading the Scriptures. Notre Dame: University of Notre Dame Press, 2008.

———. *Scripture and Metaphysics: Aquinas and the Renewal of Trinitarian Theology*. Challenges in Contemporary Theology. Malden, MA: Blackwell, 2004.

Lindbeck, George. "Atonement and the Hermeneutics of Intratextual Social Embodiment." In *The Nature of Confession: Evangelicals & Postliberals in Conversation*, edited by Dennis L. Okholm and Timothy R. Phillips, 221–40. Downers Grove, IL: Intervarsity, 1996.

———. "The Church's Mission to a Postmodern Culture." In *Postmodern Theology: Christian Faith in a Pluralistic World*, edited by Frederic B. Burnham, 37–55. San Francisco: Harper and Row, 1989.

———. "Confession and Community: An Israel-Like View of the Church." *Christian Century* 107 (May 9, 1990) 492–96.

———. *The Nature of Doctrine: Religion and Theology in a Postliberal Age*. Philadelphia: Westminster, 1984.

———. "Scripture, Consensus, and Community." In *Biblical Interpretation in Crisis: The Ratzinger Conference on Bible and Church*, edited by Richard John Neuhaus, 74–101. Grand Rapids: Eerdmans, 1989.

———. "The Story-Shaped Church: Critical Exegesis and Theological Interpretation." In *Scriptural Authority and Narrative Interpretation*, edited by Garret Green, 161–78. Reprint, Eugene, OR: Wipf and Stock, 2000.

Lohfink, Gerhard. *Does God Need the Church?: Toward a Theology of the People of God*. Collegeville, MN: Liturgical, 1999.

Long, D. Stephen. *Divine Economy: Theology and the Market*. Radical Orthodoxy Series. New York: Routledge, 2000.

———. "The Way of Aquinas: Its Importance for Moral Theology." *Studies in Christian Ethics* 19 (2006) 339–56.

Long, Stephen A. "Man's Natural End." *Thomist* 64 (2000) 211–37.

———. "On the Loss, and the Recovery, of Nature as a Theonomic Principle: Reflections on the Nature/Grace Controversy." *Nova et Vetera* 5 (2007) 133–84.

Lubac, Henri de. "Apologetics and Theology." In *Theological Fragments*, 91–104. Translated by Rebecca Howell Balinski. San Francisco: Ignatius, 1989.

———. "Apologétique et Théologie." *Nouvelle Revue Théologique* 57 (1930) 364–65.

———. *At the Service of the Church: Henri de Lubac Reflects on the Circumstances That Occasioned His Writings*. San Francisco: Communio, 1993.

———. *Augustinianism and Modern Theology*. Edited by Lancelot Sheppard. New York: Crossroad, 2000.

———. *Augustinisme et Théologie Moderne*. Coll. Théologie 63. Paris: Aubier-Montaigne, 1965.

————. "The Authority of the Church in Temporal Matters." In *Theological Fragments*, 199–233. Translated by Rebecca Howell Balinski. San Francisco: Ignatius, 1989.

————. *A Brief Catechesis on Nature and Grace*. Translated by Richard Arnandez. San Francisco: Ignatius 1984.

————. *Catholicism: Christ and the Common Destiny of Man*. San Francisco: Ignatius, 1988.

————. "Christian Explanation of Our Times." In *Theology in History*, 440–56. San Francisco: Ignatius 1996.

————. *Christian Resistance to Anti-Semitism: Memories from 1940–1944*. San Francisco: Ignatius, 1988.

————. *The Church: Paradox and Mystery*. Staten Island, NY: Alba, 1969.

————. *Corpus Mysticum: L'eucharistie et L'église au Moyen Âge. Étude Historique*. 2d edition, revised and augmented. Coll. Théologie 3. Paris: Aubier-Montaigne, 1949.

————. *Corpus Mysticum: The Eucharist and the Church in the Middle Ages; Historical Survey*. Translated by Gemma Simmonds with Richard Price and Christopher Stephens. Faith in Reason. London: SCM, 2006.

————. *The Drama of Atheist Humanism*. San Francisco: Ignatius 1995.

————. *Exégèse Médiévale: Les Quatre Sens de L'écriture*. Vol. 2/1. Théologie 42. Paris: Aubier-Montaigne, 1961.

————. "Hellenistic Allegory and Christian Allegory." In *Theological Fragments*, 165–96. Translated by Rebecca Howell Balinski. San Francisco: Ignatius, 1989.

————. *Histoire et Esprit: L'intelligence de L'écriture d'après Origène*. Théologie 16. Paris: Aubier-Montaigne, 1950.

————. *History and Spirit: The Understanding of Scripture according to Origen*. Translated by Anne Englund Nash; with Greek and Latin translation by Juvenal Merriell. San Francisco: Ignatius, 2007.

————. "Internal Causes of the Weakening and Disappearance of the Sense of the Sacred." In *Theology in History*, 223–40. Translated by Anne Englund Nash. San Francisco: Ignatius, 1996.

————. "The Light of Christ." In *Theology in History*, 201–20. Translated by Anne Englund Nash. San Francisco: Ignatius, 1996.

————. *Medieval Exegesis: The Four Senses of Scripture*. Vol. 1. Grand Rapids: Eerdmans, 1998.

————. *Medieval Exegesis: The Four Senses of Scripture*. Vol. 2. Grand Rapids: Eerdmans, 2000.

————. *Méditation sur L'église*. Paris: Aubier-Montaigne, 1953.

————. "Le Mystère du Surnaturel." *Recherches de Science Religieuse* 37 (1949) 80–121.

————. *Le Mystère du Surnaturel*. Paris: Aubier-Montaigne, 1965.

————. "The Mystery of the Supernatural." In *Theology in History*, 281–316. Translated by Anne Englund Nash. San Francisco: Ignatius, 1996.

————. *The Mystery of the Supernatural*. Translated by Rosemary Sheed. Introduction by David L. Schindler. Milestones in Catholic Theology. New York: Crossroad, 1998.

————. "Mysticism and Mystery." In *Theological Fragments*, 35–69. Translated by Rebecca Howell Balinski. San Francisco: Ignatius, 1989.

————. "Nature and Grace." In *The Word in History*, edited by Patrick Burke, 24–40. New York: Sheed & Ward, 1966.

———. "On an Old Distich: The Doctrine of the 'Fourfold Sense' in Scripture." In *Theological Fragments*, 109–27. Translated by Rebecca Howell Balinski. San Francisco: Ignatius, 1989.

———. "On Christian Philosophy." *Communio (US)* 19 (1992) 478–506.

———. "Political Augustinianism?" In *Theological Fragments*, 235–86. Translated by Rebecca Howell Balinski. San Francisco: Ignatius 1989.

———. *La Révélation Divine*. Traditions Chrétiennes. Paris: Cerf, 1983.

———. *Scripture in the Tradition*. Translated by Luke O'Neill. Introduction by Peter Casasrella. Milestones in Catholic Theology. New York: Crossroad, 2000.

———. *The Splendor of the Church*. New York: Sheed & Ward, 1956.

———. *Surnaturel: Études Historiques*, Coll. Théologie, 8. Paris: Aubier-Montaigne, 1946.

———. *Teilhard de Chardin: The Man and His Meaning*. New York: New American Library, 1965.

———. *Teilhard Explained*. Translated by Anthony Buono. Deus Books. New York: Paulist, 1968.

———. "The Theological Foundation of the Missions." In *Theology in History*, 367–427. Translated by Anne Englund Nash. San Francisco: Ignatius, 1996.

———. *Theological Fragments*. Translated by Rebecca Howell Balinski. San Francisco: Ignatius, 1989.

———. *Theology in History*. Foreword by Michel Sales. Translated by Anne Englund Nash. San Francisco: Ignatius, 1996.

———. *Three Jesuits Speak: Yves de Montcheuil, 1899–1944, Charles Nicolet, 1897–1961, Jean Zupan, 1899–1968*. San Francisco: Ignatius, 1987.

———. "Typology and Allegorization." In *Theological Fragments*, 129–64. Translated by Rebecca Howell Balinski. San Francisco: Ignatius, 1989.

Lubac, Henri de, and Angelo Scola. *Entretien Autour de Vatican II: Souvenirs et Réflexions*. Théologies. Paris: Cerf, 1985.

MacIntyre, Alasdair. *Three Rival Versions of Moral Enquiry*. Notre Dame: University of Notre Dame Press, 1990.

Maritain, Jacques. *Three Reformers: Luther, Descartes, Rousseau*. Westport, CT: Greenwood, 1970.

Marrus, Michael Robert, and Robert O. Paxton. *Vichy France and the Jews*. Stanford: Stanford University Press, 1995.

Marshall, S. L. A. *World War I*. Introduction by David Kennedy. Boston: Houghton Mifflin 2001.

Matthews, Jackson, editor. *The Collected Works of Paul Valéry*. Vol. 10, *History and Politics*. New York: Pantheon, 1962.

McCool, Gerald A. *From Unity to Pluralism: The Internal Evolution of Thomism*. New York: Fordham University Press, 1992.

———. *The Neo-Thomists*. Marquette Studies in Philosophy 3. Milwaukee: Marquette University Press, 1994.

———. *Nineteenth-Century Scholasticism: The Search for a Unitary Method*. New York: Fordham University Press, 1989.

McKenzie, John L. "The Significance of the Old Testament for Christian Faith in Roman Catholicism." In *The Old Testament and Christian Faith: A Theological Discussion*, edited by Bernhard W. Anderson, 102–14. New York: Herder & Herder, 1969.

McPartlan, Paul. *The Eucharist Makes the Church: Henri de Lubac and John Zizioulas in Dialogue*. Edinburgh: T. & T. Clark, 1993.

McQuillan, S. *The Political Development of Rome: 1012–85*. Lanham, MD: University Press of America, 2002.

Milbank, John. *Being Reconciled: Ontology and Pardon*. Radical Orthodoxy Series. London: Routledge, 2003.

———. "Henri de Lubac." In *The Modern Theologians: An Introduction to Christian Theology since 1918*, edited by David Ford and Rachel Muers, 76–92. Malden, MA: Blackwell, 2005.

———. "The Programme of Radical Orthodoxy." In *Radical Orthodoxy? A Catholic Enquiry*, edited by Laurence Paul Hemming, 34–45. Heythrop Studies in Contemporary Philosophy, Religion & Theology. Aldershot, England: Ashgate, 2000.

———. *The Suspended Middle: Henri de Lubac and the Debate concerning the Supernatural*. Grand Rapids: Eerdmans, 2005.

———. *Theology and Social Theory: Beyond Secular Reason*. Signposts in Theology. Cambridge, MA: Blackwell, 1991.

———. *Theology and Social Theory: Beyond Secular Reason*. 2d edition. Oxford: Blackwell, 2006.

———. *The Word Made Strange: Theology, Language, Culture*. Oxford: Blackwell, 1997.

Milbank, John, et al., editors. *Radical Orthodoxy: A New Theology*. New York: Routledge, 1999.

Myers, Ched. *Binding the Strong Man: A Political Reading of Mark's Story of Jesus*. Maryknoll, NY: Orbis, 1988.

Neufeld, Karl. "In the Service of the Council: Bishops and Theologians at the Second Vatican Council (for Cardinal Henri de Lubac on His 90th Birthday)." In *Vatican II: Assessment and Perspectives; Twenty-five Years After (1962–1987)*, vol. 1, 71–105. Edited by René Latourelle. 3 vols. New York: Paulist, 1988.

Nichols, Aidan. "Thomism and the Nouvelle Théologie." *The Thomist* 64 (2000) 1–19.

Oakes, Edward T. "The Paradox of Nature and Grace: On John Milbank's *The Suspended Middle: Henri de Lubac and the Debate concerning the Supernatural*." *Nova et Vetera* 4 (2006) 667–96.

Oakley, Francis. "Natural Law, the *Corpus Mysticum*, and Consent in Conciliar Thought from John of Paris to Mattias Ugonius." *Speculum* 56 (1981) 786–810.

O'Donovan, Oliver. *The Desire of the Nations: Rediscovering the Roots of Political Theology*. Cambridge: Cambridge University Press, 1996.

O'Donovan, Oliver, and Joan Lockwood O'Donovan. *From Irenaeus to Grotius: A Sourcebook in Christian Political Thought, 100–1625*. Grand Rapids: Eerdmans, 1999.

O'Meara, Thomas. *Church and Culture: German Catholic Theology, 1860–1914*. Notre Dame: University of Notre Dame Press, 1991.

Origen. *On First Principles*. Translated by Paul Koetschau and G. W. Butterworth. Gloucester, MA: Smith, 1973.

Peddicord, Richard. *The Sacred Monster of Thomism: An Introduction to the Life and Legacy of Réginald Garrigou-Lagrange*. South Bend, IN: St. Augustine's, 2005.

Pickstock, Catherine. "Reply to David Ford and Guy Collins." *Scottish Journal of Theology* 54 (2001) 405–22.

Pius XII. *Humani Generis*. Online: http://www.vatican.va/holy_father/pius_xii/encyclicals/documents/hf_p-xii_enc_12081950_humani-generis_en.html

Placher, William C. Introduction to *Theology and Narrative: Selected Essays*, edited by Hans Frei, et al., 3–25. New York: Oxford University Press, 1993.

Powell, Mark Allan. *What Is Narrative Criticism?* Minneapolis: Fortress, 1990.

Ravier, André, editor. *La Mystique et les Mystiques*. Paris: Desclée de Brouwer, 1965.

Reno, Russell R.. "The Radical Orthodoxy Project." *First Things* 100 (2000) 37–44.

Rhodes, Anthony Richard Ewart. *The Vatican in the Age of the Dictators, 1922–1945*. London: Hodder & Stoughton, 1973.

Robbins, Vernon K. "Narrative in Ancient Rhetoric and Rhetoric in Ancient Narrative." In *SBL Seminar Papers* (1996) 368–84.

Russo, Antonio. *Henri de Lubac: Teologia e Dogma nella Storia. L'influsso di Blondel*. La Cultura 40. Roma: Studium, 1990.

Saint-Simon, Henri, comte de. *Oeuvres de Saint-Simon et d'Enfantin*. 47 vols. Paris: Dentu & Leroux, 1865–1878.

Schindler, David L. "Christology, Public Theology, and Thomism: De Lubac, Balthasar, and Murray." In *The Future of Thomism*, edited by Deal Wyatt Hudson and Dennis Wm. Moran, 247–64. American Maritain Association Publications. Notre Dame, IN: American Maritain Association; distributed by University of Notre Dame Press, 1992.

Schwartz, Hillel. *Century's End: A Cultural History of the* Fin de Siècle *from the 990s through the 1990s*. New York: Doubleday, 1990.

Shanley, Brian J. "*Sacra Doctrina* and the Theology of Disclosure." *Thomist* 61 (1997) 163–87.

Smith, James K. A. *Introducing Radical Orthodoxy: Mapping a Post-Secular Theology*. Grand Rapids: Baker Academic, 2004.

Staley, Kevin M. "Happiness: The Natural End of Man?" *Thomist* 53 (1989) 215–34.

"Surnaturel." *Revue Thomiste*, special issue, 1–2 (2001).

Thibault, Pierre. *Savoir et Pouvoir: Philosophie Thomiste et Politique Cléricale au XIX Siècle* Histoire et Sociologie de la Culture 2. Québec: Les Presses de l'Université Laval, 1972.

Thiemann, Ronald F. *Revelation and Theology: The Gospel as Narrated Promise*. Notre Dame: University of Notre Dame Press, 1985.

Thomson, John A. F. *The Western Church in the Middle Ages*. New York: Oxford University Press, 1998.

Tolson, Jay. "Academia's Getting Its Religion Back." *U.S. News and World Report* (August 28, 2000) 52.

Turner, Denys. *Faith, Reason, and the Existence of God*. New York: Cambridge University Press, 2004.

Velde, Rudi A. te. "Understanding the *Scientia* of Faith." In *Contemplating Aquinas: On the Varieties of Interpretation*, edited by Fergus Kerr, 55–74. Faith in Reason. Notre Dame: University of Notre Dame Press, 2003.

Volf, Miraslov. "Theology, Meaning, and Power." In *The Future of Theology: Essays in Honor of Miraslov Volf*, edited by Miraslov Volf et al., 98–113. Grand Rapids: Eerdmans, 1996.

Von Arx, Jeffrey Paul, editor. *Varieties of Ultramontanism*. Washington DC: Catholic University of America Press, 1997.

Wagner, Jean-Pierre. *Henri de Lubac*. Initiantions Aux Théologiens. Paris: Cerf, 2001.

Wannenwetsch, Bernd. "The Political Worship of the Church: A Critical and Empowering Practice." *Modern Theology* 12 (1996) 269–99.

Ward, Graham. "Bodies: The Displaced Body of Jesus Christ." In *Radical Orthodoxy: A New Theology*, edited by John Milbank et al., 163–81. New York: Routledge, 1999.

———. "In the Economy of the Divine: A Response to James K. A. Smith." *Pneuma: The Journal of the Society for Pentecostal Studies* 25 (2003) 115–20.

———. "Radical Orthodoxy and/as Cultural Politics." In *Radical Orthodoxy?: A Catholic Enquiry*, edited by Laurence Paul Hemming, 97–111. Heythrop Studies in Contemporary Philosophy, Religion & Theology. Aldershot, England: Ashgate, 2000.

Weber, Eugen Joseph. *Action Française; Royalism and Reaction in Twentieth Century France*. Stanford: Stanford University Press, 1962.

Weigel, Gustave. "The Historical Background of the Encyclical Humani Generis." *Theological Studies* 12 (1951) 208–30.

Wells, Samuel. *Improvisation: The Drama of Christian Ethics*. London: SPCK, 2004.

Wielenberg, Erik J. *Value and Virtue in a Godless Universe*. Cambridge: Cambridge University Press, 2005.

Williams, Rowan. *On Christian Theology*. Challenges in Contemporary Theology. Oxford: Blackwell, 2000.

Witvliet, John D. "The Opening of Worship: Trinity." In *A More Profound Alleluia: Theology and Worship in Harmony*, edited by Leanne Van Dyk, 1–27. Grand Rapids: Eerdmans, 2005.

Wood, Susan K. "The Nature-Grace Problematic within Henri De Lubac's Christological Paradox." *Communio (US)* 19 (1992) 389–403.

———. *Spiritual Exegesis and the Church in the Theology of Henri de Lubac*. Grand Rapids: Eerdmans, 1998.

Wright, N. T. *Jesus and the Victory of God*. Christian Origins and the Question of God 2. Minneapolis: Fortress, 1996.

Index